ENGLISH

BEN FOGLE

ENGLISH

A STORY OF MARMITE, QUEUING AND WEATHER

WILLIAM
COLLINS

William Collins
An imprint of HarperCollins*Publishers*
1 London Bridge Street
London SE1 9GF
WilliamCollinsBooks.com

First published in Great Britain by William Collins in 2017

22 21 20 19 18 17
10 9 8 7 6 5 4 3 2 1

HB ISBN 978-0-00-822224-6
TPB ISBN 978-0-00-822225-3

Printed and bound in Great Britain by
CPI Group (UK) Ltd, Croydon, CR0 4YY

MIX
Paper from
responsible sources
FSC
www.fsc.org   FSC™ C007454

CONTENTS

PROLOGUE

There was a hubbub of excited chatter as, clutching steaming cups of tea, the women gathered around a series of small tables to admire the spoils of war. The Great Yorkshire Show had just finished and the crochet, patchwork, flower arranging and cakes had all 'come home'. There was a general chatter of approval. The room was decorated with bunting and it had the air of a village fete. This *was* Jam and Jerusalem.

I was in Harrogate, North Yorkshire, for the weekly gathering of the Spa Sweethearts Women's Institute. The WI, as it is known, was formed in 1915 to revitalize communities and encourage women to produce food in the absence of their menfolk during the First World War. Since then it has grown to become the largest voluntary women's organization in the UK, with more than six thousand groups and nearly a quarter of a million members.

The Queen herself is a member, and the WI, in my humble opinion, understands better than any other organization how the country works. Always polite, it has a reputation for no-nonsense, straight talking. The chairwoman of the WI's public affairs committee, Marylyn Haines-Evans, recently said, 'If the WI were a political party, we would be the party for common sense.' If anyone understands the quixotic essence of Englishness, it is the ladies who attend these regional WI gatherings.

I chose the location carefully too. Popular with the English elite during the nineteenth and twentieth centuries, during the Second World War, government offices were relocated from London to the North Yorkshire town and it was designated the stand-in capital should London fall during the war. It frequently wins the Britain in Bloom competition and has been voted one of the best places to live in the UK. It is what I would call a solid Yorkshire town. The combination of Harrogate and the WI is, I think, the perfect English 'brew'.

I had come along to one of the WI's evening gatherings to find out what Englishness means to them. Rather uncharacteristically, I was a little nervous as I walked to the stage in the small hall. I had brought my labrador, Storm along as an icebreaker and for some moral support, and together we made our way to the centre of the stage.

It was a relatively small gathering, perhaps fifty strong, but these women have solid values and in my mind they are the voice of England. Ignoring the jingoistic reverence that a national sporting event or royal occasion generates, I asked them what Englishness means.

'The weather.'

'Queuing.' A lot of nodding heads.

'Apologizing. We are always apologizing,' stated another woman to a chorus of agreement.

'Roses and gardens.'

'Tea.' This got the loudest endorsement.

'Baking and cakes.'

'The Queen.'

I asked them whether they would ever fly the St George's Cross from their homes. There was an audible gasp, accompanied by a collective shaking of heads.

'Why not?' I wondered.

'Because it has been hijacked by the extreme right,' answered one woman.

'It represents racism and xenophobia,' added another.

'We aren't allowed to be English, we are British.'

I asked whether we should celebrate our national identity more like the Welsh, Scots and Northern Irish. To which the whole room nodded in approval, not in a jingoistic, nationalist kind of way, but in an understated, English kind of way. It was a genteel, considered discussion of the virtues of Englishness and the erosion of our national patriotism.

'The Last Night of the Proms is as patriotic as we get,' explained another member of the group, 'but that patriotism is about the Union.'

Here England was speaking. We have a solid idea of what it is to be English, we have a grasp of some of the character traits of living Englishly, but we no longer celebrate that Englishness.

I asked if it was time to reclaim our national identity and take pride in being English. There was a round of applause.

'Reclaim the celebration of Englishness for us, Ben.'

And that is what this book is about.

INTRODUCTION

LIVING ENGLISHLY

I am standing at the top of a vertiginous hill. When I say vertigi-nous, I mean the gradient is 1:1 in places, so steep you can't stand up. A damp mizzle has descended on the valley, coating the grass in a greasy layer of moisture that has in turn soaked into the soil, turning it into an oily runway of mud.

It is the kind of mizzle that soaks you unknowingly. It has a stealthy ability to drench clothes, hair and skin before you have even noticed. Large drips of rain begin to fall from the peak of my flat cap, worn in a hopeless attempt to keep a low profile. My heart leaps and my stomach lurches as I take in the contours of the steep hill.

On this Spring Bank Holiday Monday, hundreds of people are streaming across the fields below, yomping along the narrow footpaths that bisect the fields. Next to me a German from Hamburg is busy fitting a mouth guard to his teeth, while a New Zealand rugby player is shoving shin pads down his long socks.

Along the brow of the hill, flagged by a simple plastic fence, are a further dozen nervous-looking faces from across the globe who have descended on this damp Gloucestershire hill for arguably one of the most famous eccentric sporting events in the world, the annual Cooper's Hill Cheese Rolling. To paraphrase one social commentator, it involves 'twenty young men chasing a cheese off a cliff and tumbling 200 yards to the bottom, where they are scraped up by paramedics and packed off to hospital'.

Which is about right. The steepness of the hill, combined with the undulations and the enthusiastic adrenalin of young men being cheered on by a crowd of thousands of spectators, leads to broken legs, arms, necks, ribs and even backs as a handful of brave souls chase a 9lb Double Gloucester cheese downhill at 70mph.

Why they started doing it, nobody really knows, although there are theories. The most colourful is that it has pagan origins. The start of the new year (spring) was celebrated by rolling burning brushwood down hills to represent rebirth and to encourage a good harvest. To enhance this the Master of Ceremonies also scattered buns, biscuits and sweets at the top of the hill. Cheese rolling is said to have developed from these rituals, although the earliest record of it dates back only to 1826.

During rationing during and after the Second World War a wooden cheese was used, with a small triangle of actual cheese inserted into a notch in the wood. In 1993, fifteen people were injured, four seriously, and in 2011, a crisis hit when the cheese rolling was cancelled after the local council decided to try to impose some order on this typically ramshackle English event. The council stipulated that the organizers should provide security, perimeter fencing to allow crowd control and spectator areas that would charge an entrance fee. The official competition was cancelled and the event went underground … which meant it continued as normal, but without any official organization, and with no ambulances.

Since then, the event has continued to grow, courtesy of a clandestine group of anonymous 'organizers', their identities shrouded in secrecy to avoid prosecution. Cooper's Hill Cheese Rolling continues to attract thousands of spectators and dozens of competitors from all over the world.

And now I find myself on the top of the famous hill next to an assortment of adrenalin junkies, waiting to take part myself.

'You gonna do it?' smiles a young lad holding a beer.

'Maybe,' I shrug. 'You?'

'No way mate, I'm not mad,' he smiles.

A couple of local men with a semi-official air and wearing white coats are milling around.

'Are you an organizer?' I ask a man busy organizing.

'Nah,' he replies with a smile, 'no organizers here.'

Another man in a white coat is busy with a bag of cheeses, a slight giveaway as to his official status. 'Are you an organizer?' I ask.

'No, mate,' he replies as he unpacks the cheese.

'You're not going to race the cheese, are you?' asks an athletic-looking woman.

I shrug my shoulders.

'Well, I'm the only medic here,' she replies with a slight look of concern.

Hundreds and thousands of people continue to envelop the hill, which is now thronging with people of all ages, here to witness the unofficial official cheese-rolling championships. It seems incredible that the event has seemingly been so well organized when there are no official organizers. Without structure, money or a committee, the event has somehow managed to corral spectators, crowd control and competitors. It is perhaps a fine reflection of Englishness that the entire event is so beautifully managed.

Back to the top of the hill and my heart is pounding as I wait for the count to begin, images of broken bones racing through my mind.

'I broke my neck racing the cheese last year,' smiles a young girl. 'I can't decide whether to race it again this year,' she adds.

'I'll count to four,' instructs the official-looking unofficial. 'We will release the cheese on three, you run on four.'

I look around at the nervous faces beside me as people dig their heels into the slippery slope. The hill is so steep and the mud so ice-like that it is difficult not to let gravity take its course even while sitting. Every so often one of the competitors slides a couple of metres down the slope, before struggling back up.

Next to me is Chris, the multi-winning champion who is also a serving soldier. 'Any secrets or advice?' I ask nervously.

'Just go for it. Commit to the cheese,' he smiles, 'and keep the body loose.'

So worried have the army been about his participation and likely injury that they urged him not to compete, even changing his shift to coincide with the morning of the event. But wild dogs wouldn't keep Chris from competing in his beloved event. He is the joint world champion cheese-roller, winning two cheeses – an honour he carries with pride.

The huge round cheese – its edges encased in wood to protect it from breaking up as it bounces down the hill – is rolled one-handed into position next to me by another Unofficial in a white coat and bowler hat, clutching a beer in his other hand.

'For Dutch courage,' smiles a man wearing a luminous yellow jacket that bear the words 'Fuck Health and Safety', offering me a bottle of whisky. I take a swig and hold my breath.

'One, two ...'

'Three.' And with that the cheese begins to roll, picking up speed in microseconds.

'Four ...' There is a slight delay and then my feet begin to turn.

I take one huge stride before the gooey mud takes over. My legs are swiped from under me and I land with a heavy thud on the mud, before picking up speed as gravity does her thing. There is no stopping me now as I struggle to regain my balance, but my bottom clings to the mud like a bobsled to the icy track, following the contours of a small water channel. All around me I am aware of tumbling legs as competitors cartwheel, slip and stride down the vertiginous slope. I hear the roar of the spectators as I momentarily regain my balance and take another stride before slipping forwards, head first through a patch of stinging nettles and then over a small hillock. I am fleetingly airborne before roly-polying sideways over my arm and back onto my bottom.

Once again I take to my feet as the hill begins to flatten out. And now I face one of the biggest dangers of all … the local rugby team.

They have traditionally been used to slow competitors down and prevent collisions with the crowd gathered at the bottom of the hill. For 'slow down' read 'tackle to the ground', often with low leg tackles. I have been warned about the rugby team and now, on my legs once again and out of control, I find myself hurtling towards two enormous rugger buggers.

'It's Fogle' is the last thing I hear before four arms envelop the lower part of my body and I come to a grinding halt in a heap at the bottom of the hill.

I lie there in a daze for a moment before another hand hauls me to my feet. I am a muddy mess, my arms covered in long scratches and grazes, my legs in large stinging-nettle welts, but apart from a throbbing pain in my right arm, I am not only alive but appear to be intact. Which is more than can be said for my fellow competitors, one of whom lies prostrate and unconscious at the bottom of the slope as a small crowd of concerned Unofficials gather around.

I catch a glimpse of Chris parading the cheese in front of the gathered world media. The event will be beamed around the world, from the *Today Show* in America to the front page of Australian newspapers. Somehow I have survived the cheese rolling and lived to tell the tale.

In many ways, cheese rolling in all its glorious absurdity defines us as a nation. It is daft, eccentric and gloriously pointless. There is no particular reason to do it, but it has become a rich part of our heritage, though no one really knows how or even when. We love to laugh at it even though it can cause serious injury. It involves stubborn, stiff-lower-jawed participants happy to tumble head over heels through mud and nettles and risk their lives in a hapless and, let's be honest, hopeless task to chase a cheese at 70mph.

It defies rhyme or reason. It isn't sexy or cool or clever. It is muddy and hurty, but it has an essential 'Englishness' about it …

This book has been a little like a chameleon. It has changed and morphed as I have travelled the length and breadth of England. A bit like us when we dress for the English weather, this book has never been quite sure what clothes to put on. So, as part of my researches, I have walked the quicksands of Morecambe Bay with the Queen's Guide and climbed Helvellyn with the Fell Top Assessor. I have chased cheeses down Gloucestershire hills and danced with Morris dancers in Rochester. I have been fortunate to walk the grounds of Buckingham Palace and to exercise the horses of the Royal Household Cavalry on their summer holiday in Norfolk. I have sat through rain-drenched hours of missed play at Wimbledon and squelched through the mud of Glastonbury. I have walked the corridors of No. 10 Downing Street with prime ministers and I have served tea at Betty's Tea Room in Harrogate. Each one quintessentially English, but what do they say about us as a nation?

After all, to the outside world, we are British. I remember once flying to New York and at immigration faced the frankly terrifying border guards at JFK airport.

'What is your nationality?' he asked.

'English,' I replied.

'You can't be English,' he answered flatly.

'But I am,' I continued foolishly.

'You can be British, but there's no such thing as being English,' he scowled.

What's more, English and Englishness have become so politically incorrect. The words have been hijacked by UKIP and the BNP, becoming something that many of us feel squeamish about. We are unsure if we are even allowed to call ourselves English. We are, of course British, a part of a unique union of nations that make up Great Britain. We are *not* English, although we may be Scottish or Welsh or Northern Irish.

More often than I can remember during the research for this book, I've been told that I'm British not English. 'I'm writing a book about Englishness,' I would explain; there would be a pause, a head tilt and then,

'Don't you mean Britishness?'

'No,' I'd reply, 'I mean Englishness.'

'I think you mean Britishness,' they'd inevitably repeat, adding in a whisper, 'Don't forget the other nations.'

And when I went onto social media to ask people for ideas on what are our English traits, the most common reply was 'Don't you mean British traits?', followed by a stream of abuse from Welsh, Scots and Northern Irish incensed that I could be so callous as to write a book exclusively about Englishness.

But this book is about Englishness – or, as I decided to describe it to myself, living Englishly.

I am no social scientist or historian. I have no academic credentials in 'Englishness'; in fact the subject has already been tackled by people far more learned and academic than myself – both Jeremy Paxman and Kate Fox have written brilliantly about Englishness. But what I do have is a burning passion, a drive and, most importantly, a pride in my identity. I love to celebrate this identity in all its quirkiness.

Cheese rolling is a good example of a national trait that rather accurately describes the character of Englishness – eccentricity. The dictionary definitions are pretty concise: according to the *Collins English Dictionary*, 'Eccentricity is unusual behaviour that other people consider strange.' The *Oxford English Dictionary*, meanwhile, defines 'eccentric' as '(of a person or their behaviour) unconventional and slightly strange.'

And, like a moth to a light, I have long been attracted to eccentricity. The child of an actress, it is fair to say that I grew up around a fair amount of oddball behaviour. My mother would often meet me at the school gates wearing a wild wig, heavy make-up and with some new and unrecognizable accent as she immersed herself in whatever her current role happened to be.

My immediate reaction was one of embarrassment. Like many children, I wanted to be a sheep and follow the crowd. I didn't want to be different, to stand out.

But as I became older I found myself drawn to the unusual. Strange places and people. I remember meeting the Englishwoman who ran Helga's Folly in Sri Lanka, and who walked around wearing black lace escorted by a dozen Dalmatians; or the British spy living in the Costa Rican jungle with tales of tea with Colonel Gaddafi and riding in tanks with Saddam Hussein; or peculiar aristocrats like Lord Bath and his dozens of 'wifelets'.

I found myself drawn to eccentric landscapes like Dungeness with its crazy, Daliesque architecture, or competing in an array of eccentric fixtures from the Brambles cricket match in the middle of the Solent to the World Stinging-Nettle Eating Championships.

Does that make me an eccentric? I don't think so, but there is most certainly one within. The joy of eccentricity is that you don't care. Look at the Fulfords, the aristocratic family made famous by Channel 4's *The Fu@£ing Fulfords* for an example of really not giving a F@£k. I am pretty confident that I will eventually become a bow-tie-wearing eccentric surrounded by dozens of dogs. It really is only a matter of time.

Eccentricity aside, I consider myself a proud Englishman. I was born in Marylebone, London, the capital of England. I am a Land Rover-driving, Labrador-owning, Marmite-eating, tea-drinking, wax-jacketed, Queen-loving Englishman. And yet technically I'm not. I'm actually an imposter. My grandfather was Scottish and my father is Canadian. In all honesty, I am a mongrel. A mixed breed with no obvious authority to write a book about Englishness, And yet I have lived my life being described as the quintessential Englishman. Over time some of those traits and characteristics have perhaps become exaggerated. I blame travel. Despite my childhood adoption of a few Canadian pronunciations, my accent and dialect has changed according to my location. Believe it or not, I haven't always sounded like this. Like what? you might ask. Well, for those who have never heard me talk, I am a little bit Posh. Correction. I'm not posh but I sound posh. RP – Received Pronunciation – is the official term. IT MEANS I PRO-NOUNCE EVERY WORD AND SYL-A-BYL CLEARLY.

The first changes to my accent came when I went to live in Ecuador, South America. For the first time, I became proud of my heritage. Subconsciously it was probably also an effort to distance myself from America and Americans. I lived with a beautiful family called the Salazars, and Mauro, my Ecuadorian 'father', was obsessed with all things English. 'Tell me about hooligans?' he would ask over a plate of beans and rice. 'And what about the Queen?' He was obsessed with Benny Hill and Oasis and *Four Weddings and a Funeral*.

He would spend hours quizzing me on the motherland, and I suppose I began subliminally to morph into a sort of Hugh Grant caricature. Several further years in Central and South America and I became fixated on my heritage, hoarding jars of Marmite and boxes of PG Tips. It was only when I returned to give a talk at my former school in Dorset that one of my teachers commented on the changes to my accent.

I genuinely believe that it is all the time away, overseas, exploring and adventuring that has given me time to think and explore my national identity. Sometimes, when you are too close to something, it is difficult to reflect honestly; often, we don't like what we see.

Let's be frank: England itself doesn't have a glowing halo when it comes to colonial and imperial history. Indeed, we are rightly embarrassed by much of our past. And now we face turbulent times in which we, as the wider nation, have been forced to ask ourselves who we are. What began with an emotionally charged independence referendum for Scotland ended with Great Britain's decision to leave the European Union. In the light of all of that, what does it mean to be English?

It is a loaded subject and a loaded book to write, full of pitfalls and taboo subjects that cause upset and irritation. It is why I occasionally feel I should never have written it. It is the reason I have agonized over it. It has given me sleepless nights.

Of course, it is easy to paint a national character with brush-strokes of stereotyping, and I will make no apology for my effort to explore many of these traits. After I had got beyond the stream of abuse from Scots, Welsh and Northern Irish occasioned by writing a book about Englishness, the character traits people suggested most often on social media were queuing, Marmite, umbrellas, the Queen, tea, fish and chips, Wimbledon, not complaining, bad teeth, dry humour, wax jackets, muddy Glastonbury, politeness, and the weather.

All of them iconically English, but it is the weather that has fascinated me the most. It is such a huge part of our national identity. It dominates our conversations. It is the subject of endless fascination and has, in my humble opinion, been the catalyst for so much of what makes England and the English what we are.

Again, if I'm honest I wanted to write a book about the weather. I wanted to explore our complex relationship with the weather – something we love to hate. The more I explored and researched, the more I became convinced that it is indeed the weather that has come to define us as a nation. Almost everything, every national trait and quirk and foible, can be attributed in some form to the weather. Okay, sometimes the link can be pretty tenuous, but it's always there. So, often in this book, the chapters will explore a topic and our climate will be lurking in the background, lighting the subject with its changeable, unpredictable presence.

When I was a young boy, there was a song that we used to play over and over. It was one of my mother's songs from the film *Half a Sixpence*, in which she starred alongside Tommy Steele. I can still remember every word:

> If the rain's got to fall, let it fall on Wednesday,
> Tuesday, Monday, any day but Sunday
> Sunday's the day when it's got to be fine,
> 'Cause that's when I'm meeting my girl.
>
> If the rain's got to fall, let it fall on Maidstone,
> Kingston, Oakstone, anywhere but Folkestone,
> Folkestone's the place where it's got to be fine.
> 'Cause that's where I'm meeting my girl.
>
> What could be wetter or damper
> Than to sit on a picnic hamper
> Sippin' a sasparella underneath a leaky umbrella?
>
> If the rain's got to fall, let it fall on Thursday,
> Saturday, Friday, any day but my day.
> Sunday's the day when it's got to be fine,
> 'Cause that's when I'm meeting my girl.

The weather is a fundamental part of who we are. It has been estimated that weather-obsessed British people spend on average six months of their lives talking about whether it's going to rain or shine, according to a survey published recently. Speculation about whether it's going to be wet, complaints about the cold and murmurings about the heat are also the first points of conversation with strangers or colleagues for 58 per cent of Britons, the survey recorded. Another study found that Britons talk about the weather for about two days (forty-nine hours, to be exact) every year and the subject comes up more often than work, what is on television, sport or gossip.

Nineteen per cent of over-65s questioned also believe they can predict the weather as well as a professional weatherman. We are a nation whose starting and ending points are the weather.

The more I roamed England, the more I turned the nature of the book over in my head. Then one day, as I walked through the rain along Blackpool beach, I thought to myself, 'That's it. This is an honest portrait of my own experiences of Englishness over the years. The weather seeps into every corner of our English personality but the book is actually about understanding Englishness. It's about Marmite, umbrellas, wonky teeth, sporting innovation and heroic failure. It's about bad food and royalty and Hugh-Grant type characters. It's as diverse as the nation itself.'

And what about the divide? Is there really such a thing as one Englishness? We might be a tiny island, but geographically and socially we are arguably one of the most diverse nations in the world. There is the obvious North/South divide, but there are more nuanced differences across the counties that make up England.

Shortly before I handed in my manuscript, my editor emailed me. 'Do you think you could call it British?' he asked. My heart sank, but it also gave me the resolve to lift my head and puff out my chest.

I am English (sort of) and I am proud of it, and this is my story of Living Englishly.

CHAPTER ONE

WHATEVER THE WEATHER

'Sunshine is delicious, rain is refreshing, wind braces us
up, snow is exhilarating; there is really no such thing as
bad weather, only different kinds of good weather.'
John Ruskin

Millbank Studios, opposite the Houses of Parliament, was a hive
of political activity as I made my way into the entrance hall.

'Hello Ben,' smiled a smart-looking man in full naval ceremonial dress.

'Hello sir.'

It was Lord West of Spithead, former First Sea Lord and Chief
of Naval Staff. During my Royal Naval Reserve days, he was kind
of a big deal. He also happens to be the father of my great friend,
Will.

'What are you doing here?' he enquired. 'About to climb
Everest?'

'I'm here to be a weather presenter.' At which point I think I lost his attention and he marched off towards Parliament with a wink.

I was ushered down a narrow corridor, through a high-security door and into a large TV studio, ITV Weather's dedicated meteorological nerve centre. I had decided that any quest in search of Englishness had to start with a visit to the place we go for our daily weather fix.

'Hello Ben,' smiled Lucy Verasamy. 'Cup of tea?' she asked (obeying rule one of Englishness).

There was no need for weather small talk here. Lucy is weather. She lives the weather and she loves the weather. 'What percentage of your life do you spend talking about the weather?' I asked.

'About fifty per cent,' she smiled.

When it comes to dinner-party conversation, Lucy's job must make her the best guest. All her weather small talk is big talk. She knows everything about it. She positively oozes weather fanaticism, speaking at 100mph. I thought I was good at talking until I met Lucy.

'Do you want to see the studio?'

I felt like a child in a sweet shop. I'm sure I'm not supposed to be this thrilled by a weather studio, but apparently I'm not alone. 'People do get pretty excited,' she admitted as we walked into a large empty room with a huge green piece of fabric hanging from the wall. 'Same one Harry Potter's cloak was made from,' she winked.

She walked onto her presenting mark and immediately an image of her standing in front of a large map of the British Isles appeared on one of the monitors. This is the picture of the professional weather presenter we're used to seeing.

Given that we can now access the weather from multiple sources, I wondered what the role of a weather presenter is in 2017.

'You can get weather apps, weather online, weather in social media, in the papers, on the radio,' she explained, 'but the weather presenter's role is to interpret that data and translate it for our viewers.' A digital weather report can't predict humidity, hay fever risk and all the other important effects of the conditions on our lives.

'What's the most common question?'

'"Is it going to snow at Christmas?" followed by "Will it be a hot summer?"'

You can't say we aren't predictable.

Of course, all weather presenters are now marked by the most notorious weather-presenting 'moment' on 15 October 1987, when Michael Fish got the forecast wrong in spectacular style. 'Earlier today a woman rang the BBC and said she'd heard there was a hurricane on the way. Don't worry. There isn't,' he announced cheerily during the weather slot on the *One O'Clock News* that day. That night, force 11 winds gusted across the south of England for several hours, uprooting 15 million trees and causing total mayhem. Fish's legendary 'blooper forecast' has since had more than half a million hits on YouTube.

In a typically English way, Fish has lived up to the 'gaffe' – though he maintains he was talking about a different storm system over the North Atlantic which didn't reach England, not the depression from the Bay of Biscay that caused the damage. He makes regular appearances on comedy shows, reliving the 'hurricane blooper' with self-deprecating humour. Thanks to the bankability of weather as a topic of interest to the English, the controversy has spun its own cultural sideshow. The term 'the Michael effect' was coined for the tendency ever since of weather presenters to predict a worst-case scenario in order to avoid being caught out. Fish appeared as guest presenter of the weather news on the twentieth anniversary of the Great Storm. A clip of his original bulletin was immortalized and given global exposure as part of a video montage in the opening ceremony of the London 2012 Summer Olympics.

Back in the 1980s and early 90s, weathermen really were a big deal. Ulrika Jonsson began her career as a 'weather girl', becoming the nation's sweetheart. Michael Fish's weather rival was John Kettley, and together they were immortalized in a 1988 novelty hit by A Tribe of Toffs from Sunderland, 'John Kettley is a Weatherman':

> John Kettley is a weatherman
> a weatherman
> a weatherman
> John Kettley is a weatherman
> And so is Michael Fish

'People still talk about Michael Fish,' Lucy marvels, 'even people who weren't born till after the storm.' It's one of my first observations about our obsession with the weather that weather forecasters can become national treasures. Lucy trained under the eye of another great weatherman, Francis Wilson. Amongst Francis' many accolades is he was the first to use computer-generated graphics on British television.

'Have a go on the weather map,' Lucy says. 'Use the map, but engage with the audience,' she explains as I stand in front of the invisible map 'hidden' in the green screen. I glance at the monitor and there, in full Technicolor glory, is my face and arms, gesticulating to the map.

'We are one of the few live TV broadcasts not to use autocue,' she says with pride.

Behind me on the television monitor is a map of Britain with moving weather arrows to show the direction of wind, and large green patches to show the rain and showers. More easily identifiable are the yellow and orange circles showing the temperature – the deeper the orange, the hotter the forecast temperature.

'It will begin cool in the south before getting warmer.' My attempt at presenting makes me feel slightly fraudulent. And then I remember that ITV Weather alone has 15 million viewers a week and realize the responsibility of the job.

The problem with Britain is that most of the big weather is in the north, while the majority of the dense populations are in the south. The result for a weather presenter can be arms waving wildly high and low on the map, like some Karate Kid impersonation. 'Francis always told me not to look like I was dancing or chopping with my arms,' Lucy explains.

'People love to grumble about the weather,' she smiles, 'too hot, too cold, too windy. I suppose it plays up to our national stereotype of a nation of grumblers.' Interestingly, she attributes the vast number of weather apps now available to our eternal search for 'the right weather': if people don't like a weather prediction, they will look for one that suits them. Trying to tame the untameable weather.

Lucy explains that there are several features that make the English weather what it is, changeable and famously unpredictable. As part of the United Kingdom, England lies between latitudes 50 and 56 degrees north. An island country, it sits on the western seaboard of the continent of Europe, surrounded by sea. The English live at a point where competing air masses meet, creating atmospheric instability and unsettled weather. In *The Teatime Islands*, my first book, I described England/Britain from the perspective of a faraway outpost as 'this small rainy island in Western Europe'.

On the other side of the country, our geographical position on the edge of the Atlantic places us at the end of a storm track, a relatively narrow area of ocean down which storms travel, driven by the prevailing winds. As the warm and cold air fly towards and over each other, the earth's rotation creates cyclones and the UK bears the tail end of them.

What makes our climate so mild is the Gulf Stream, which raises the temperature in the UK by up to 5°C in winter. It also adds moisture to the atmosphere, which makes it much harder to predict the weather as it adds to the number of variables that need to be forecast.

These variables mean vastly unpredictable weather. I can remember both snow at Easter and also such heat that the chocolate eggs were melting. November can be hotter than June, and winter often doesn't arrive until February. We are more likely to have snow at Easter than Christmas. We can wear T-shirts in November. It's all topsy-turvy, and that is what we *love* to talk about. Even within England, some regions are more susceptible than others to certain kinds of weather as the air masses jostle for dominance. North-west England is buffeted by the maritime polar air mass, which can bring frequent showers at any time of the year. North-east England is more exposed to the continental polar air mass, which brings cold dry air. The south and south-east are closest to the continental tropical air mass, which carries warm dry air. The south-west is the area most exposed to the maritime tropical air mass, which ushers in warm moist air. Wet, dry, warm, cold, it is a proper maelstrom. 'There's a lot of weather about today,' meteorological sages like to say mysteriously, as if the skies are full of gods of the elements whimsically calling the shots with thunderbolts and winds, lightning and storms. No wonder so many folk sayings 'reading the weather' remain popular. 'Red sky at night, shepherd's delight. Red sky in the morning, shepherd's warning' first appears in the Bible in the Gospel of Matthew but has led to variations such as 'Red sky at night, sailor's delight. Red sky in the morning, sailor's warning'. 'Rain before seven, fine by eleven' is another which emphasizes the variability of the weather systems passing over our green and pleasant land.

Lucy has presented hundreds if not thousands of weather reports over a decade. 'The thing about being a weather girl is that the weather always leads,' she smiles. 'We are merely the messengers, we can't change the weather.'

While it's fair to say I will probably never become a weatherman, at least Lucy has a warm studio in which she can shelter from the worst of the elements, which is a lot more than can be said for what is arguably England's most extreme forecasting job, that of the Fell Top Assessor. This was the next port of call in my English weather odyssey.

A bitter wind ripped across the car park as I made my way to the waiting Land Rover. It was midwinter and I was joining a man with one of the most unusual weather jobs in England.

I have always loved the Lake District. I will never forget the first time we went there as a family. I couldn't believe that England had such a magical, watery landscape. I still get that childhood excitement whenever I visit as I hurtle back to my childhood. It is the location of *Swallows and Amazons*.

But today I was in the Helvellyn range of mountains, between Thirlmere and Ullswater, ready to climb Helvellyn itself. It is a dramatic, rugged mountain – at 3,117ft the third-highest point in England – and from its summit, on a clear day, you can see Scotland and Wales. Alfred Wainwright, the celebrated fell walker and guide book author, described one ridge to Helvellyn Plateau as 'all bare rock, a succession of jagged fangs ending in a black tower', which makes the fact that there have been a number of fatalities on the mountain over the years understandable.

The rocks of Helvellyn were forged in the heat of an ancient volcano some 450 million years ago. It inspires poetry as well as respect for its dangers. Coleridge and Wordsworth both wrote about it. This is the final stanza of Wordsworth's poem 'To ——, on Her First Ascent to the Summit of Helvellyn':

> For the power of hills is on thee,
> As was witnessed through thine eye
> Then, when old Helvellyn won thee
> To confess their majesty!

The mountain has attracted lots of odd adventurers. In 1926, one man landed and took off from the summit in a small plane. Today, though, Helvellyn is arguably best known for one of the strangest weather-forecasting jobs in the world: that of the Fell Top Assessor, whose role is to assess both meteorological and ground conditions to provide an accurate local forecast for the estimated 15 million visitors to the Lake District National Park each year. The key is to check the ground underfoot and predict avalanche risks.

Dressed in multiple layers against the bitter wind, soon we were in the cloud as the temperature plummeted and the trail became increasingly icy. Thick grey cloud clung to the Cumbrian valleys. Drystone walls disappeared into the gloom as we began our hike. We were forced to strap crampons to our boots as we ascended the snow and ice. Gripping my ice axe in one hand, we beat into the wind that had dropped the temperature to a freezing minus 9°C. Ice formed on my eyelashes as we continued past half a dozen hardy mountaineers.

Soon we had reached the summit, where the Fell Top Assessor's real work begins. He pulled his tiny notebook from his jacket and assessed the conditions. Tiny horizontal icicles, known as hard rime, had formed on every surface, including us. These miniature formations of spiky ice grow into the wind, giving an indication of the prevailing winds on the summit. Wind speed and wind chill measured, within minutes he had gathered the necessary data, and after a quick mug of tepid tea from a Thermos flask, we began our descent.

Every day, come rain or shine, wind or snow, storm or hurricane, the Fell Top Assessor climbs the peak to report on weather conditions from the summit. That's *every* day. Working seven days on and seven days off, the two assessors will take it in turns to make the daily climb, often braving temperatures as low as minus 16°C. It is estimated that the fell top assessors climb the equivalent of Everest every two weeks.

Unsurprisingly, candidates must have 'considerable winter mountaineering experience and skills, preferably with a mountaineering qualification', according to the job description, which continues, 'You will provide information and advice to other fell users to ensure safe and responsible use of the mountain. You will also identify and carry out basic rights of way maintenance on the routes.' Other skills required include the ability to write concise reports, assess snow and ice conditions and use a map and compass.

Jon Bennet, who has been a fell top assessor on Helvellyn for eight years, says: 'Fell top assessing is the best job, and to be out in the hills doing something as worthwhile as this is a perfect combination.' The job is not without its perils, however, as several walkers have lost their lives on the peak in recent years.

In October 2016 Robert Pascoe, a 24-year-old RAF engineer, was killed when he lost his footing while walking with a companion on the Striding Edge side of Helvellyn and fell 650ft down the mountain. In 2010, Alan Burns, thirty-nine, from Preston, Lancashire, suffered fatal head injuries in a fall from Swirral Edge. Three days later, Philip Ashton, forty-three, from St Helens, Merseyside, fell from the same ridge while walking with friends and died later in hospital.

Yet Helvellyn is one of the most popular fells with walkers in winter and summer, attracting ramblers and experienced mountaineers who come to enjoy the views and the diverse topography. And the Striding Edge route to the summit is one of the busiest.

And as far as jobs go, being the Fell Top Assessor probably beats sitting in front of a computer screen for eight hours a day. At least, that's what the adventurer in me thinks. More generally, the job tells me that English people are prepared to go to any extreme to provide others with the most precise information about the weather.

'What's the weather like?' asked my mother as I clung to the side of a tiny rowing boat in the middle of the Atlantic Ocean. I was on a satellite phone, 1,500 miles from land, and my mother was asking about the weather.

'Warm, a little rain, beautiful cloud formations,' I answered. 'What about you? Is it cold?'

'Freezing, I had to scrape a thick layer of ice off the car.'

'We're expecting rain later.' I replied.

I was six weeks into a gruelling and frankly rather dangerous bid to row across the Atlantic Ocean, and my rare link to the outside world via satellite phone was dominated by chats about the weather. How English is that?

We *love* to talk about the weather. It's all about the weather. I have lost count of the number of conversations I have had around the world that have been about weather. And now here I was on one of my most dangerous trips, and my mother's main concern was the prevailing weather conditions.

The first time I met the Queen (apologies for the humble brag there – very unEnglish, maybe it's the Canadian part of me coming out), it was at Windsor Castle. It was December and I was, quite honestly, a little nervous. She had gathered the great and the good from the world of rural and agricultural life to celebrate the countryside.

'What am I going to talk to her about?' I worried as I made my way to Windsor. There were so many things I could tell her, about the places I had been and the adventures I had experienced. I would tell her about Antarctica, and of the time I met a tribe in the jungles of Papua New Guinea. Perhaps I would recall meeting the Prince Philip Island cult, or the time I met some of her Labradors.

'It's terribly cold, Ma'am, isn't it?' I smiled as I shook her gloved hand.

'Warmer than last December. Though we could do with a little rain,' she replied.

We both nodded, and she headed off to chat to the next guest.

And that just about sums it up. My first opportunity to chat to Her Majesty, and I talked about the weather.

I have found myself in the most unlikely situations around the world discussing the nuances of the English weather. And here's the thing: we don't really have weather. As Lucy Verasamy told me, it can be a little rainy, a little windy, sometimes a bit sunny – but let's be honest, the strangest thing about the English weather is that it's all a little *meh*. Compared to other countries it really is quite benign.

If you doubt me here, just take a trip to the Andes, or Borneo or even the US, and you will see what I mean by BIG weather. I'm talking about hurricanes, tornadoes, freezes, heatwaves. In England we have variables, but most of our weather-related conversations revolve around too much rain, or too little rain, or it being too warm, or too cold. And that is about it. It amazes me that we are capable of talking about the weather so fluidly and constantly when it varies so little.

Visitors from abroad are thoroughly bemused by the English fixation with the weather – because the only extreme aspect of our weather is its changeability. The conditions our climate might usher in from one day to the next induce inordinate anxiety, even though we technically 'enjoy' a temperate climate, with temperatures rarely falling lower than 0°C in winter or rising higher than 32°C in summer. English weather plays out its repertoire of conditions right in the middle of the range of potential hazards – certainly without the blizzards, tornadoes, hurricanes, killer heatwaves and monsoons that plague other geographical zones. We don't have to batten down storm hatches, switch to snow tyres or build homes to strict storm mitigation codes (as they do in New England). We don't have companies offering storm-chasing adventure holidays. It is said that, on average, an English citizen will experience three major weather events in their lifetime. The singular characteristic of the English weather is that it changes frequently and unexpectedly.

And this leads on to another point about our relationship with our weather: our propensity to complain about it. This is at odds with the Blitz-like spirit of 'mustn't grumble', but we do. I think we have a tendency to be a pessimistic nation, particularly when it comes to the weather. Is there such a thing as ideal weather for the English? Isn't it always too hot or too cold, a bit grey or intolerably windy, unbearably humid or relentlessly drizzly? It's rarely right.

How many times have you heard someone saying the weather is perfect? Even on those rare cloudless, windless summer days of unbroken blue sky, there is often some reason to lament the weather: 'It's too hot', 'The grass is turning brown', 'We need rain', 'Careful or you'll get sunburn'. You get the point.

But somehow the weather is part of our psyche. It may have something to do with our geographical location in the North Atlantic and the resulting propensity for it to rain.

Here are some English weather stats. The hottest recorded temperature was 38.5°C (101.3°F) in Faversham in Kent on 10 August 2003. The hottest month in England is August, which is usually 2°C hotter than July and 3°C hotter than September. The sunniest month was over 100 years ago, when 383.9 hours (the equivalent of thirty-two 12-hour days) of sunshine were recorded in Eastbourne, Sussex in July 1911. The lowest August temperature was minus 2°C on 28 August 1977 in Moor House, Cumbria. Highest rainfall in 24 hours was 10.98in (279mm) on 18 July 1955 in Martinstown, Dorset. The largest amount of rain in just one hour was 3.62in (92mm) in Maidenhead in Berkshire on 12 July 1901. The lowest temperature recorded in England was minus 26.1°C at Newport in Shropshire on 10 January 1982.

Wherever I am in the world, I am asked about the weather at home. I never know whether this is genuine curiosity about the renowned unpredictability of English weather or a reliable conversational gambit – an ice breaker, so to speak – because it is assumed that anyone hailing from England is totally fixated on the weather. As Professor Higgins told Eliza Doolittle when he launched her into society in the film *My Fair Lady*, it is advisable when making conversation to 'stick to the weather and everybody's health'.

It's true that the English always hope for a White Christmas or a Summer Scorcher, and worry about a Bank Holiday Wash-Out or a Big Freeze. Weather warrants capital letters. It has status in everyday life. But the obsession is not just with the big picture; it is about the minutiae of each day's conditions. There is no doubt that the English are genetically tuned to be on tenterhooks as to (a) what the weather is looking like each morning and (b) whether conditions are exactly as have been forecast.

We secretly like the fact that our weather continually takes us by surprise, often several times in the course of one day. The changeability of the weather has been a source of marvel, anxiety and unfailing interest since the year dot. In 1758 Samuel Johnson wrote an entire essay entitled 'Discourses on the Weather'. 'It is commonly observed,' he pointed out, 'that when two Englishmen meet, their first talk is of the weather; they are in haste to tell each other, what each must already know, that it is hot or cold, bright or cloudy, windy or calm ...' He went on to explain that

An Englishman's notice of the weather is the natural consequence of changeable skies and uncertain seasons. In many parts of the world, wet weather and dry are regularly expected at certain periods; but in our island, every man goes to sleep, unable to guess whether he shall behold in the morning a bright or cloudy atmosphere, whether his rest shall be lulled by a shower or broken by tempest.

So, long before our national addiction to social-media alerts, breaking newsflashes and live online updates, the English had the weather to spice up conversation on an almost minute-by-minute basis.

Enter a particularly English social stereotype: the weather obsessive. An article in *Country Life* in 29 August 2012 surveyed the type, which has existed since medieval times. 'Who, from the hotly contended field, takes the Golden Barometer as Britain's most possessed weather obsessive?' asked Antony Woodward.

Would it be William Merle, the so-called Father of Meteorology, who had the curious idea of keeping a daily weather journal in 1277, persisting doggedly for 67 years? Or William Murphy Esq, MNS (Member of No Society), Cork scientist and author of little repute, whose 1840 Weather Almanac (on scientific principles, showing the state of the weather for every day of the year), despite correctly predicting the weather for only one day, became a bestseller?

How about Thomas Stevenson, one of 'the Lighthouse Stevensons', who measured the force of an ocean wave with his 'wave dynamometer' before going on to devise the Stevenson Screen weather station? Admiral Beaufort, perhaps, whose eponymous wind scale sailors still use? Or the artist John Constable, whose 'skying' cloud paintings ushered in a new scientific approach to the depiction of the heavens? Dr George Merryweather, inventor, is surely a contender for his 12-leech 'tempest prognosticator'. Then there's poor Group Capt J. M. Stagg, on whose knotted shoulders rested the decision of whether to go, or not to go, on D Day. Or perhaps it's the humble Mr Grisenthwaite, who's assiduously kept a two-decade lawn-mowing diary (and why not?) that was, in 2005, accepted by the Royal Meteorological Society as documentary evidence of climate change?

In all honesty, I'm surprised that there aren't more examples of English people obsessed with our weather.

And the funny thing is, we still look to the weather for daily interest – even more so, now we have a myriad of forecasting apps, widgets and websites with names like Accuweather, Dark Sky, Raintoday, Weather Bomb, Radarscope and so on. Rather than eradicating uncertainty about how the day will pan out, forecasts with detailed features surely useful only to a few – such as hourly UV level predictions and dew point information – simply add more variables to a reliable topic of conversation.

'Lovely day, isn't it?'

'Yes! It's 17°C, but at 3 p.m. it will feel like 12°C because of an east wind blowing in with a chill factor of minus 5!'

Amateur meteorology is a quintessentially English hobby, requiring kit, dedication and lots of specialist vocabulary. All over England people have set up independent weather stations in their own back gardens with hygrometers, anemometers and sunshine recorders. To join this club you need a Stevenson Screen, a sort of box which is the standard means of sheltering instruments such as wet and dry bulb thermometers, used to record humidity and air temperature. Every aspect of its structure and setting is specified by the World Meteorological Organisation, which states for example that it should be kept 1.25m above the ground to avoid strong temperature gradients at ground level. It should have louvred sides to allow free passage of air. Its double roof, walls and floors must be painted white to reflect heat radiation. Its doors should open towards the pole to minimize disturbance when reading in daylight, and so on. As one observer has quipped, 'It's like bee-keeping without the bees. The Stevenson Screen even looks like a beehive.'

Often, weather watching is done for a purpose. Pilots, especially of gliders and microlights, need to find optimum windows for their sport. Ditto sailors. Surfing has introduced a whole new meteorological community: wind and waves can be constantly monitored via mobile phone and laptop before the dash down to find ideal surf at West Wittering or Newquay.

One thing the English weather can be relied upon to do is to throw up all sorts of dramatic variations, such as the infamous 'wrong kind of snow'. This phrase became a byword for euphemistic excuses after the broadcaster James Naughtie interviewed British Rail's Director of Operations, Terry Worrall, asking him to explain how a period of light snowfall could have caused such severe disruption to services in February 1991. The laughable exchange went like this:

> WORRALL: 'We are having particular problems with the type of snow, which is rare in the UK.'
> NAUGHTIE: 'Oh, I see, it was the wrong kind of snow.'
> WORRALL: 'No, it was a different kind of snow.'

Despite this attention to every nuance of different types of inclement weather, the English always seem to be endearingly ill-prepared for a change in conditions. There is an almost annual fuss about why the gritters haven't treated the roads before icy conditions strike. Who has a can of de-icer to hand on the first few days it's forecast to freeze? And who is ever dressed appropriately for weather different from that seen from the window first thing in the morning? We are as addicted to weather-watching as we might be to a long-running soap opera, only in this case the drama comes from being caught out by a sudden shower or ambushed by a freak hailstorm. In July 2006, higher than average temperatures caused a series of power blackouts in central London, closing shops and businesses in the West End, due to the unforeseen amount of electricity used by air conditioners. That could only happen in England. Our weather may have prompted the invention of waterproof outerwear and the Wellington boot, but we rarely seem to be prepared. Perhaps it's a case of hope over expectation? In Wimbledon, we host the world's greatest tennis tournament, the only Grand Slam contested on grass – a surface which means play has to stop with every raindrop, unlike the clay of Roland Garros where play continues in drizzle. We persist in picnicking in less than ideal weather. Why not? It's what we do. We're English!

Even when prevailing conditions tend to be overcast (England has an average of one in three days of sunshine), the topic itself is never dull. What other country's newspapers print daily photographs of morning mist, evening cloud formations, thunderous skies marbled with lightning or spectacular moody sunrises? What other language has so many weather-based phrases? The

English can be 'under the weather' or 'as right as rain', 'snowed under' or 'on cloud nine'; we have 'fair-weather friends', we 'sail close to the wind', find 'every cloud has a silver lining' and, if we're lucky, rejoice in 'a windfall'. Or so many ways of describing cold: chilly, nippy, fresh, freezing, icy, parky, raw, snappy, numbing, cool, crisp, brisk, bleak, wintry, snowy, frosty, icy-cold, glacial, polar, arctic, sharp, bitter, biting, piercing? And that's without all the regional dialect or slang. What other nation's government would commission a survey to find out how often the average citizen mentions the weather? (YouGov in 2011 found that the average Briton comments on the weather at least once every six hours.) Where else is the population so pinned to its meteorological environment?

Well, perhaps there is one reason. The English can be thankful to the weather for many random legacies that affect aspects of our lives.

It was weather that inspired the most popular hymn in the English language, 'Amazing Grace'. An intense Atlantic storm in March 1748 so terrified slave-ship master John Newton when travelling aboard a slave trader en route to Ireland that he prayed for divine mercy. Twenty years later, Newton, now a minister and ardent abolitionist, referred to his 'great deliverance' and described his salvation in a hymn co-written with the poet William Cowper:

> Amazing grace! (How sweet the sound)
> That sav'd a wretch like me!
> I once was lost, but now am found,
> Was blind, but now I see.

It was prolonged snowfall in 1908 that resulted in the invention of the windscreen wiper. Gladstone Adams was travelling back to his Newcastle home after driving down to Crystal Palace Park to support Newcastle United against Wolverhampton Wanderers in the FA Cup final. The snow was so heavy he had to continually pull off the road to clear snow from his windscreen. Furious, he folded down the windscreen and arrived home frozen, vowing to invent some mechanical means of keeping the windscreen clear. Three years later he patented a design: it was never built, but the prototype is on display at Newcastle's Discovery Museum.

We owe so much to unpredictability and variety. Would Turner, perhaps the greatest English artist, be so celebrated as a painter of light and atmospheric effects if he lived in a country without so much fog, light rain, storms and volatile cloud formations? Would the Glastonbury festival be the renowned event it is without the mud and the fashionable way with wellies? The iconic cover of the Beatles' 1969 *Abbey Road* album – with Paul, John, Ringo and George filing across a zebra crossing – would not include the quirky touch of a barefoot McCartney had he not whimsically decided to discard shoes and socks due to the sweltering heat on the day it was shot.

The Norman Conquest, 1066 and all that, might never have happened: stormy weather in the Channel allowed William to land unopposed. Wind and a violent storm saved us from invasion by sinking the Spanish Armada in 1588.

The weather throughout history has given telling insights. On 9 February 1649, for example – the day Charles I was due to be beheaded – it was so cold that the Thames had frozen. Records reveal that Charles was led to the scaffold wearing two shirts. He had taken the precaution so that he would not shiver in front of the huge crowd, giving the impression that he was afraid. 'I would have no imputation of fear,' he said. 'I do not fear death.'

I'm not done with the weather in this book. There is still so much to explore, but so far I think we can safely say that as a nation we love to talk about the weather. Or perhaps we love to grumble about it. Our forecasters are household names and often national treasures, and we have people so dedicated to giving us the most accurate information that they'll risk life and limb in the process. The weather seeps into our national fabric, from our language to our inventions to our history.

No one has put it quite as well as the New Zealand band Crowded House, who might be commenting on the New Zealand weather but it rings so true about our weather:

'Everywhere you go, always take the weather with you ...'

CHAPTER TWO

THE SHIPPING FORECAST

'And now the Shipping Forecast, issued by the
Met Office on behalf of the Maritime and
Coastguard Agency at 05:00 today.'

I am in Central London. It's 4.30 a.m. and the sun is beginning to
rise on England's capital city. The sky is streaked with long red
wisps of orange and red on a canvas of pale blue sky. Heavy grey
smudges of rain hang across the horizon, dropping midsummer
rain. Flocks of green parakeets dance from tree to tree in Regent's
Park as I head towards Portland Place and one of the most iconic
components of our establishment, the BBC.

I have worked for the BBC for nearly two decades and many
of its programmes are rightly considered national treasures: *The
Archers, Blue Peter, Desert Island Discs* … but for me it has always
been the Shipping Forecast, the five-minute weather update for
mariners, that symbolizes all that is great about this institution.

I can remember as a child hearing the forecast, marvelling at the often alien-sounding names and wondering what it all meant. The curious mix of words: Viking, Dogger, German Bight. They were so strange and exotic and mysterious. I was enthralled, and that fascination has lasted a lifetime – at home I still have a large map on which each area is labelled and marked off.

I have visited all of the regions; I have experienced the best and the worst of the weather, on land and at sea. But I had never visited the home of the Shipping Forecast … until now.

Chris Aldridge, the senior announcer at BBC Radio 4, invited me to sit in one morning. And so it was that, long before London had woken, I found myself journeying across the deserted city to Broadcasting House. Chris has been reading the shipping forecast for over twenty years and calculates that he has intoned the names of the familiar locations over three thousand times.

Broadcasting House was deserted except for a couple of security guards in the lobby. 'Hi Ben,' grinned Chris as he ushered me up through the doors. 'Sorry about the early start.' Up on the fourth floor, the *Today* programme office was a hive of activity as they prepared for their Monday morning show. Justin Webb and Sarah Montague sat in silence in the middle of the office preparing their scripts,

'Morning.' I smiled, trying to look cool and unflappable. 'Nice weather!' I added. What was I doing talking about the weather with the country's premier news presenters? The Radio 4 *Today* programme is another BBC institution and I was a little in awe.

'Here we go,' said Chris, settling me into the small studio, where a bank of televisions were broadcasting various news channels. In the middle was a huge digital clock. It read 5.13 a.m.

'This is Matt, our producer,' he introduced me. 'And this is Stav.' Stavros Danaos, one of the BBC's weather forecasters, sat at the microphone clutching his notes and the all-important forecast.

5.20. 'A minute to broadcast,' announced Matt through the headphones.

Stav cleared his throat as Chris introduced the Shipping Forecast.

There is not one individual who is *the* voice of the Shipping Forecast. I knew that there must be more than one because I had heard both male and female presenters reading the forecast, but I was surprised to hear that there are as many as twenty who rotate.

The complexities of the data to non-mariners mean that new presenters must take a special Shipping Forecast course to learn the significance of each piece of information, ensuring the correct intonation. 'You must learn not to say "Gale 8" with a rising intonation on the 8,' explained Chris as Stav prepared to deliver his missive to mariners across the British Isles, 'On the Beaufort Scale, 8 *is* a gale, therefore it's important not to read it with a raised intonation, but to lift the 9 afterwards.'

Stav's smooth voice delivered the information with confidence and authority. It was strange hearing it produced in such neutral surroundings, given all the years of listening to it while being buffeted by gales.

And now the shipping forecast issued by the Met Office, on
　　behalf of the Maritime and Coastguard Agency, at 0505
　　UTC* on Monday 3rd July 2017.
There are warnings of gales in Trafalgar.
The general synopsis at midnight:
High Scandinavia 1038, expected Norwegian Sea 1036 by
　　0600 tomorrow. Low 200 miles west of Sole 994 expected
　　Fitzroy 1001 by same time.
The area forecasts for the next 24 hours:
Viking, North Utsire, North South Utsire: Variable 3 or 4.
　　Slight, occasionally moderate. Fair. Good.
South Utsire, South Forties: Easterly or northeasterly 5 to 7.
　　Moderate or rough. Showers. Good.
North Forties, Cromarty: Easterly 4 or 5, occasionally
　　6 in south. Moderate, occasionally rough. Showers.
　　Good.
Forth, Tyne, Dogger: East or northeast 5 or 6. Moderate.
　　Showers. Good.
Fisher: Northeast 5 to 7. Moderate or rough. Showers.
　　Good.
German Bight, Humber: Northeast 5 or 6. Slight or
　　moderate. Showers. Good.
Thames, Dover: Mainly east or northeast 4 or 5, occasionally
　　6 later. Slight or moderate. Showers. Moderate or good.
Wight, Portland: East 4 or 5, occasionally 6 later. Slight or
　　moderate. Showers. Good.

---

* *UTC stands for Universal Co-ordinated Time – the new international term for
GMT.*

Plymouth: East or southeast 5 to 7. Moderate or rough.
Showers. Good.

Biscay: Southeast backing east 5 to 7, perhaps gale 8 later.
Moderate or rough. Occasional rain or showers. Mainly
good.

South Fitzroy: Southerly at first in east, otherwise westerly
becoming cyclonic later, 5 or 6. Moderate or rough,
becoming rough or very rough. Occasional rain or
thundery showers. Good, occasionally poor.

North Fitzroy, Sole: Southeasterly backing easterly 6 to gale
8, occasionally severe gale 9, becoming cyclonic 5 or 6 for
a time in west. Rough or very rough, occasionally high
later. Occasional rain. Good, occasionally poor.

Lundy, Fastnet: Southeast backing east 5 to 7. Moderate or
rough. Showers. Good.

Irish Sea: East or northeast 5 or 6. Slight or moderate.
Showers. Good.

Shannon: Southeast 7 to severe gale 9, backing east 5 to 7.
Rough or very rough. Occasional rain. Good, occasionally
poor.

Southwest Rockall: Southeasterly 5 to 7. Rough or very
rough. Fair. Good.

Northeast Rockall, Malin, Hebrides, Bailey: Southeasterly 5
or 6. Moderate or rough. Fair. Good.

Fair Isle: Easterly or southeasterly 3 or 4, occasionally 5 in
southwest. Slight or moderate. Fair. Good.

Faeroes: South or southeast 4 or 5, occasionally 6 later. Slight
or moderate, becoming moderate or rough later. Mainly
fair. Good.

Southeast Iceland: Southerly or southeasterly 5 or 6.
Moderate or rough. Occasional rain, mainly in west, fog
patches at first. Moderate or good, occasionally very poor
at first.

Once Stav had finished, Matt's voice came through the headphones, 'Listen to this,' and with the click of a button, the clean,
clear forecast became slightly distorted with the crackle of inter-
ference. 'You're hearing it through a shortwave transistor radio
we have hidden in the depths of the BBC,' he explained. 'We use
it to ensure we are still broadcasting and to check what the listeners are hearing.'

I loved the idea that a tiny old-fashioned radio, gathering
cobwebs somewhere in a largely forgotten office, was still in use
while the rest of the building hummed with the latest in broadcasting equipment.

Even though most modern ships have on-board technology
that gives the same information, even though much of the listening audience has no need of maritime weather bulletins, the
Shipping Forecast retains its unique, otherworldly authority no
matter which BBC reader intones the strict 370-word summary.
It's also a pointer to many of our seafaring traditions and accom-
plishments. Take the Beaufort Scale as an example – another of
England's meteorological gifts to the world, born from our rich
weather patterns and unique maritime heritage.

The scale was devised in 1805 by Francis Beaufort, a Royal
Navy officer on HMS *Woolwich*. Measurements of wind speed at
the time were highly subjective, so the reports were unreliable.
Beaufort devised a way of standardizing the strength of the wind,

at first simply in terms of its effects on the sails of the Royal Navy's frigates: from 'just sufficient to give steerage' to 'that which no canvas sails could withstand'. As steam power arrived, the scale was changed to reflect the prevailing sea conditions rather than the effect on the fast-disappearing sails. In 1946, tropical cyclones – forces 13–17 – were added to the scale.

The shipping forecast itself can be traced back to 1853, when Captain Robert Fitzroy – the captain of HMS *Beagle*, made famous by Charles Darwin – was tasked with finding a way to predict the weather in order to reduce the growing number of Royal Navy and trading vessels lost around Britain's coast. He set up fifteen weather stations around the coastline which together started to provide a version of the weather forecast by 1861. In 1911 the information was sent in Morse code to ships and then, sixty years after those fifteen weather stations were set up, in 1921, it was broadcast on the radio, marking the birth of the Shipping Forecast.

Fitzroy's original weather stations were based on locations and geographical features. North and South Utsire, Wight, Lundy, Fastnet, Hebrides, Fair Isle, Faeroes and Southeast Iceland were all named after islands, many of which I have been to – including the notoriously stormy Rockall, which true to form was lashed by gales. I still feel sick just thinking about it. German Bight was formerly known as Heligoland, an island that once belonged to Britain before we swapped it and the Caprivi Strip – a small protrusion of land in Namibia – with the Germans in exchange for Zanzibar.

Forties, Dogger, Sole and Bailey were named after sandbanks, while Thames, Humber, Shannon, Cromarty and Forth carried the names of rivers. Dover and Portland were called after the respective towns. Biscay and Irish Sea are named after, well, seas. Finally, Finisterre, Trafalgar and Malin are all headlands.

Perhaps the biggest controversy to hit the Shipping Forecast came in 2002 when the Met Office agreed to change the name of Finisterre to Fitzroy, after the forecast's founder. Finisterre is also used by the Spanish meteorological office in its shipping forecast to refer to a different, much smaller area.

So controversial was the decision that the United Nations World Meteorological Organisation (can you believe such a thing actually exists?) was called to adjudicate. They ruled that the name change was unlawful. The British press were furious that another nation would meddle in our shipping affairs, and the name stuck.

As an island and a seafaring nation, we are particularly proud of our coast and the waters that surround us. The weather and the oceans have played a pivotal role in our history and lives. And the people who work the waters and the coastline – like fishermen and lighthouse keepers – have always struck me as playing a rich and important part in our national identity.

My own relationship with the ocean goes deep. Despite my central London roots I have spent a great deal of time on or next to the ocean, from a year marooned on a deserted island in the Scottish Outer Hebrides to several months rowing across the Atlantic, not to mention a spell flirting with joining the Royal Navy when I was a student. A keen sailor, I have also spent many years aboard yachts all around the English coastline.

While studying at Portsmouth University on the south coast I enrolled in the University Royal Naval Unit. I was enthralled by naval history and would often disappear into another world as we held formal dinners below deck on HMS *Victory* in Portsmouth Harbour. The Royal Navy and Portsmouth were steeped in a rich and tangible maritime history. I became a midshipman officer aboard HMS *Blazer*, a small grey P200 Fast Patrol Boat into which we somehow managed to cram nearly a dozen people per voyage.

It was a baptism of fire for a lazy university student. I would spend my week drinking, sleeping and generally missing lectures, and weekends washing the heads (toilets) with a toothbrush and being shouted at by higher ranks. HMS *Blazer*'s permanent crew were technically lower ranking than us, but we all knew where the authority lay and the regular sailors took great pride in making life as much of a misery as possible.

Truth be told, I loved the regimen of life aboard a naval vessel. In spite of the storms and the language and the discipline and the sleepless night shifts and the impossible navigation, there was something rather marvellous and English about the Navy. We took our small grey war vessel on foreign deployments as far afield as Norway and Gibraltar, where we would often host foreign powers' First Sea Lords. I wondered frequently whether they ever realized we were mere university students dressed in our finest officers' jackets. I shall never forget my time in Dartmouth at the Royal Britannia Naval College. It still gives me tremendous pride that I played a tiny part in our rich naval heritage.

Throughout all of these maritime experiences, there has been one constant: the Shipping Forecast. I have listened to the Shipping Forecast in most of the regions included in the report.

I have been on fishing trawlers, naval warships, yachts and remote islands, listening in to London. Often, the contrast between the conditions in the sea areas referred to and the calm of the BBC studio in which the report is read could not be more marked. There was always something reassuring about the smooth tones of the BBC reader's voice as it crackled through the ship's radio delivering the update from the Met Office, but I often wondered whether the reader had any idea under what conditions the words were being listened to.

While I endured gales, rain and storms, I would imagine the calmness of London. The way the reader announced storm force winds without a hint of worry or drama was always a comfort. The report was utterly literal. Fact. No hype or drama. No jeopardy – that was hidden within the forecast in the numbers of the Beaufort Scale. You never wanted to hear of anything above a 10. The Shipping Forecast above all had the ability to transport me to a different place, more often than not a slightly nicer, calmer one.

There is a school of thought that the Shipping Forecast is much more than purely weather information. Some consider it poetry; others a national anthem of sorts. However you see it – and poets, musicians, rock bands, comedians, film makers, video game designers continue to draw inspiration from it – the BBC broadcast attracts hundreds of thousands of daily listeners who have no technical need to know their Dogger from their Lundy.

It is treasured just as it is – from its idiosyncratic vocabulary, whereby winds are either veering (changing clockwise) or backing (changing anti-clockwise), to its sense that there is, beyond the individual stresses and concerns we might ponder as we lie tucked up cosily in bed, a truly wild maritime world out there.

Some fans go as far as to describe it as an adult lullaby, a soporific comfort that helps them nod off at the end of a long day. There is no doubt that it has evolved into a quirky but much-loved national institution, as intrinsic as the Houses of Parliament or fish and chips.

In the opening ceremony for the 2012 London Olympic Games, the Shipping Forecast was played with the accompaniment of Elgar's 'Nimrod' to represent Britain's maritime heritage. Such is its popularity, the BBC iPlayer website retains a collection of humorous and lyrical clips, even a quiz. It's been read by playwright Alan Bennett. Its form and formulaic language have been borrowed to create a rap version called 'Snoop Doggy Dogger' and applied satirically to the world of politics and sport. Artists, musicians, writers, comedians and even politicians have lined up to both satirize and pay tribute to its distinctive tones: these include Seamus Heaney, Blur, Stephen Fry, Frank Muir, Radiohead, British Sea Power and Carol Ann Duffy. And there have been a few celebrity readings, such as that by former Deputy Prime Minister John Prescott, who read the forecast in 2011 to raise awareness of Red Nose Day. When it came to his native Humber, he deliberately dropped the 'H' and said: "Umber, as we say it up there.' Once, in 1995, a plan was mooted to move the late-night broadcast back by twelve minutes – prompting a fierce debate in Parliament and fierce newspaper outrage. The Shipping Forecast remained anchored in the schedule at 0048. Everyone, it seems, loves the Shipping Forecast.

How can I sum up the forecast's appeal to those who don't technically need it? Mark Damazer, the Controller of BBC Radio 4, nails it: 'It scans poetically. It's got a rhythm of its own. It's eccentric, it's unique, it's English. It's slightly mysterious because nobody really knows where these places are. It takes you into a faraway place that you can't really comprehend unless you're one of these people bobbing up and down in the Channel.'

Zeb Soanes, a regular Shipping Forecast reader, who once fulfilled a listener's wish by delivering the forecast from the top of Orfordness lighthouse, touches on its emotional pull: 'To the non-nautical, it is a nightly litany of the sea. It reinforces a sense of being islanders with a proud seafaring past. Whilst the listener is safely tucked up in their bed, they can imagine small fishing boats bobbing about at Plymouth or 170ft waves crashing against Rockall.'

The purpose of the Shipping Forecast is to warn against the hazards of hostile weather. And as such it taps into an ancient impulse. Throughout history, the English have scanned the horizon along the country's 2,748 miles of coastline on the lookout for perils. We can call upon Shakespeare to express in the most lyrical terms how geography – a sense of place and its attendant climate – makes a people who they are. John of Gaunt's speech in *Richard II* beautifully crystallizes the English view of their 'scep-tre'd isle':

> This fortress built by Nature for herself
> Against infection and the hand of war,
> This happy breed of men, this little world;
> This precious stone set in the silver sea,
> Which serves it in the office of a wall,
> Or as a moat defensive to a house.

There hasn't been a successful invasion of our shores since 1066 – for 950 years – but still we keep an eye out to guard against threats. These are much more likely to be incoming weather formations than armadas or invading fleets. Our island existence depends on keeping a watchful eye over our waters. The Shipping Forecast subliminally reassures us that someone is doing that.

The English language is full of vocabulary, phrases and idioms that reveal its people come from maritime stock. For example: the Romans arrived in AD 53, and stayed not just as imperial administrators, but also as traders and tellers of stories of the Christian 'cult' of Jesus alongside their pagan deities. A few centuries later, when Christianity had become established, the main body of the churches built all over the country at the centre of communities became known as the nave, from the Latin for ship, *navis*. The name came as a natural transfer of associated ideas. Like ships that introduced the religion, naves contain a body of people.

Until mass air travel became the norm in the late 1950s, and the Channel Tunnel opened in 1994, marine transport was the only way for anyone to reach the English or for the English to reach the rest of Europe and the world. That's why maritime trade and the Royal Navy have always had such great importance. We send boats and ships out on missions (naval, commercial, leisure) and receive incoming vessels only by invitation or by arrangement with the harbourmaster.

And as a nation, we spend a lot of time out on the water. In fine weather there's nothing the English like more than pootling around in a dinghy or on a raft, feeling the sea air on their face on a bracing coastal walk, or enjoying a bucket and spade holiday on a stretch of sand. To live in a cottage by the sea has long been a

dream of those approaching retirement. The fashion for afford-
able package holidays by the seaside was consolidated when Billy
Butlin established a chain of hotels at locations such as Bognor,
Blackpool, Skegness, Barry Island, Ayr and Clacton. Our
top-rated chefs prize seaweed as 'sea herbs' and fight to stop all
our hand picking of our own supplies. As no one lives more than
a hundred miles from the coastline and many rivers have tidal
reaches, the screech of seagulls is as familiar as the siren call of
the fair-weather ice cream van. The hinterland behind the coastline is dotted with woods, hollows and tunnels romantically
suspected to have once served as hiding places for smugglers'
contraband. Nautical novels are noted bestsellers, from C. S.
Forester's Hornblower books to Patrick O'Brian's twenty-volume
Aubrey–Maturin series of novels, set in the early nineteenth
century and following the lives and careers of Captain Jack
Aubrey and his friend, naval physician Dr Stephen Maturin.

So many quintessentially English passions are built on
sea-based stories, from the rock music popularized by pirate
radio in the 1960s – broadcast from offshore ships or disused sea
forts, providing music for a generation not yet served by legal
radio services – to the notion of an ocean cruise as the dream
once-in-a-lifetime holiday. Personal challenges and stories
revolve around the sea too: to swim the English Channel, to row
across the Atlantic, to circumnavigate the British Isles. We are
bound to the sea in a way that infuses our whole national
mindset.

Take the fast-food dish we gave to the world: fish and chips.
Piping hot fish and chips wrapped in newspaper, doused in salt
and vinegar, is what foreigners think we eat outside as a comfort

on cold and wintry days. And even today, with the invasion of fast food from America and elsewhere, it is estimated there are still eight fish and chip shops for every McDonald's.

Finally, it is impossible to document our English maritime heritage without mention of the Royal National Lifeboat Institution. As a child I can remember my pride in raising money for the iconic RNLI. I had one of their famous lifeboat donation tins, which I used to fill over the course of the year. It is almost impossible to visit any beach or coastal village in England without seeing the famous RNLI flag, although I'm sure few of us notice it, because it's so familiar.

The RNLI has saved more than 140,000 lives since 1824. Today it is staffed almost exclusively by 4,600 volunteers – who provide search and rescue at sea as well as lifeguard cover at over 150 English beaches. Their work is invaluable in sustaining our proud island nation status.

Back at Broadcasting House, Chris explains why he thinks the Shipping Forecast is so popular. 'Many of the names are unfamiliar to people apart from the context of the Shipping Forecast, so it turns our landscape into a slightly ethereal world, inhabited by communities we are connected to but know nothing about. It's something that binds us together when so much divides us.'

I'm struck by how true this is. The Shipping Forecast is many things to many people – essential information, a lullaby to send them to sleep, a poem, a song, a comfort in times of stress or danger at sea. Perhaps above all, though, it reminds us who we are: an island people in the Atlantic who naturally, instinctively, look to sea.

CHAPTER THREE

HEROIC FAILURES

If you can keep your head when all about you
Are losing theirs and blaming it on you;
If you can trust yourself when all men doubt you,
But make allowance for their doubting too:
If you can wait and not be tired by waiting,
Or being lied about, don't deal in lies,
Or being hated, don't give way to hating,
And yet don't look too good, nor talk too wise …
Rudyard Kipling, 'If'

'Success is overrated. We all crave it despite daily
evidence that our real genius lies in exactly the opposite
direction. Incompetence is what we are good at.'
Stephen Pile, *The Book of Heroic Failures*

Heroes come in all shapes and sizes, but for me there is one hero who defines Englishness. He's not a lantern-jawed explorer or a brave soldier but a builder and plasterer from Gloucester, Michael Edwards. I have come to meet him in a small coffee shop on Stroud High Street.

With a rucksack slung over one shoulder, the now clean-shaven Edwards is still instantly recognizable. Nearly thirty years ago, he became an unlikely national hero when he finished last in the 70m and 90m ski jump at the Winter Olympics in Calgary, Canada.

Eddie looks thinner than I remember him, but then maybe it was all the padding he had to wear during those jumps. Without his moustache he looks slightly younger. He is fit and healthy-looking as he takes off a small day pack and apologises (English tick) for being a little late.

I'm actually quite star-struck; you see, I really am a child of the Vancouver games. It hit the sweet spot during my adolescence and Eddie 'the Eagle' Edwards, as he became known, was the hero of the day. I can still remember sitting on Mum and Dad's bed watching with bated breath as he took to the ski jump. The whole nation held its breath. We never expected him to do well, but as with the weather, we were forever hopeful. Eddie offered us the exoticism of snow and winter and cold combined with his 'bloke next door' derring-do. He was a cross between Shackleton and Benny Hill.

That winter he gave the nation hope. A one-man army batting above his weight. A nation weighed down with sporting failure could only ascend.

'I've just been on a cruise,' he said, explaining his tan. I asked him what he thought it was that made him stand out from the crowd. 'Being the underdog,' he replied, 'they liked the pluckiness'.

I wonder whether he felt fairly portrayed by the press. Was he, is he, the hapless, clueless builder? He smiles and winks. I can only assume from his demeanour that he played the game well: an 80s Joey Essex.

The English are always better when disarmed. We are not as generous with the bravado and arrogance of winners. We prefer modesty and understatement. It is a peculiarity of the English and Eddie is the benchmark. He doesn't have the presence that some great people carry with them but he exudes an eccentric swagger. He is certainly brave, but in many ways Eddie is the perfect example of the Englishman. Slightly wonky-toothed. Plucky. Bold. Eccentric. Hapless. Failing. Odd. He is a jar of Marmite and the weather in one. Cloudy with a chance of Marmite showers. He has that English charm. A walking apology.

We sit largely unnoticed as we sip our tea (English tick) in Stroud Costa Coffee. Me and this goliath of Englishness.

Eddie the Eagle defines a unique type of heroism that defies the norm and is English to the core: his oversized milk-bottle glasses and helmet tied with string were the exact opposite of the typical profile of the Winter Olympics competitor. Yet perhaps for that reason, he captured the world's imagination with his nerve and fearless attitude. Above all, his fame was not based on success but failure. Eddie the Eagle was for a time the most famous failure in England. As a sporting and academic failure myself, for a time he gave me hope: he was the little guy taking on the world in a series of terrifying jumps.

Edwards had a dream from childhood about being an Olympian. As a teenager he became obsessed with downhill skiing after going on a school skiing trip. He achieved some success despite having no money – he was self-educated, working class and about as different from the British Olympic establishment as you could get. Defeated by money, he remained determined to wear the British Olympic tracksuit. Effectively shunned by the Olympic movement, he had a brainwave and decided to enter the ski jump; he had never jumped before, but Britain had no competitors. So, if he achieved the qualifying distance, he would be a shoo-in for the team in Calgary in 1988. He qualified … just. But if he thought he'd won over the establishment he was wrong; they continued to oppose his participation in the Games, considering him a national embarrassment. Happily, the huge worldwide television audience, me included, thought differently and he became a global sporting phenomenon.

Despite his last-place finishes in both the 70m and 90m competitions, cheering the plucky underdog became a national pastime. Edwards epitomized everything we English love about an amateur hero: he simply played the game, with no care about whether he won or lost.

When he came home, his face was everywhere and his earnings were huge. Over time, the bookings fell away – and this is what I love about his story. He went back to his plastering job, which he still does part time today.

Edwards tried to qualify for the next three Winter Olympics, but failed – thanks to a rule specifically designed to keep amateurs like him out – often hurting himself in the process. Over the course of his career, he fractured his skull twice and broke his jaw, collarbone, ribs, knee, fingers, thumbs, toes, back and neck. 'I think the only bones I haven't broken are my shoulder, hip and thigh,' he says.

He retired at the age of thirty-four in 1998. In a further twist to his amazing story, a trust he'd set up to hold and manage his earnings failed and he was declared bankrupt in 1992. Again, a huge setback only spurred him on. He was fascinated by the legal process and decided to retrain as a lawyer. He went back to school, gained his qualifications – starting with GCSEs – and finally obtained a law degree from De Montfort University in 2003, fifteen years after the Calgary Winter Olympics.

He says he has always believed that with 'resistance and tenacity you can achieve anything'. 'We are a resilient nation,' he says, 'but we are moving towards the US mentality' of success marked by medals rather than just participating and doing your best. The last few Olympic Games, the Tour de France, golf and now the America's Cup have all transformed the English sporting reputation from hapless failure to hero and the Eddies of this world have been replaced by bleached-toothed sporting machines.

Eddie is still very much in demand. A regular on the speaking circuit, he has even had a Hollywood film made about his life. As we say farewell I wonder whether this kind of English sporting hero has become an endangered species in a country that has pulled up its socks when it comes to sport. In my mind, though, Eddie will remain my own sporting hero, taking on the establishment and winning.

* * *

In many ways, Eddie the Eagle was merely following the centuries-old recipe created by our rich history of explorers who specialized in that plucky derring-do, have-a-go attitude. As a tiny island nation we have produced some of the world's greatest explorers and adventurers; but what defines many of the great English expeditions is failure. We take on a challenge knowing that it is doomed to fail but press on regardless. Shackleton, Scott, Fawcett, Mallory … the long list of heroic failures seems to define a unique kind of Englishness. Is that dogged determination in the face of adversity part of the romance, the danger and exhilaration of treading the fine line between success and failure? A little like our sport and even our weather, we appear to have an inevitable resignation to being doomed to failure.

This admiration of failure goes hand in hand with the fact that we have never been particularly good at celebrating success. I'm not sure if it's pessimism, guilt or jealousy, but we have a strange relationship with high achievement. We often describe it as tall-poppy syndrome, the phenomenon whereby we will root for individuals until their stem – success – becomes too tall, and then we cut them down to size.

As an island nation, more used to looking to the horizon to ward off invaders, England took a surprisingly long time to use her maritime expertise to explore the world beyond our borders. Portugal and Spain were pioneers in undertaking voyages in the so-called Age of Discovery of the fifteenth and sixteenth centuries. They established vast and enviably wealthy empires, prompting England – in a race against France and the Netherlands – to sail forth to claim colonies and set up trade networks of their own in the Americas and in Asia. Then, in the sixteenth century, along came Sir Francis Drake, Sir Martin Frobisher and Anthony Jenkinson, and the English adventurer was born, ushering in an era of investigation around the globe which has had a lasting effect on the society in which we live today. Explorers raised anchor and set off with an ambitious to-do list. They were determined to discover new lands, to further scientific enquiry, to bring home new mineral and agricultural resources, to map the world in greater detail – and to make a name (and fortune) for themselves. The dangers were real; the adventure exhilarating. Such hazardous missions were open to all social classes. A roll call of the best-known explorers shows that few survived to reminisce about their forays in pipe and slippers. They leave a colourful legacy of heroes, perilous challenges and mysteries …

Arguably our earliest pioneer was Captain James Cook. He was born in 1728 in a small village near Middlesbrough, the son of a farm worker. One of the few naval captains to rise through the ranks, Cook's achievements are pretty impressive. Between 1763 and 1767 he was responsible for charting the complex coast-line of Newfoundland aboard HMS *Grenville*. On an expedition commissioned by the Royal Society of London for Improving Natural Knowledge, he commanded HMS *Endeavour* to witness the transit of Venus across the sun – a rare event visible only in the southern hemisphere – sailing to Tahiti via Cape Horn. Once the astronomer, Charles Green, had made his observations they sailed on to New Zealand and then became the first Europeans to navigate the length of Australia's east coast. Cook claimed the region for Britain and named it New South Wales.

In 1772, a year after his return home, Cook set out on a second voyage to look for the southern continent. They nearly succeeded but had to return before discovering it because of the extreme cold. For his final voyage, he set out to discover the fabled North-West Passage, which the world's navigators and cartographers presumed was the link between the Atlantic and the Pacific Ocean. He was unsuccessful and ended up landing on Hawaii, where he was stabbed by an islander and died on 14 February 1779. Despite a lifetime of success, his untimely death seems to me to mark the beginning of the era of heroic failures.

While Cook circumnavigated the globe, nearly a century later a new generation of explorers would begin a new land grab for some of the last unexplored corners of the planet, the polar regions.

I took on my own ocean in 2005 when I teamed up with the double Olympic gold rowing champion James Cracknell to row the Atlantic. Ocean-rowing is a peculiarly English occupation that has escalated in popularity over the last decade. Goodness knows why. Rowing a tiny 21ft boat made of plywood and stuck together with glue nearly 3,500 miles across the Atlantic has to count as the most miserable seven weeks of my life.

What makes it so English? Well, the slowness and monotony have an appeal a little like that of cricket; the challenge itself is both eccentric and utterly pointless; and it is far from glamorous or sexy. In many ways, ocean-rowing epitomizes so many English traits. There's a certain 'because-it's-there' feeling to the whole enterprise.

So why did I choose to do it? Well, I think my Englishness played a part.

Growing up, I relished the stories of those great earlier explorers and pioneers. A particular favourite was Captain Robert Falcon Scott, who was born in 1868 in Plymouth, Devon. He led two expeditions to the Antarctic. On the *Discovery* expedition in 1901–4 he broke a new southern record by reaching latitude 82°S and discovered the Polar Plateau. Then in 1910 he set off for the Terra Nova Expedition, which was to end infamously in tragedy. He reached the South Pole on 17 January 1912 a month after Roald Amundsen's Norwegian expedition. They perished on the return journey having missed a meeting point with the dog teams. Temperatures suddenly dropped to -40°C as they trudged northwards.

In a farewell letter to Sir Edgar Speyer, treasurer of the fund raised to finance the expedition, and dated 16 March 1912, Scott wondered whether he had missed the meeting point and fought the growing suspicion that he had in fact been abandoned by the dog teams: 'We very nearly came through, and it's a pity to have missed it, but lately I have felt that we have overshot our mark. No-one is to blame and I hope no attempt will be made to suggest that we had lacked support.'

On the same day, one of his companions, Laurence Oates, who had become frostbitten and who had gangrene, voluntarily left the tent and walked to his death. Scott wrote down Oates's last words, some of the most famous ever recorded: 'I am just going outside and may be some time.' If ever there was an English way of dying, surely that was it?

I was always taken by the tragic tale of Captain Scott, so perhaps it is no surprise that when I finally got a chance to take part in a race to the South Pole, once again James Cracknell and

I teamed up for an escapade which I recounted in *The Accidental Adventurer*. In a gratifyingly English outcome, we were pipped to the finish by the Norwegian team, by the tiny margin of four hours. Heroic failures to the last.

Born around the same time as Scott was another plucky Englishman, George Herbert Leigh Mallory. He took part in three British expeditions to Mount Everest in the early 1920s. First was the 1921 reconnaissance expedition, which reached 22,500 feet (6,900m) on the North Col. In the second, a year later, the team including Mallory got to 27,320 feet (8,320m) but could not summit. But it was his 1924 summit attempt with climbing partner Andrew 'Sandy' Irvine that is most deeply shrouded in mystery. Both men disappeared as they attempted to become the first to stand on top of the world. They were last seen about 245 vertical metres from the summit. The fate of the climbers remained a mystery until 1 May 1999, when a research expedition sponsored by the BBC to find the climbers' bodies came across Mallory's corpse at 26,755 feet (8,155m). Irvine's body remains somewhere up there. Did they reach the top? The subject remains one of intense speculation and continuing research. Whatever the answer, Mallory and Irvine only added to the public's enduring love of the heroic failure.

When you're going into the unknown, it's quite possible that you'll disappear and, if you're English, the odds are that bit shorter. Perhaps one of the greatest explorer mysteries is that of Lieutenant Colonel Percival 'Percy' Harrison Fawcett, born in 1867 in Torquay, Devon.

His upbringing was about as English as you could get. He was educated at Newton Abbot Proprietary College; in 1886, he joined the Royal Artillery and was stationed in Ceylon (as it then was). He studied mapmaking and surveying and joined the Royal Geographical Society. Military life bored him and after a spell working undercover for the British Secret Service in North Africa, he received a commission from the RGS to use his survey-ing skills to settle a border dispute between Bolivia and Brazil. He arrived in La Paz in June 1907, aged thirty-nine. Fantastic stories started to trickle back to London. He claimed to have shot a giant 62ft anaconda, as well as many other animals unknown to zool-ogists – including a 'cat-like' dog and a giant poisonous Apazauca spider. He made seven expeditions through the jungle and his adventures became the inspiration for Sir Arthur Conan Doyle's *The Lost World*. After volunteering to serve in the First World War he returned to South America with his eldest son, Jack, in 1925. Before the war, he'd heard local legends about a lost city called 'Z', somewhere in the Brazilian jungle. It became an obses-sion. He was convinced the city existed in the Mato Grosso region and he, his son and Jack's best friend, the heroically named Raleigh Rimell, plunged into the jungle. They were never seen again. Percy left instructions with his wife that, if they should disappear, no one should come after them; but ever since hundreds of expeditions have taken place with the sole purpose of locating this true English heroic failure.

It continues to surprise me the astonishing rate at which we have generated great adventurers compared to the size of our nation. Take a look at the current generation of great English explorers: Colonel John Blashford-Snell, Sir Ranulph Fiennes, Sir Chris Bonington, Sir Robin Knox-Johnston and Dame Ellen MacArthur, to name just a few. We are celebrated for our explorers, but I think somehow we tend to celebrate those who have a go and fail spectacularly rather than those who easily come out on top.

A. A. Gill wrote in his book *The Angry Island: Hunting the English*:

> For the English, real character is built not by winners, but by losers. Anyone can be a good winner … It is in losing that the individual really discovers what they're made of, and it was in coming a good second that the kernel of the truth in the lesson of sport lay, because winning a game of muddied oafs or flannelled fools is transiently unimportant, but being able to cope with failure and disappointment, to turn around the headlong impetus of adrenalin, effort, expectation and hope, and still shake hands with your opponent and pick up the bat or the boot the next day – that's the proving and honing and the toughening of character.

We are perhaps the world leaders in heroic failure, and we're actually happy with that.

CHAPTER FOUR

STRAWBERRIES AND CREAM

In my navy blue linen suit I felt positively bland amidst the riot of colour. Pink jackets with white braid, candy-striped jackets in yellow, purple and green, camouflage jackets, floral jackets, red school blazers, blue blazers, salmon-pink trousers, canary-yellow trousers and purple caps. One man wore luminous green trousers, below which could be seen one velvet orange shoe with yellow laces, the other shoe in velvet green with red laces. Some had eschewed colour for white loafers, white shirt, and cream-coloured trousers and jackets. Bowler hats, top hats, Panama hats and straw boaters competed alongside various sporting caps of every shade and hue imaginable.

There were W. G. Grace lookalikes with long beards and double-breasted white blazers alongside hipster toffs and moustachioed dandies with walking sticks and old rowing ties, old boys' rowing hats in an equally garish cacophony of colours, and some older men in full naval uniforms. Everyone swigged merrily from champagne flutes or glasses of Pimm's along the bustling banks of the Thames. Meanwhile, the competitors – tall, gangly young rowers – marched around in candy-striped Lycra and Henley tops in a rich palette of pastels. The women, in dresses that came below the knee, wore an assortment of hats in every shape and size, but alongside the rainbow of gentlemanly sartorial splendour, they all looked rather drab.

Once a year Henley-on-Thames plays host to the biggest rowing regatta in the world and arguably the poshest event in England. It is an A–Z gathering of every public schoolboy in the land. While Ascot is all about the ladies and their hats, Henley is about the gentlemen and their outlandish blazers and trousers. Rowing club colours on a blazer or cap are encouraged, as is the wearing of straw boaters. And here, in the colours of the blazer, is where English eccentricity comes into play. The pastel rainbow-striped blazer of the Cambridge Archetypals stands out a mile. Entitlement to wear it is legendary: you have to row in the Boat Race three times, get a third-class degree and have spent three nights in jail. Another exquisitely exclusive tale belongs to the chaps entitled to wear the Hampton Curtains blazers, tailored from brown burlap fabric adorned with lions and crests which was cut down from Hampton School's Great Hall. Only ten of these garments exist, because they can only be worn by those who have won the triple crown of junior rowing – that is, the Schools Head of the River race, the National Schools Regatta and the Princess Elizabeth Plate at Henley.

Toffs have always had a soft spot for bright, garish colours. Only in England could the upper/middle-class penchant for wearing red trousers lead to the creation of a website, Look at my

F****** Red Trousers, which is 'a collection of photographs in celebration of the vibrant and burgeoning red-trousered communities of London and the home counties'. In some ways, I suppose, red trousers might arguably be seen as a part of our national dress – it definitely is for toffs, at any rate. Henley is the opportunity for the great and the good of the upper middle classes to show off their peacock-like plumage in all its multicoloured glory. If Skittles could be people, they would be Henley's racegoers.

While the riverbanks hummed with thousands of spectators, the real action of course belonged to the Thames itself. The river had been divided into two sections: one side for the racing, the other for the spectators' boats. Hundreds in every shape and size punted, rowed, paddled, steamed and motored up and down. Tiny wooden skiffs were overladen with blue-blazered passengers, all sipping on glasses of Chablis. Small skiffs had been converted into mobile picnic sites, and beautiful old craft glided elegantly along, laden with with impossibly posh-looking people sitting in wicker chairs. A beautiful old steamer puffed past in a huge plume of white vapour, a full brass band playing 'God Save the Queen'. I passed two Canadian canoes lashed together with huge planks of wood onto which a table and chairs had been set for a full silver service lunch, complete with candlestick holders and wine bucket.

Nervous-looking crews rowed up the outside of the river alongside the flotilla of other vessels on their way to Temple Island, from where all the races start. All along the shore, thousands of cheering old boys plonked themselves down in deckchairs with livery that matched their jackets. Floating precariously along on tiny man-made islands were the course officials, marooned like posh Robinson Crusoes.

We had been invited as guests of Sir Steve Redgrave. If there is a sport that represents the very essence of Englishness, it must surely be rowing. And if there is a sportsman who defines stiff-upper-lipped Englishness, it is Sir Steve Redgrave. I have been fortunate to know Steve since I teamed up with his one-time rowing partner James Cracknell for the race to the South Pole and the hellish crossing of the Atlantic in a rowing boat.

After lunch we made our way back down the riverbank, picking our way through the crowds of rosy-cheeked men with over-hanging bellies telling stories of their school days. 'One of the privileges of being chairman is that I can send you out in the umpire boat,' Sir Steve said before ushering us to a long, sleek skiff, umpire flag hanging limply from the stern.

The man in charge was none other than Sir Matthew Pinsent, the third of the Oarsmen Foursome and another English national treasure. Matt was wearing a blue rowing blazer with an Afghanistan Olympic tie that he had been given by the visiting Olympic squad. The last time I had seen him was in some half-finished hotel in the Russian winter resort of Sochi, where we were both working as commentators for the Winter Olympics.

Having boarded, we meandered our way upriver past the dozens of craft towards the start line. On one beautiful wooden launch I noticed the familiar features of Prince and Princess Michael of Kent. His marvellous beard was twitching in the wind as our wake splashed against the side, nearly causing them to spill their drinks. I suppose the umpire boat had the river's superiority.

Two miles further down the course we reached the start. The race was the 3.20 Fawley Challenge Cup between Gloucester Rowing Club and Malvern Preparatory School from the USA. Henley attracts teams from more than twenty-five countries, all in search of rowing glory. Joining us in the boat were the rowing coaches from the respective schools.

'You can take photographs,' explained Matt, 'but you mustn't communicate, talk, nor gesture to the teams.'

He stood at the front of the skiff in his blue rowing hat, red flag held aloft in his hand. 'Attention, GO!' The two four-man boats dipped their oars into the water and began to pull down the course.

The crowds roared their approval as the two rowing boats raced alongside one another. 'Malvern!' Matt shouted through the loud hailer. 'MALVERN!' he repeated, holding his flag to the right. They were veering to the left. There was a clash of oars as the boats came too close, but the rowers remained focused on the race, not missing a stroke as they continued past the halfway point, then alongside first the bandstands and then the stewards' enclosure. I spotted the familiar faces of James Cracknell and Sir Steve keeping a close eye on the race. The boats slipped through the water towards the matriarch of rowing craft, the magnificent *Gloriana*, which cast a majestic shadow on the water and seemed to bestow a blessing on the whole occasion.

Henley is almost a character of Englishness. It is an essential fixture in what's known as the English Summer Season – or simply The Season, to those who are involved. I got my first taste of this annual upper-middle-class jolly after landing a job at

Tatler, that quintessential English magazine. By a complete fluke I ended up being picture editor there, having started as PA to Giles Coren and the late A. A. Gill. *Tatler* covers The Season avidly and I had a year of attending all the main events.

The Season originated in the eighteenth century, when members of the aristocracy traditionally kept a house in London. Fans of *Downton Abbey* will know that the Crawley family would regularly decamp to Grantham House, their grand townhouse in St James's Square. The purpose behind The Season's calendar of events – which started in April and went on until 12 August – was to entertain the families of the well-to-do while Parliament was sitting. As a result, most of the 'fixtures' were within a carriage ride of London and the organizers, in that very English way, collaborated to make sure that there were no date clashes.

Historically, The Season provided celebrations of the arts: opera at Glyndebourne, music at the Proms concerts, fine art at the Royal Academy Summer Exhibition and drama at West End theatres. It included horticulture with the Chelsea Flower Show (to ensure landowners were up to date with the latest hothouse plants and fashionable shrubs). It celebrated equestrianism with a full line-up of showpiece events featuring flat racing, National Hunt racing, three-day eventing and show jumping: Royal Ascot, the Cheltenham Gold Cup, Badminton, the Grand National, the Royal Windsor Horse Show, the Epsom Derby and Glorious Goodwood. The jewels in the crown of the calendar were of course Trooping the Colour in Horse Guards Parade and the Order of the Garter service in Windsor.

In addition there was a huge variety of traditional upper-class sporting events, which provided days of jollity and plenty of excuses for partying as men competed in the Boat Race, Henley Royal Regatta, Guards polo, the lawn tennis championships at Wimbledon, Cowes Week and the Lord's Test match. The traditional end of The Season was the Glorious Twelfth of August, which marks the beginning of the grouse shooting season. Society would retire to the country to shoot birds during the autumn and hunt foxes during the winter, before coming back to London again with the spring. For many years The Season ran like that, requiring huge household expenditure on the latest fashions and armies of cooks to provide exquisite feasts and picnics.

The clothes are still a vital ingredient, and the dress codes for the events add an interesting dimension – and some confusion. At Wimbledon, players must still conform to strict rules regarding clothing:

The following refers to all clothing, including tracksuits and sweaters, worn on The Championship courts both for practice and for matches.

1. Competitors must be dressed in suitable tennis attire that is almost entirely white and this applies from the point at which the player enters the court surround.
2. White does not include off white or cream.
3. There should be no solid mass or panel of colouring. A single trim of colour around the neckline and around the cuff of the sleeve is acceptable but must be no wider than one centimetre (10mm).
4. Colour contained within patterns will be measured as if it is a solid mass of colour and should be within the one

centimetre (10mm) guide. Logos formed by variations of material or patterns are not acceptable.

5. The back of a shirt, dress, tracksuit top or sweater must be totally white.

6. Shorts, skirts and tracksuit bottoms must be totally white except for a single trim of colour down the outside seam no wider than one centimetre (10mm).

7. Caps, headbands, bandannas, wristbands and socks must be totally white except for a single trim of colour no wider than one centimetre (10mm).

8. Shoes must be almost entirely white, including the soles. Large manufacturers' logos are not encouraged. The grass court shoes must adhere to the Grand Slam rules (see Appendix A below for full details). In particular shoes with pimples around the outside of the toes shall not be permitted. The foxing around the toes must be smooth.

9. Any undergarments that either are or can be visible during play (including due to perspiration) must also be completely white except for a single trim of colour no wider than one centimetre (10mm). In addition, common standards of decency are required at all times.

10. Medical supports and equipment should be white if possible but may be coloured if absolutely necessary.

In 2017, three players were instructed to change their underwear because they contravened rule 9. The All England Club even provided suitable attire for two of the competitors. The all-white dress code is so instilled in the minds of the tennis-loving English public that a confused ticket-holder telephoned the Championships' public relations office one year to ask if it was all right for her to come as a spectator in a sundress made of white fabric with 'just a few light sprigs of flowers'.

Many events of the Season have traditional expectations, if not diehard rules, with regard to dress for ladies and gentlemen. At Royal Ascot, for example, hats are obligatory. If permitted to enter the Royal Enclosure (there are also, of course, strict regulations qualifying entry to that most exclusive enclave), gentlemen are required to wear either black or grey morning dress, including a waistcoat, with a top hat. There are also rules about how to handle the hats: another rule states that a gentleman may remove his top hat within a restaurant, a private box, a private club or that facility's terrace, balcony or garden. Hats may also be removed within any enclosed external seating area within the Royal Enclosure Garden. Ladies must wear hats and not show bare midriffs or shoulders.

In the stewards' enclosure at Henley Royal Regatta, gentlemen must wear a jacket and tie. A lady's skirt hem must reach below the knee and is checked before entry by the stewards' officers. Hats are encouraged but 'not required' for ladies. When a student protested at being denied entry to the stewards' enclosure for failing to meet the dress code, saying she had worn the dress 'in the Royal Enclosure at Ascot and nobody said anything', a spokesman defended the dress code by saying, 'The intention is to maintain the atmosphere of an English garden party of the Edwardian period by wearing a more traditional dress.'

Not all dress codes are about showiness. At polo matches, for example, it is usual for gentlemen to wear a blazer and white trousers, but ladies should wear sensible flat shoes, as the tradition of 'treading in the divots' precludes the wearing of heels. The tradition, by the way, is that at half-time in the match, the spectators are allowed onto the field to stamp down any ridges and divots created by the ponies' hooves so that the ball will travel smoothly in the second half.

The Chelsea Flower Show, the Royal Horticultural Society's flagship garden show, held over five days in May in the grounds of Chelsea Royal Hospital, is an annual favourite of the Queen's. She has only missed the show twice during her reign. The event attracts the world's specialist horticulturalists, celebrity garden designers and vendors of every imaginable (and never before imagined) plant-related accessory. Visually beautiful and laden with a thousand floral displays, the show makes a lovely day out, embracing artistry and practicality, the elite and the cottage gardener. Where else do you find fanatics of the hosta, of carnivorous plants from around the world or of esoteric specimens of the bearded iris; or discover the latest in luxury pergolas, garden clogs and wind-powered kinetic sculptures? The Chelsea Flower Show is said to attract more FTSE 100 chief executives than any other of The Season's social events, but the only formal day requiring something dressy is Monday, the day of the Queen's visit. Otherwise women tend to wear a flowery dress to mark the occasion, offset with sensible shoes – especially necessary at 4 p.m. on the last day when the Chelsea Bell signals the 'sell-off' and visitors stampede to buy from the show displays.

Glyndebourne Opera has also become a summer institution. The English country house, dating from the sixteenth century and occupying a site of bucolic beauty near Lewes in East Sussex, has hosted an annual opera festival since 1934. Anxiety about what to wear is part of the fun for women, though the English summer chill often means a picnic rug around the shoulders is a popular accessory. Initially, the productions were staged within the house, but in 1994 the much-loved and homely auditorium was replaced by a state-of-the-art, acoustically impressive free-standing opera house bolted on to the side of the main building and seating 1,200 people in comfort.

The origins of the festival are worthy of an operatic score themselves. John Christie, grandfather of the current custodian Gus Christie, inherited the estate in 1920. In the course of renovating and doubling the length of the south façade of the house, he added a vast room to accommodate one of the largest organs in the country outside a cathedral. After the Second World War, Christie gave sections of the soundboards, pipes and structural parts to the rebuilt Guards Chapel at Wellington Barracks in Birdcage Walk, which had been destroyed in the Blitz; the case and console remain at Glyndebourne. Christie loved music and regularly held amateur opera evenings in the organ room. At one of these soirees in 1931, he met his future wife, the Sussex-born Canadian soprano Audrey Mildmay, a singer with the Carl Rosa opera company. After a whirlwind romance, they married on 4 June 1931 and returned from honeymoon – where they had attended the Salzburg and Bayreuth festivals – with the notion of bringing professional, small-scale opera to Glyndebourne.

The combination of amazing music and a beautiful setting, complete with formal gardens, a large water-lily pond and sheep grazing in the surrounding fields, is glamour incarnate, but not without some eccentric English touches. Most opera-goers travel between Lewes train station and Glyndebourne in a double-decker jalopy provided by the festival, often joined on the way back by members of the cast and orchestra to catch the last train.

It is perhaps a sign of the times that Debrett ('the recognized authority on etiquette, influence and achievement since … 1769') now runs a half-day programme called 'The British Social Season Course' for … corporate hospitality. How best to impress your VIP guests? A day at Ascot, Wimbledon or Henley is the answer. 'Brand ambassadors are often expected to know the intricacies of the British social Season – the events, traditions and dress codes,' runs the Debrett blurb. 'As a result of this programme, you will be able to share subtleties and insights with your clients, facilitate confident conversations and put them at ease. It will also enable you to assess a client's need for guidance and impart advice with grace and discretion.'

As well as headaches about what to wear, the other perpetual cause of anxiety is, of course, the weather.

The Season brings extreme weather pressure points. There are certain days of the year when concern about the likelihood of fine weather reaches a hysterical peak: will rain threaten the immaculate preparations of garden designers showing at the Chelsea Flower Show? Will the sun shine for the traditional 2 p.m. Royal Procession of four open carriages that carry the Queen and her family to the Royal Enclosure at Ascot? Will stilettos and suede brogues bear up to a day on the grassy riverbanks of the enclosure at Henley Royal Regatta? There is frantic checking of forecasts and weather apps in the weeks, days, hours and minutes before each event; essential clothing adjustments are made right up to the last moment.

For top designers planning the ultimate garden display, the weather at Chelsea is a key factor. Even in a year of average conditions, horticulturists suffer nightmares as they nurture and coax flowers that normally bloom in summer to reach show-stopping perfection in May. In recent years, 2012 probably ranks as the worst on record, with the run-up blighted by torrential downpours, night time frosts and an unusual lack of sunlight, growers warned of a shortage of roses, tulips, irises, geraniums, foxgloves, rhododendrons, wisterias, azaleas, peonies, delphiniums, lupins and euphorbias. The *Evening Standard* reported that 'One designer admitted she's "having a nervous breakdown" as her roses and irises refuse to bloom. Another fretted that a trailing nasturtium, supposed to be the centrepiece of a display, is three feet shorter than intended.

'Former gold medal winner David Domoney, working this year with Alan Titchmarsh on a new series of ITV's *Love Your Garden*, said entrants should try everything from hairdryers to heat lamps to keep plants in good health. Growers are resorting to swathing plants in protective fleece at night and faking sunlight using sodium lamps …'

Of course Wimbledon, or The Championships at the All England Lawn Tennis and Croquet Club, to give the world's most prestigious tennis tournament its full and proper name, is arguably the most weather-wary sporting event in the world. This is because its USP is so wholly reliant on the weather. It is the only one of the four major tennis tournaments known as the Grand Slams to be contested on grass, so play on its much admired, immaculate emerald sward can only occur when there is not a single drop of drizzle, rain or precipitation falling on the ground of this very English corner of London.

In a world of all-weather surfaces, acute psychological rivalries and punishing professionalism, Wimbledon gives equal billing to its traditions of strawberries and cream, Pimm's, an English garden party atmosphere and all-white clothing rule. The addition of a retractable roof on Centre Court – with one due to be added to No. 1 Court – has reduced stress about rain preventing play, but Wimbledon wouldn't be Wimbledon without the daily greeting: 'Ladies and gentlemen, may I have your attention please? May I have your attention please? The latest update from the Met Office indicates a band of cloud …'

For an immediate immersion in quintessential Englishness, a visitor should join the Queue at Wimbledon. And yes, it must have a capital 'Q', for it is not only a proper noun but a proper institution, a social event in itself that incorporates overnight campers and dedicated tennis fans intent on a fun time, rain or shine. It snakes up Church Road and around Wimbledon Park, overseen by a benign army of honorary stewards. The Queue has its own set of rules, and you can bet your life there will be much tutting if you transgress any one of them.

Just before Wimbledon in The Season comes Royal Ascot. It was founded by Queen Anne in 1711 and boasts excellent horse racing, but the real sport lies in spotting how flamboyantly the challenge has been met of wearing the most eccentric hat or providing the most indulgent car-park picnic. Those attending for the first time can never quite believe the daily fairy-tale frisson of watching the Queen, her family and distinguished guests arriving in a procession of horse-drawn open-top carriages. The raising of the Royal Standard signals the start of each race day. Bookies take bets on the Queen's hat colour, and wardrobe etiquette is scrupulously observed. In the Royal Enclosure, morning dress is required but 'no cravats'. They are for weddings, don't yer know!

The Season brings out the eccentric customs and fashions of upper-class society. It includes some of the most famous of our sporting and cultural events and, if you want to be exposed to extreme Englishness, or have three months of living Englishly, you'd be hard pressed to find a better means of doing so.

As the Summer Season comes to an end, we enter the so-called Silly Season: where the English love of a good headline collides with a beautiful storm of ridiculousness. News stories about saucily shaped vegetables and silhouettes of religious leaders appearing on pieces of toast feature daily.

WOMAN FINDS A HAT IN A TREE

SHOCK AS POPE STEPS DOWN TWO YEARS AFTER BRUM VISIT

NEW FOOTPATH GATE 'TOO NOISY'

WARNING OVER DANGEROUS CUPCAKES

WHITSTABLE MUM IN CUSTARD SHORTAGE

GRASS GROWING FAST AFTER RAIN

POODLE HOLDS CLUE TO DEATHS

POSTMAN BEATEN BY LAVENDER BUSH

BUILDERS THWARTED BY FISH-EATING SPIDERS

CHEEKY SEAGULL NABS CRISPS

YAWNING ALMOST KILLED A MAN

PATIENT GETS PILLOW CASE INSTEAD OF GOWN

The Brighton *Argus* once carried the cover headline KITTEN CHOKES ON MOUSE. But my favourite is from the *Cambridge Evening News*: KITTEN THAT LOOKS LIKE HITLER – pictures.

So consistent are the August Silly Season news stories that it is possible to guarantee a number of topics including sharks spotted off Cornwall, crop circles in Dorset, photographs of – depending on what kind of weather we've been having – an empty or overflowing reservoir, a story titled 'Who's running the country', accompanied by photographs of our MPs on holiday, and some animal story.

There was much mourning, both in fishing circles and beyond, in August 2009 when Benson the carp passed on. Britain's largest specimen was a star in the carp world and had been caught and returned to the water sixty-three times. So named because of a hole in her dorsal fin shaped like a cigarette burn, she was found dead at the tender age of an estimated twenty to twenty-five years old (carp normally live for around four decades). The tabloids were joined by the posh papers in asking who killed Benson. 'Even the *Wall Street Journal* has been in touch,' said Tony Bridgefoot, owner of Bluebell Lakes near Oundle, where Benson lived and died.

In August 1998, under the headline DIVE! DIVE! DIVE!, a Tynemouth policeman told the papers about the dive-bombing herring gulls that were driving his family to distraction. 'We had almost become prisoners in our own home,' Robert Lephard reported. 'Sometimes it was like a scene from Hitchcock's *The Birds* just trying to get to the car.'

In 2009, killer chipmunks were all the rage in Fleet Street, invading Britain from mainland Europe. The *Sun* reported that young mum Roxanne Whelan was attacked by one in her garden when she popped out for a smoke, and the *Daily Star* even managed to shoehorn a bit of anti-French sentiment into its coverage, reporting that 'Dodgy French street sellers are flogging them to unsuspecting Brits at £10 a go as pets. But the rodents are actually vicious Siberian chipmunks that can kill.' Expert Guy Bruel advised: 'The public must be on its guard.'

In 2005, the *Sun* picked up a story from the *South London Press* that squirrels in Brixton were turning on to crack thanks to addicts burying their stashes in gardens (adding that crack-crazed squirrels are a common sight in the US). Even the *Guardian* got in on the act, launching its own search for the drug-hoover rodents. 'I've just seen one jump down from an old sunflower by the Seventh Day Adventist church,' it quoted one Reg Throssell as saying. 'I locked eyes with it and it stared back at me really confidently. It was scavenging and it looked scrawny.'

Crop circles are the great silly-season standby, but in 2000 the *Daily Mail* found a different angle. Its two-page spread, headed CROP CIRCLES ARE MESSAGES FROM ALIENS (ACCORDING TO A CAT), was about a giant circle in a wheat field in Wiltshire, in which the paper's science correspondent (!) asked, 'A message from aliens – or are the hoaxers having a field day again?' An 'expert' opined that the circle was located on one of the energy lines that apparently criss-cross the planet; the evidence consisted of her friend taking a Burmese cat into the circle and reporting: 'The animal seemed to know it was something extraordinary.'

But the grandaddy of political summer-holiday stories occurred in 1973 when Harold Wilson, then leader of the Opposition, was saved from drowning in the Scilly Isles. Slipping into the sea from a rubber dinghy, he was growing weak after half an hour in the water before he was rescued by the Wolff family. Though it seemed that Wilson tried to keep it quiet, the story soon came out – SCILLY SECRET FLOATS TO THE SURFACE was one headline. Wilson's press secretary, Joe Haines, tried to have the blame put on Paddy, Wilson's golden labrador, for knocking him into the drink. But as was later recalled by the bestselling novelist Isabel Wolff, who was in her teens at the time, Paddy was innocent.

But the winner must surely go to the *Sun*, which on a particularly quiet news day dedicated a front cover to the actor Richard Wilson. Under the front-page headline VICTOR MELDREW FOUND IN SPACE, the paper reported that astronomers had found a constellation that, when its dots were joined, made the face of his best-loved character.

This was on the front page of a newspaper read by two million people. Only in England …

CHAPTER FIVE

MAD DOGS AND ENGLISHMEN

'That so few now dare to be eccentric,
marks the chief danger of the time.'
John Stuart Mill, *On Liberty*

I have always loved eccentrics. We all know at least one person
we can describe as 'alternative'. They range from the slightly
quirky bow-tie wearing sort, like the politician Neil Hamilton,
right up to eighteenth-century Shropshire squire Mad Jack
Mytton, who rode a bear into dinner parties.

If you think about it, eccentricity is very unEnglish. Englishness
is about not making a scene, about not boasting or being different. And yet eccentricity bucks those character traits and allows
us the option to be very noticeable. Visiting American friends
always comment on the middle-class obsession with Boden floral
shirts. 'You'd never get away with that at home,' they marvel at an
eye-dazzlingly bright pink floral shirt.

Eccentricity and Englishness go together like fish and chips. You only need to look at some of our place names. Like Barton in the Beans, Droop, Upper Snodsbury, Nether Wallop, Crudwell and Puddletown, the last of which is not to be outdone by Tolpuddle, Affpuddle and Briantspuddle – which incidentally is just down the road from Throop. There's Matching Tye, Westward Ho! – complete with exclamation mark – and Blubberhouses in North Yorkshire; Mumford Sock in Somerset; Wetwang in East Yorkshire; and my personal favourite, Great Snoring in Norfolk.

Although eccentricity is found throughout England's social strata, it has to be said that the aristocracy have traditionally been gold medallists when it comes to sheer oddness. My personal favourite is Lord Bath, with whom I worked for nearly a decade at his magnificent stately pile, Longleat, in Wiltshire.

Longleat is one of the finest Elizabethan houses in England. It was built by Sir John Thynne, Member of Parliament and steward to Edward Seymour, 1st Duke of Somerset, whose descendants became the Marquesses of Bath. Longleat is still the seat of the Thynn family today. The house was designed by Robert Smythson and took twelve years to build, being largely completed in 1580. The 900 acres of parkland that surround it were designed by Capability Brown and there are a further 100,000 acres of woods and farmland. In 1949 it became the first stately home to open to the public, and most significantly it also boasts the first safari park to be established outside Africa.

The safari park opened in 1966 as the result of a gentleman's agreement between the then Lord Bath (the 6th Marquess) and Jimmy Chipperfield of the famous Chipperfield's Circus family. The latter dynasty goes back more than three hundred years, making the Chipperfields one of the oldest circus families in Europe. The idea of a safari park within the grounds of the stately home was embraced by Lord Bath, who was even then exhibiting early signs of eccentricity, but he was slower to grasp the concept of a drive through a safari park. When Chipperfield put the idea to him, he looked puzzled and said, 'Won't the cages have to be awfully big if cars are to drive into them?'

'No sir, it's the people who are going to be in cages – their cars – and the lions who are going to be free,' Chipperfield replied.

At the outset, fifty lions, all extras from the film *Born Free*, were brought in to roam the 100-acre reserve. Three thousand cars visited the park on the first weekend and within five months the capital cost of the venture had been repaid.

The Lions of Longleat were thus born. But there is another attraction that has a far more interesting history than the Lions, and that is the 'Loins of Longleat', as the press have dubbed him. Alexander George Thynn, the 7th Marquess of Bath, is as much a part of Longleat as the lions and is arguably one of the country's most colourful and eccentric characters.

Tall and broad, he has a tremendous presence. Slightly dishevelled with his huge white beard and long curly hair, he looks a little like a cross between a Johnny Depp in *Pirates of the Caribbean*, Henry VIII and Father Christmas. Combine that with his bohemian values and you have quite a winning combo. He also has a very individual dress sense that usually involves a combination of floral waistcoat, velvet trousers, a beret, cowboy boots and a colourful 'Technicolor dream' coat. His style has been described as Kabul Chic, although I always found it more Captain Jack Sparrow.

I have always loved his style and his individuality and though he is undoubtedly eccentric, he is also far more complex than that implies. He is ranked 359th in the *Sunday Times* Rich List, with an estimated wealth of £157 million, and yet he drinks wine from wine boxes and he sent his children to state school. He is married but he doesn't believe in monogamy. He is aristocratic but he doesn't like conservative conformity. He stood for election in 1974 in an attempt to devolve power to Wessex, and sat in the House of Lords as a Liberal Democrat.

Married to Hungarian actress Anna Gyarmathy since 1969, he has two children. The rest of his private life is open to speculation, often fuelled by the irascible Lord himself. While Lady Bath may be the supreme chatelaine of the main house, dotted around the vast estate in various cottages are a handful of the famous 'wifelets' or mistresses.

A prolific painter, he has covered the walls of much of the historic house with his own creations – at one time his efforts covered nearly a third of the entire wall space. Using a porridge-like combination of oil and sawdust, he has created murals of every shape, size and colour imaginable. They stare out from the walls and ceilings like naive 3D art. In addition to the murals, there are around 150 portraits of the Marquess's royal ancestors. These are accompanied by sixty-eight paintings of various wife-lets, adorning the staircase known as Bluebeard's gallery. 'Some people have notches on their bedposts,' Lord Bath explained the first time he showed me the collection, 'I prefer to paint them. Far more flattering, I think you'll agree.' He is particularly fond of the Kama Sutra room, which is stuffed with pornographic illustrations. The murals are his proudest achievement. Due to their highly flammable nature they became a unique fire risk, and the local fire brigade were forced to change their entire fire drill in case of a fire at Longleat to cope with the tons of high-risk artistic materials on display.

When his son, Ceawlin, and his new wife Emma took over Longleat, there was a huge falling out when Ceawlin decided to remove the murals from the walls. Ceawlin and his father haven't spoken for years as a result.

The house is open to the public – all, that is, except for Lord Bath's private apartments. In these the rooms are interconnected and include a modern kitchen, its shelves stacked with tins of processed foods, and a futuristic dining room, a little like the starship *Enterprise* from *Star Trek*. Hidden at the top of the house are the collections of his late father, Henry Thynn, the 6th Marquess, including a collection of Hitler paintings and Nazi memorabilia. At prep school, Alexander tried to please his father by being as good a fascist as possible. As a prep school prefect, he once punished some boys by putting them under the floorboards with a table on top. He then wrote to his father boasting of what he had done. Henry responded by reporting him to the headmaster for bullying.

Like all good English aristocrats, Lord Bath was never far from his most loyal companion, a yellow labrador called Boudicca. They were inseparable, 'Boody-boo, Boody, Boody-boo,' he would boom in his bass voice. The house staff used to joke that they would have to follow his lordship wherever he went to prevent a trail of destruction caused by the ever-excitable Boudicca as her tail knocked against priceless artefacts. It always reminded me of the scene in *Mary Poppins* where the staff of 17

Cherry Tree Lane have to hold on to all the family's possessions each time the retired Captain fires his cannon.

Alexander George Thynn, 7th Marquess of Bath, is a classic English eccentric. Aristocratic, gloriously unconcerned with social norms – of the aristocracy or any class – he simply does his own thing in his own very unusual manner.

A little closer to home, about ten years ago I hired a woodworker to help me build some shelves in my London office. It soon transpired that this was no ordinary woodworker. Mark McGowan was also an artist, or to be precise, a mix of artist, performer and eccentric. While Tracy Emin and Damien Hirst would firmly fall within the eccentric artist category, there are others who extend the classification further and one of those is Mark McGowan.

Over the course of the shelf-building, he revealed his bizarre stunts to me. He finds a cause – often these are what is euphemistically called 'niche' – and tries to find an eye-catching means of bringing it to people's attention. Sometimes the causes themselves are a little obscure. He once nailed his toe to a gallery wall for eight hours in a surreal protest against fallen autumn leaves, because … well, I didn't really follow his train of thought if I'm honest.

Another issue that captured Mark's imagination was student debt (he is a graduate of Camberwell School of Art). 'I once rolled a peanut across London with my nose,' he announced one day while sawing a piece of wood. He had apparently hit upon the idea of pushing a monkey nut with his nose along the pavement for seven miles from Goldsmiths College to 10 Downing Street. Twelve days and eleven monkey nuts later, he arrived at the famous black door and was greeted with a cup of tea. How English is that whole scenario?

Flushed with success, he followed up his monkey nut roll with a protest at people taking stones from Brighton beach. For this he tried to cartwheel the sixty miles from Brighton to London. But simply cartwheeling would have not made the point sufficiently clear. So he strapped 12lb rocks to his feet and stuck eighteen sticks of Brighton rock to his face. He had to abandon the feat after four days. I love the fact that he managed even that long.

He next took up the cause of cleaners, rolling five miles on the pavement from Elephant and Castle to a gallery on Bethnal Green Road. Again, that wasn't quite enough, so he wore yellow Marigold gloves and sang 'We Wish You A Merry Christmas' as he rolled along the London streets.

But arguably his most inspired 'performance' took place when he spent twelve days in a bath of baked beans and tomato sauce. Not odd enough? He also had two chips up his nose and seven pounds of sausages tied around his head. Why?

'Because I wanted to turn myself into a full English breakfast,' he told confused onlookers. Still confronted by confused faces, he explained his logic a bit further. A visiting friend from Italy had criticized the English diet. 'I took him to a traditional English pub but he started to complain when he saw the menu,' Mark revealed. 'There were things like eggs, chips and beans or steak and mushroom pie with chips and beans, but he didn't seem impressed by the cuisine. I suppose he would have preferred mozzarella.

'It got me thinking about how much some people criticize our food – even blaming a good old fry-up for obesity. We don't support our culture enough, so I thought I would celebrate a part of it by turning myself into a full English breakfast.' He added, 'I suppose I am the British alternative to David Blaine, but sitting in a plastic box is nothing compared to what I will be doing.'

McGowan follows a long tradition of eccentrics. Perhaps the earliest we have detailed records of was John 'Mad Jack' Mytton. He was born at the end of the eighteenth century and inherited a huge fortune at the age of two. Mad Jack didn't worry too much about his education from that point onwards. He was expelled from Westminster School for fighting with one of the masters and then was kicked out of Harrow for putting a horse in his tutor's bedroom. He left Cambridge without a degree having shipped two thousand bottles of port into his rooms.

Money, drink and animals seem to have played a large part in his behaviour, which became increasingly eccentric as he grew older. Deciding he wanted to be an MP, he offered voters £10 each to vote for him – spending the equivalent of £750,000 in the process. Having attended the House of Commons for half an hour he declared that the debates were boring and promptly left.

Mad Jack had a weakness for animals, keeping two thousand dogs and feeding his favourites steak and champagne. There are numerous stories of bets and madcap stunts, including an attempt to find out whether a horse pulling a trap could jump over a toll-gate (it couldn't), riding a horse into the Bedford Hotel in Leamington Spa, up its grand staircase and onto the balcony and over the diners below, out through the window and on to the Parade for a bet, and asking a passenger whether he'd ever been thrown out of a horse-drawn gig. When the passenger said he hadn't, Mad Jack exclaimed, 'What!! What a damn slow fellow you must have been all your life!' and drove the carriage up a slope, tipping both himself and the passenger out. One of the quotes I like about Mad Jack, which is so English, is that it was said of him, 'Not only did he not mind accidents, he positively liked them.'

Mad Jack led a dissolute and reckless life which ended, as such lives often do, very young. He died in King's Bench Prison in Southwark, rather sadly described by his biographer as a 'round-shouldered, tottering, old-young man bloated by drink, worn out by too much foolishness, too much wretchedness and too much brandy'. He was only thirty-five.

Another favourite – and a much gentler type – was Gerald Hugh Tyrwhitt-Wilson, 14th Baron Berners, who was born in 1884. He showed an early sign of his eccentric mind when, having heard that a dog would learn to swim if you threw it in the water, he tried to teach the family pet how to fly by hurling it from his bedroom window. He was a genuinely talented artist and composer, which might explain why his Rolls-Royce contained a small clavichord, a keyboard which could be stored beneath the front seat, and why he dyed the doves on his estate many colours. He apparently also drove around his estate wearing a pig's head.

He built a 140ft tower called Farringdon Folly, to which he attached a sign at the bottom that read 'Members of the Public committing suicide from this tower do so at their own risk'. When it came time for his own end, in 1950, he wrote his own epitaph, which read:

Here lies Lord Berners
One of the learners
His great love of learning
May earn him a burning
But, Praise the Lord!
He seldom was bored.

And one of my favourite nuggets about this lovable eccentric is that his doctor never sent a bill, saying that treating Berners and having his company had been payment enough.

The old aristocracy supplied many of England's most bizarre eccentrics, because to have a really odd lifestyle you require a large personal fortune and the arrogance to ignore the reactions of your fellow countrymen.

Animals and eccentrics seem to go hand in hand. Baron de Rothschild lived in a grand house in Buckinghamshire where he drove a carriage drawn by four zebras. Francis Henry Egerton, the 8th Earl of Bridgewater, preferred dogs to humans and insisted that they eat with him each day at an enormous dining table. Each dog wore a starched white napkin around its neck throughout the meal. Waiters attended one dog each and served them from silver dishes.

Lord Rokeby, who was born in 1713, would spend hours in the sea off the beaches of Kent. He was obsessed with water and often his servants would have to pull him out unconscious. He built a huge water tank at his home in order to be able to float for hours on end, eating in the water when he was hungry. His beard grew down to his waist and would spread out on the surface of the water as he lay there.

Lying around seems to go hand in hand with aristocratic eccentrics. Lord North returned from honeymoon in October and announced to his new wife that he was going to bed. After a few days she asked a servant why he was still under the covers, and received the reply that Lord North always stayed in bed from 9 October to 22 March. When she asked her husband about this, he replied that no Lord North had got out of bed between October and March since his ancestor had lost the American Colonies.

In more recent times, Sir John ('Jack') Leslie became known as the Lord of the Rave after getting into electronic dance music very late in life. At the age of eighty-five he celebrated his birthday by going clubbing in Ibiza. When he was asked about it, his enjoyment came through loud and clear: 'People were worried at first and said these discos might be rough but they are the absolute opposite. Everyone is so nice to me. The boys keep bringing me pints for some reason and the girls keep taking me out to dance and kissing me. It's wonderful. The people are fantastic and it seems to amuse them I'm there. They say they hope they're like me at eighty-five. One boy threw his arms round my neck and told me I was his idol.

'It is such fun watching people dancing and the music gets in your bones and makes you get up and dance,' Sir Jack once said, 'I get up and I leap around just as I feel like. When I hear the boom boom it electrifies me. I can leap up and down, and it's as if my ankles were electrified.'

The 5th Duke of Portland, William John Cavendish-Bentinck-Scott, was known as the 'gentle mole' because he loved to dig tunnels all over his estate, Welbeck Abbey in Nottinghamshire. He is said to have been the inspiration for the character of Badger in Kenneth Grahame's *Wind in the Willows*. Famously reclusive, the Duke was, like the Badger, gruff and sullen when he did come across other human beings. His obsession with tunnel-building supposedly came about because he wanted to block off access to his estate and when objections were made, he hit on the idea of making underground walkways. The tunnels themselves were wide enough for three people to walk abreast and lit by gas lights. One tunnel struck out for a mile and a quarter in the direction of Worksop.

The greatest achievement of his excavations was what was supposed to be the ballroom, but ended up housing his extensive art collection. The dimensions alone are staggering – it was 158ft long, 63ft wide and 22ft high. It might seem peculiar that such an anti-social man would build a ballroom; he had no desire for human company. However, it seems that his motivation for building was in fact quite generous. It is estimated that he employed as many as 1,500 artisans and labourers and spent £100,000 a year in the local economy. His eccentricity made the community thrive.

For all that, he never invited anyone over. 'He preferred to use the ballroom as a solo roller-skating rink,' according to one observer.

English eccentricity is a reflection of our individuality. As an island nation we have had to be unique and loud in order to stand out in the world. Wealth and genes, it seems, can serve to make us even more individual than normal. And just as with our heroic failures, we are intensely proud to lead the world in producing Grade A loons.

John Stuart Mill, who is quoted at the head of this chapter, hated any kind of tyranny, and particularly despised the sneering, curtain-twitching, self-elected arbiters of social conformity. For him, they were tyrants responsible for 'enslaving the soul'. Instead, Mill saw eccentric behaviour – so long as it harmed no one – as not only a matter of personal freedom, but a boon to society.

Eccentricity touches almost every aspect of Englishness, a juxtaposition of the staid, stiff-upper-jawed Englishman. At once contradictory and contrary, we want to conform and yet we prefer to march to the beat of our own drum.

Maybe the English just like to be different.

CHAPTER SIX

WELLIES, WAX, BARBOURS AND BOWLERS

Do we have a national dress? There are traditional costumes for so many countries which have become clichés – the Lederhosen-wearing Germans, stripy Breton-topped French, lumberjack-shirted Canadians – but it's difficult to pinpoint a national 'look' for the English. There are clothing items that are considered quintessentially English, though, and they all help protect us against our most common weather feature: the rain. In this chapter, I want to have a look at some of them.

The first is something I genuinely think I could not live without: the wax jacket. I love wax jackets. I love them so much, I wanted to write a whole book about them but my publisher wasn't sure there was a market.

I got my first wax jacket when I was 16. It was a green Barbour Bedale. It was several sizes too big, but I love that jacket and I have been addicted ever since. I still have it and count it among my collection of about twenty – although that might be a conservative estimate. And honestly, the more weathered and battered, the better.

In my mind, there can be fewer items of clothing that define a nation more. They are heavy, stiff and unflattering, and yet, a little like a Land Rover Defender, there is something deliciously utilitarian and 'everyman' about them. They are loved by farmers, supermodels and royalty alike.

To understand the story of the wax jacket we really need to explore the story of waterproof clothing in general; I should probably admit here to owning more than a hundred waterproof jackets (I told you I was a little bit weird). Perhaps this will be the marker of my developing eccentricity.

It is no surprise that as a nation England should excel in outdoor wear: as a nation obsessed with the weather, we have been forced to create barriers against it. A kind of climate armour.

The story of our contribution to keeping people dry begins in Roman times. A letter written almost 2,000 years ago by a Roman officer on sentry duty on Hadrian's Wall told of a revered garment that protected against the chill. Flavius Cerialis described an overcoat made of wool – a long hooded garment known as the 'birrus Britannicus'. Made with untreated wool, it was waterproof and doubled up as a blanket. It was to become the Barbour of its day, a fashion item among Romans, exported in large numbers. Two hundred years later the Emperor Diocletian lists the 'birrus Britannicus' when detailing the most superior goods traded across the Empire. It was the only British export to make the list. The cost was 6,000 denarii, said to be the equivalent of three months' pay for a teacher, 300 kilos of pork or 500 litres of everyday wine.

So even in Roman times, we had an international hit on our hands. The development of today's wax jacket, though, dates back to the 15th century, when sailors applied fish oils and grease to their heavy sailcloth. They did this because they noticed that wet sails were more efficient than dry ones; however, if the water soaked into the cloth, the weight slowed the ships down. By greasing them, the sails retained their increased efficiency but not the extra water weight. However, the oil tended to yellow with age – the reason for sailors' waterproofs still being predominately yellow – and tended to stiffen up too much in the cold.

Fast forward to the mid-nineteenth century and the sail cotton was impregnated with paraffin or a natural beeswax, either through application, or it was woven in.

From the leftover caps of material the sailors and sailmakers would cut themselves waterproof overalls and capes to keep dry. Several companies cooperated to create paraffin-impregnated cotton, which produced a highly water-resistant cloth, breathable, but without the stiffness in the cold or yellowing with age. Woven by the sailmaker Francis Webster, it was taken to Lancashire to be dyed black or olive, and then to London for ammonia treatment. The cloth was then returned to Lancashire for waxing, and then back to Webster's in Arbroath for storage, sales and distribution across the British Empire.

Waxed cotton became an instant success with the commercial shipping industry, and Webster's as primary manufacturers began thinking of other markets for the product. One of the early adopters was J. Barbour & Sons in the outdoor industry, producing waxed jackets for farmers and gamekeepers.

Barbour wasn't the only company developing new ways of protecting the English from the elements. The Mackintosh or raincoat (abbreviated as mac or mack) is a form of waterproof raincoat, first sold in 1824. The Mackintosh is named after its Scottish inventor Charles Macintosh. Although the Mackintosh coat style is common, a genuine Mackintosh coat is made from rubberised or rubber-laminated material.

Clothing manufacturers like Mackintosh used sophisticated scientific research to create garments that worked in different kinds of weather – reflecting the subtle differences in our climate. From early on they produced coats that were either showerproof (to ward against light drizzle – that kind of English dampness that gradually seeps into your clothes) or waterproof (to protect against a proper downpour).

In 1823, Charles Macintosh patented a double-textured fabric sandwiched around a layer of rubber. The Mackintosh became the synonym for the raincoat and a staple of the English wardrobe. Its popularity really took off during the Second World War, though, when it was adopted by the British armed forces as their first-choice waterproof. Since then, Mackintosh has been through many changes and has had different owners, but the classic coat is still undeniably an essential element of English fashion culture.

Another of the most recognisable modern English fashion brands is Burberry. With an estimated retail value of over 150 billion Euros, Burberry has come a long way from its origins as a Victorian outfitter's shop in Basingstoke, Hampshire.

Thomas Burberry was born in 1835 in Brockham Green, Surrey. After serving his apprenticeship at a local draper's shop,

Burberry opened his own small clothing outfitters in Basingstoke in 1857.

Burberry had a good head for business and by 1861 the census reveals that he was employing seven men, three boys and seven women in his shop. Burberry began researching and experimenting with materials to produce fabrics which were weatherproof and suitable for the population around Basingstoke – mainly farmers and landed gentry who either worked outdoors or enjoyed fishing, hunting and riding.

In 1880 his research yielded a weatherproof and tear-proof fabric which he called gabardine. The material was light and breathable, but managed to protect from the worst of the English weather.

Burberry took off. It opened a shop in Haymarket, London in 1891 and followed that with outlets in Reading, Manchester, Liverpool and Winchester. Abroad, the products were sold through agencies in Paris, New York and Buenos Aires.

Showing a very modern knack for the celebrity endorsement, in 1911 Burberry became the official outfitter for Roald Amundsen, the first man to reach the South Pole, and Ernest Shackleton, who led a 1914 expedition to cross Antarctica. He also marketed his products to the armed forces, and they were famously worn by Lord Kitchener and Lord Baden Powell. Thomas Burberry didn't retire until 1917 – an incredible life's work. His two sons took over the business and trademarked the now famous Burberry check design.

One of the last products Thomas saw go into production was the trench coat. Patented by Burberry in 1912, it was an unbuttoned style made from gabardine and fastened with a belt. The trench coat was adapted to serve the needs of the military in the early 20th century and was worn in the trenches of the First World War by British soldiers. Epaulettes displayed an officer's rank, while the belt's metal D-rings were used to attach equipment. After the war, the trench coat became popular with civilians. More recently it has been sported by Alexa Chung and Rosie Huntington-Whiteley on numerous occasions, and other style-setters spotted wearing the celebrated classic include Jessica Chastain, Poppy Delevingne and Clémence Poésy; Burberry's Autumn/Winter 2014 campaign saw Cara Delevingne, Malaika Firth and Tarun Nijjer modelling the trench, proving the brand is fast becoming much-coveted by a new generation.

Of course, the most famous wax jacket of all is the Barbour.

The manufacturer of functional and elegant outerwear is based in a factory in Simonside in South Shields, northeast England, and has been steered by the Barbour family for five generations. Their classic jackets are still manufactured by hand and they make more than 100,000 per year. Quintessentially English, they even do a range of dog coats (tartan, quilted, polar, wax, waterproof) and accessories (bandannas, collars, leads, duvets, beds).

I went to visit one day. It was my first trip to a textile factory and it was brimming with activity as hundreds of women worked on an assortment of sewing machines of every shape and size. There were zippers and liners and buttons and hoods all being hand processed through buzzing, whirring machines.

I could just about make out wax pockets and the famous tartan liners being carefully cut to size on huge tables. It was all very labour-intensive. With dozens of different jackets in multiple sizes and colours, creating a garment is a complex jigsaw puzzle of manufacture. Luckily enough many of the workers were second or third generation, so they have the process in their genes.

In one corner of the factory was a large pile of jackets all carefully returned, often at vast expense, to be repaired and rewaxed.

Away from the buzz and hum of the work floor, the Barbour headquarters were relatively spartan and quiet. Huge photographs of old adverts and photographs hung from the walls, a reminder of the company's rich heritage.

Helen Barbour sat, cuppa in hand, new puppy on the table, in the 'Brand Room'. The tiny dog raced across the vast wooden table and then proceeded to pee in the middle of it. 'I am so sorry', she apologized, clearing the mess up.

On a large rail were a collection of antique and vintage jackets that charted Barbour's history. The Barbour began its life as fishermen's overalls; a collection of old catalogues offered a little porthole into the original provenance of the South Shields garment. Sou'wester and yellow fishing trousers were produced to protect the early fishermen from the worst of the North Sea conditions. The brand found a market and the factory has been at its current site ever since, producing up to 3,000 waxed jackets a week.

Helen has a warm, welcoming manner and is passionate about the brand. It was her mother, Dame Margaret, who took over in the 1960s after the death of her husband John Barbour. The family worked in every department and even modelled their products.

'That's me', smiled Helen, flicking through an old 80s catalogue in which a young Helen is seen modelling the wax jacket in full glory. I asked Helen when the brand went from function to

fashion. She balks at the word 'fashion' but concedes to the power
of the late Princess Diana.

'It was the first official photograph of Diana with Charles – she
was wearing a Barbour,' she reminisces. 'The business finally
started to make some money.'

The company has retained a strong relationship with the royal
family, and, while they must still buy their jackets, Barbour hold
three royal warrants from the Duke of Edinburgh, the Queen and
the Prince of Wales. Dame Margaret revealed on *Woman's Hour*
that the Queen was so attached to her old faithful Barbour that
she refused to part with it even when offered a free replacement.
I can sympathize. I have dozens of old Barbours, all of which have
stood the test of time, and all of which, like a fine wine, have
improved with maturity. It's one of the many great things about
Barbour jackets – each jacket holds its history in its folds, creases,
tears and fading. They are like memory boxes.

I asked Gary, the Design and Development Manager, if there
was any one particular jacket that had surprised him by its
popularity.

'We made a special Beacon Sports jacket,' he explained. 'It was
a short run and the jacket didn't sell well, but one caught the eye
of the wardrobe department on the James Bond film *Skyfall*. They
ordered 25 for the shoot.'

Demand suddenly went through the roof. It became known as
the 'Barbour Skyfall', selling for more than £400 a pop.

After the Princess Diana boost, the publication of the *Official
Sloane Ranger Handbook* by Peter York in 1982 ensured that the
Barbour established itself as the must-have accessory for every
Sloane in London and the Home Counties. Sales boomed and

its appeal spread to unexpected parts of our culture. This culminated when the Barbour became 'festival cool'. It was the time of 'Cool Britannia', and Kate Moss was seen in a Barbour in the rain at Glastonbury. Lily Allen and Alexa Chung caught on and changed this functional bit of clothing into a fashion essential. But what the new stars of today have not recognized is that for a countryman's Barbour to be cool, it must be old. Some years ago, for example, the *Daily Telegraph* diary column impertinently suggested that the Barbour belonging to the former Chancellor of the Exchequer Kenneth Clarke was 'knackered'.

The backlash was immediate. 'Barbours, like decent port, mature with age,' wrote Jonathan Young, editor of *The Field*. Another correspondent, Terence Branch, said: 'Like an old soldier, a Barbour never dies, it only fades away.'

It is for these sentimental reasons that a Barbour is forever. It is a family friend that is rarely thrown away but instead tossed into a corner when it has begun to reach the end of its useful life. It goes into semi-retirement as an emergency coat for a guest or something to chuck in the back of the car for the dog.

When the *Telegraph* ran a competition to find the country's oldest Barbour they were inundated with thousands of entries with many jackets more than half a century old, but the prize incredibly went to a cape dating back to 1921, which just goes to prove a Barbour jacket never dies.

'We mend and rewax 24,000 jackets a year,' marvelled Helen. Gary began to pull some vintage jackets from the rail: 'This one was bespoke made for a Falklands soldier,' he beamed as he proudly showed me a tattered jacket covered in extra pockets.

'It was customized by Captain Mick Cotton who served in the 2nd battalion of the Parachute Regiment. We used a Durham jacket and added pockets and D rings and arm pouches.'

The jacket was also fitted with stud fasteners and the lower arms had extra patches of wax sewn on for additional reinforcement.

He delved into the pockets and pulled out two small cylinders. 'It still has his ear plugs.'

Many will argue that the true personalization of a Barbour lies in the contents of its pockets, a virtual time capsule of the wearer's year. I could only imagine the horrors this jacket must have experienced in the theatre of the Falklands war.

There are few brands that can boast both the Queen and the Arctic Monkeys among their fans, but the Barbour transcends fashion. I sometimes think that it is the garment equivalent of the Land Rover: it is boxy and practical; both are beloved of royalty and it is an English trademark product, recognized all over the world. Like the English, it has been born out of function to became the textile manifestation of the national spirit. Hardwearing, durable and stiff-upper-lipped.

Kate Moss wasn't just responsible for helping to save the wax jacket. She gave the Wellington boot a boost, too.

Owning a pair of wellies is a British institution. No good Englishman or -woman is complete without a good pair of gumboots.

The legacy of the Wellington boot began in 1817, when the Duke of Wellington requested that the famous London shoemaker George Hoby of St James design something that could be worn in battle but that could also be used for evening wear

– certainly a highly practical request. He wanted the design modeled on his military Hessian boots.

Hessian boots, named after German mercenaries who fought alongside the British in the American War of Independence (1775–83), were made of soft, highly polished calfskin. They were knee-high, with a low heel and semi-pointed toe suitable for stirrups and were decorated with a tassel cut into the front. Standard-issue footwear for light cavalry regiments, especially hussars, they became widely worn by civilians too.

These first boots, the Duke's namesake style made by Hoby, were made of soft calfskin leather, cut close to the calf, and were designed as a fashion item. The heels were stacked around an inch and the tassel removed. The boot was appropriately hard-wearing for riding, yet smart enough for informal evening wear. The boot was dubbed 'the Wellington' and the name stuck.

In 1856 the North British Rubber Company, later to become known as Hunter Boot Ltd, was founded. Using the newly patented vulcanization process for rubber, the company manufactured rubber boots and overshoes, alongside waterproof clothing, tyres and other durable rubber products.

In 1916, after the outbreak of the First World War, the company was commissioned by the War Office to produce sturdy rubber boots as standard winter kit to protect soldiers from 'trench foot', a medical condition caused by prolonged exposure to damp in the flooded trenches. The mills operated around the clock to produce the immense quantities of boots required: 1,185,036 pairs were made to meet the British Army's demands.

During the Second World War, Hunter Boot Ltd was again requested to supply vast quantities of Wellington and thigh boots.

By the end of the war, the Wellington had become popular among men, women and children for wet weather wear. The boot had developed to become far roomier with a thick sole and rounded toe. Also, with the rationing of that time, labourers began to use them for daily work. The Original Green Wellington, now known as the Original Boot, was introduced by Hunter in 1956.

The year 2005 is recognized as the year that the Hunter brand exploded in popularity, coinciding with their expansion overseas to America. The year also marked the 50-year celebration of the iconic Original Boot. Hunter celebrated by introducing seven new colours. Kate Moss famously wore a pair to Glastonbury that year.

A global flagship store on Regent Street, collection catwalks at London Fashion Week and collaborations with names like Jimmy Choo don't provoke particularly powerful images of tramping through mud and wading through water with a pair of wellies. Town has very clearly met Country, however. Hunter acknowledge their heritage with a great amount of pride and consistency in design.

From boots back to jackets. Like Barbour and Burberry, Belstaff is a heritage brand symbolic of rugged allure with a history of adventure, exploration, aviation and motorsport which has taken it onto catwalks around the world. Started in the mid-1920s, it became beloved of the riders of motorized bicycles and the bikers haven't looked elsewhere for jackets ever since. The reason for their popularity? Harry Grosberg, the company founder, had researched and developed a material that was windproof, rain-proof and resistant to heavy friction. Shown off by two male style icons – Peter O'Toole in *Lawrence of Arabia* and Steve McQueen in *The Great Escape*, the Belstaff jacket is now commonly seen on celebs such as Angelina Jolie, Hilary Swank, Brad Pitt and Johnny Depp. The Stoke-on-Trent manufacturer produced 40,000 of the Black Prince jackets a year during the Second World War. The jackets disappeared in the 1990s, but a change of ownership and employing talent from other iconic English brands has seen Belstaff back-motoring.

In 1571, during the reign of Elizabeth I, Parliament legislated to support the wool industry by encouraging the use of wool in products. All men of the age of six had to wear a woollen 'bonnet' during religious ceremonies. 'Persons of degree' were excluded from this requirement but anyone else not complying was fined three farthings, a huge amount of money for the working class.

The law remained for the best part of three decades and by the time it was repealed, the cloth cap (or Tudor bonnet) had become a symbol of respectability, of people prepared to obey the law and of course of the successful upper middle class. In short it became a symbol of aspiration.

The Tudor bonnet was so popular that it is still used in various forms for PhD graduation ceremonies from universities across the country (and abroad – another sign of global influence).

Men were still wearing the cloth cap by the beginning of the twentieth century and it was here that it started to span the complex English class system: it became popular with golfers.

Yet cloth caps were also a symbol of the working class in the iconic photographs of the construction of the Queen Mary at John Brown and Co. shipbuilders in Clydebank. The government had invested in shipbuilding during the Great Depression and every head of those hardworking shipwrights can be seen in a cloth cap.

Nowadays, the cloth cap looks as natural on the head of Prince Charles and David Beckham as it does on Andy Capp and Del Boy in *Only Fools and Horses* – it's like the Land Rover in its ability to adapt to all social classes.

Another English staple is the cardigan. Cupboard count: five. My wife calls them my 'grandpa' cardigans and the garment has undeniably developed a reputation as representing the slightly older generation.

We can thank James Thomas Brudenell, the Seventh Earl of Cardigan, for the iconic garment, but he was no old fogey. Indeed, he is the villain in many of George MacDonald Fraser's *Flashman* novels. Described as a pompous bully and a military incompetent, he was mistakenly ordered into action with the Light Brigade to charge the Russian guns during the Crimean War. The battle turned him into a national hero and it immortalized the woollen 'cardigan' he wore in battle.

Soon after his return to England, rumours began to circulate that he had in fact fled the battlefield, that he was a coward and a cad.

No one will ever know what really happened, but the battle of Balaclava was immortalized in Tennyson's poem 'The Charge of the Light Brigade', and Lord Cardigan left us this strange woollen garment.

* * *

Perhaps the most iconic item of clothing associated with England is the bowler hat. Loved by Sir Winston Churchill and fictional characters like Mr Banks in *Mary Poppins*, Charlie Chaplin's tramp, Laurel and Hardy, and John Steed from the *Avengers*, the Bowler hat became synonymous with businessmen in the City of London during the mid-twentieth century.

The hat originated in London in 1849 when the city's most famous and oldest hatters, Lock & Co. of St James's, were asked by politician Edward Coke to come up with a hat that would both protect his head while he was riding and not fall off. Lock & Co. asked the hat-making brothers William and Thomas Bowler to design something for them.

The brothers delivered a hat that had shellac (a natural resin) on the top for protection and didn't reach as high as the top hat. It fitted snugly around the temples, making it sit firmer on the head as well.

Coke was very happy with the hat, paid 12 shillings for it and created a global market for the London hat makers. Bowlers were adopted throughout Great Britain, Europe and North America, and even became part of the national dress of Peru. Lock & Co. are still going and estimate they sell 4–5,000 bowlers a year at £300 each.

The bowler hat of course goes hand-in-hand with the brolly.

I will admit here that I hate umbrellas. In fact, I loathe the things. I'm not sure what it is but they have always rubbed me up the wrong way. When I went onto the BBC's Orwellian comedy show *Room 101*, in which guests can banish their most hated aspects of society, I nominated the umbrella.

To be honest I find them slightly terrifying, mainly because so few people adhere to umbrella 'etiquette': they march down the street, completely unaware of the metal points that protrude from the corners.

Perhaps it is just me, but most people who use umbrellas seem to be shorter than me, which means I navigate a forest of spikes at face level, threatening to take my eye out. I have been known to suggest an umbrella 'driving licence', whereby people are taught how to use umbrellas correctly and safely while in crowds.

No one is sure of the origin of the umbrella. It is likely that it evolved from a basic shelter of leaves carried by primitive man. The rain umbrella – the one we English were more likely to need – was introduced by a merchant called Jonas Hanway in the 18th century. He'd seen umbrellas (Latin 'little shade') being used to protect ladies from the sun during a business trip to Persia. When he got back to grey and wet London, he had a shade constructed of animal ribs and stretched fabric which he used as a shield against the rain. For thirty years he was alternately shunned and ridiculed by society. Bystanders stood in shock at the social faux pas of walking with what at the time was seen as a symbol of weakness. The umbrella was 'un-English', it went against our stiff upper lip. We just braved the rain. People jeered the weak Hanway.

Taxi drivers, Hansom cab owners and sedan-chair carriers all hated him, fearing his invention would take away their business; there are reports of him being pelted with rubbish by 18th-century cabbies to add injury to the insults. Hanway persisted even when a Hansom cab driver tried to run him over. According to reports, Hanway gave him a 'good thrashing' with his hefty little shade. It seems that the umbrella has always been used as a bit of a weapon.

Twenty years after Hanway's death, the Duke of Wellington was carrying an umbrella, and it has since become one of the essential accessories of the traditional 'gentleman'.

The development of the umbrella was quick; Wellington's version had a rapier sword masked in the handle, ready for any impromptu street duels. By the middle of the nineteenth century the trademark 'U'-shaped handle was added, and the materials used were getting lighter by the decade.

It seems I am not alone in my dislike of umbrellas, though. Joseph Kennedy, the American Ambassador to the Court of St James's, loathed any mention of umbrellas.

His son, the future President John F. Kennedy, is said to have inherited his father's hatred of them.

According to historians, it was this 'umbrella phobia' that prompted Louis Steven Witt to take an umbrella to Dealey Plaza on 22 November 1963, with the intention of mocking the President as his car passed. No one knows if President Kennedy saw the umbrella. If he did, it would have been the last thing he ever noticed because, just as his car passed, he was shot dead.

The 'Umbrella Man' has triggered countless conspiracy theorists convinced that the umbrella was part of the assassination plot, used to signal his death. In 1978, Louis Steven Witt revealed himself as 'Umbrella Man', explaining to the House Select Committee investigation into the assassination of President Kennedy that: 'In a coffee-break conversation, someone mentioned that the Kennedys loathed umbrellas and all they represented.'

'You were opening the umbrella to use it as a symbol to catch the President's eye?' asked his inquisitor.

'Yes, sir.'

Perhaps this was the beginning of the end. The umbrella has become something of a pariah in recent years. While a staple of the gathering queues at Wimbledon, they have, like the bowler hat in James Bond films, become devious weapons.

One was infamously used as a real weapon in 1978, when the Bulgarian government killed the dissident journalist Georgi Markov by jabbing him with a ricin-tipped specimen on Waterloo Bridge.

And I still loathe umbrellas.

CHAPTER SEVEN

THE SILLY SEASON

'What do you call an Englishman in the knockout stages
of the World Cup? The referee.'

My mother always wanted me to be a cricketer. There have been
two cricketing highlights in my life. The first was when I accidentally managed to get into an English expat team playing an international match against Costa Rica; and the second was the time
I played in a match in the middle of the Solent amidst ocean-
going container ships and yachts.

On the latter occasion, dressed in my finest starched cricket
whites, fold marks still visible from the sporting shop shelf
from which I had bought them the day before, I made my way to
the ferry for the short journey across the Solent to the Isle of
Wight.

Cowes was already a hubbub of activity as sailors readied their
yachts for a day's sailing. I was here for a very different sport.

Down in the marina I joined a modest crowd boarding a flotilla of yachts, ribs, tenders, canoes and every other assortment of tiny ocean-going craft imaginable. As the vessels filled they set off in a small armada for the middle of the Solent.

Here, bang in the centre of one of the world's busiest shipping lanes, several dozen craft bearing hundreds of people bobbed around in the calm waters. There was no sight of land for many miles, just a busy expanse of water littered with boats. It was certainly an unusual beginning for a cricket match.

The date and time of this bizarre spectacle are dictated by the tide. For 364 days each year Bramble Bank lurks beneath the surface of the sea, halfway between the northern coast of the Isle of Wight and the mainland, a navigational hazard for any unwary skipper. Hundreds of ships have run aground here, most notably the *Queen Elizabeth II* in 2008 on her final visit to Southampton before retiring.

Each September, when the tide reaches its lowest ebb, there is one day when the water rolls back to reveal a thin stretch of golden sand in the middle of the maritime version of the M25. And in that short window, this sliver of land, roughly 200 yards long, becomes the world's oddest cricket pitch as a match is played in front of hundreds of fans. This is the annual Brambles cricket match. This is extreme cricket.

While some believe that it was prisoners from Parkhurst who were the first to play cricket on the bank, encouraged to do so by a governor who thought that escape would be impossible, the exact provenance is thought to be via a boatbuilder called Uffa Fox. A friend of the Duke of Edinburgh, Fox arranged a cricket match between 'his' team and one from the Holmwood Hotel in

Cowes. It became an annual event until Fox's death in 1972, before being resurrected by another sailor named Tom Richardson.

In 1983 Richardson was sailing back from Cowes with two friends, Tony Lovell and Chris Freer, when they saw four boats aground on Bramble Bank. 'We agreed it would be fun to play cricket on the bank again, and so the following year we challenged the Island Sailing Club.' Matches have been played every year since, some soggier than others. And in the case of Brambles, I don't mean the rainy kind of soggy. In 2008 a particularly high tide meant the waves never sank below the players' knees, but the game went ahead anyway.

Today the match is held between Island Sailing Club and Hamble Sailing Club. There are no rules and no real winner. Scoring is arbitrary. One year the Island team was fined 200 runs for not turning up in whites.

No risk of that for me, I thought, as we floated on top of the still waterlogged cricket strip. It really was an extraordinary sight to behold as dozens of boats circled on the spot, waiting for low water. Soon bubbles could be seen on the surface of the water surface and, like something from the scriptures, the waves began to part, revealing a tiny patch of damp sand. 'Sand! Sand!' came the war cry.

Vessels jostled into position as the strip began to grow, and before long spectators and players were cascading into the shallow water. Stumps were inserted, tables, parasols and deckchairs appeared. It was still early morning as Budgie Stratton from the Victory pub set up the Brambles Bar on one corner of the sandbank.

The game would best be described as organized chaos, as both sides took turns to bat amidst a very close crowd of increasingly inebriated spectators. The first ball from the opposition was hit clean into the air, one brave fielder from my team diving head-first towards the shallow waters at the edge of the sandbar, narrowly missing the ball and a passing oil tanker. It was a truly surreal experience as tankers and container ships honked their horns in approval as they sailed just a few yards beyond our game of cricket.

As I took to the wicket, bat in hand, the tide had already begun to turn. I rolled up my white trousers and focused on the ball. I thought back to all those cricket lessons with Viv Richards at Lord's cricket ground. Now was the moment to make my mother proud as the bowler raced in my direction and the ball hit the saturated sand.

It bounced and hurtled towards me. I focused on the ball as it swerved towards my bat. Wood struck leather and the ball flew heroically through the air towards the open water beyond. The crowd erupted as one luckless fielder was forced to swim for the ball. The tide was coming in fast and feet had now disappeared beneath a brownish film of water as the sand was reclaimed by the tide.

'The tide's coming in, clear the bank,' came the holler, and as quickly as it had appeared, the sandbank disappeared beneath the waves once more as dozens of people gathered up stumps and deckchairs and tables and dived back onto the armada of tiny vessels that had been anchored like ponies to the edge of the sandbank.

By the time the last of the players was back onto the boats he was up to his waist, as the umpire announced that Island Sailing

Club were the winners and we all headed back to Cowes for tea and trophies.

The Brambles cricket match is English sporting eccentricity at its most ridiculous. One of this year's competitors summed it up rather nicely, I thought, as 'Quintessentially English madness on a beautiful summer's evening.'

While my mother wanted me to be a cricketer, I had my sights set on becoming an international worm charmer.

The World Worm Charming Championships have been held annually near Willaston in Cheshire since July 1980, when a local farmer's son, Tom Shufflebotham, successfully charmed 511 worms out of the ground in thirty minutes. The championship's eighteen rules are strictly enforced by the International Federation of Charming Worms and Allied Pastimes (IFCWAP), a body that also regulates such sports as underwater Ludo and indoor hang-gliding. Tom Shufflebotham's 29-year world worm charming record was finally broken in 2009 by ten-year-old Sophie Smith, whose team successfully charmed 567 worms to the surface.

The key to worm charming is to try and fool the worm into thinking it's raining. Since the rules stipulate that worms must be charmed without the aid of water, the most popular technique is 'twanging', which involves planting a pitchfork into the soil and then rocking, hitting or twanging it. The movement sends reverberations down into the soil, encouraging the worms to think it is raining. Other less orthodox approaches have also been adopted, including playing rock guitar or xylophone, and even tap dancing to the *Star Wars* theme. Some competitors have employed rather unscrupulous tactics such as hiding worms up their trouser legs or chopping them in half to double their number – both practices in contravention of international worm charming law.

WORLD WORM CHARMING RULES

Each competitor to operate in a 3 x 3 metre plot.

Lots to be drawn to allocate plots.

Duration of competition to be 30 minutes, starting at about 2 p.m.

Worms may not be dug from the ground. Vibrations only to be used.

No drugs to be used! Water is considered to be a drug/ stimulant.

Any form of music may be used to charm the worms out of the earth.

A garden fork of normal type may be stuck into the ground and vibrated by any manual means to encourage worms to the surface.

Garden forks to be suitably covered to prevent possible injury when being transported to and from the competition. No accidents please!

Each competitor to leave his/her fork in allocated plot on arrival.

A piece of wood, smooth or notched, may be used to strike or 'fiddle' the handle of the garden fork to assist vibration.

Competitors who do not wish to handle worms may
appoint a second to do so. The second shall be known
as a 'Gillie'.
Each competitor may collect worms from his/her own plot
only.
Worms to be handled carefully and collected in damp peat
and placed in a suitable, named container provided by
the organizing committee.
A handbell to be rung about five minutes before the start
of the competition.
Competitors to keep clear of competition plots until given
the instruction 'Get to your Plots'.
The competitor who 'charms' the most worms to be the
winner.
In the event of a tie, the winner to be decided by a further
five minutes' charming.
Charmed worms to be released after the birds have gone
to roost on the evening of the event.

After seeking some local advice I headed into town to stock up
on provisions. I bought a worm bucket, a small set of bells, a
child's trumpet, a tambourine, a toy car, a tin whistle, a pitchfork
and an alarm clock. I wasn't sure how I was going to use my eclectic mix of tools but I was desperate to win.

I returned to a carnival of all things worm. There were children dressed as worms, dads dressed as worms, mums in army
camouflage and various worm-charming contraptions that would
wow Caractacus Potts. Recreating the sounds of thunder,

lightning and the pitter-patter of raindrops were all the worm-bait you needed. There were bicycles mounted on blocks with the rear wheels removed and replaced by two sticks with big boots on the end of each one. As the bicycle was pedalled, the boots thumped in turn against the ground. 'Just like thunder,' smiled the inventor. There were old lawnmowers that had been adapted Heath Robinson style to 'twang' the soil with each movement rather than chop the grass. My personal favourite was a stereo with its speakers facing the ground and a playlist called simply 'Rain'.

I gathered my worm tools and headed into the arena. There was a roar from the crowd. This must be what it is like to be an England player walking into Wembley Stadium, except I was in a Cheshire field. Still, it felt good.

We were each given a three-square-metre plot of ground that had been carefully marked out with ropes, and we had half an hour to charm as many worms to the surface as we could. Having stepped into the ring, I sat cross-legged on my little patch of soil and planned my tactics, eyeing up the competition. There were nearly a hundred competitors including worm-charming veterans.

'Focus, Ben,' I muttered to myself.

'... five, four, three, two, one ...' *Brrrrrrrrrrr!* the klaxon sounded.

I knelt on the dry grass, picked up the tambourine and started tapping it rhythmically against the ground. Nothing. Not a worm in sight.

I took the tin whistle, placed its end against the soil and blew tunefully. Nothing. Blew ... forcefully. Still nothing.

I jangled bells and tooted on the trumpet. Still not a worm in sight.

Every so often I would hear a great cheer as a worm was carefully extracted from the ground. 'How are they charming them?' I fumed.

I patted the ground with the tambourine and blew again on the tin whistle. In desperation, I resorted to a sort of rain dance, tapping my feet against the ground in simulation of rain.

Each new cheer drove my increasingly frantic attempts on. I lay on the ground and held my hands to my mouth. 'Wormy, here wormy worm worms.'

Nothing.

Just as despair was beginning to set in, I caught a glimpse of something in the green grass, a flicker of brown. It was the unmistakable body of a worm. I froze, my heart began to pound. I had to get it before it disappeared back into its hole. Slowly I lowered my hand. I practised the 'chopstick' movement with my thumb and forefinger and … snatch! I snapped at the ground. My fingers locked around its slippery body but it was thin, really thin. Too thin.

I had overestimated the power of my squeeze and the worm snapped in two, leaving me with a writhing half-worm between my fingers, in direct contravention of the spirit and practice of international worm charming.

'You killed it!' frowned the director.

'No, I doubled it,' I corrected her as I placed it in the bucket. At least I was off to a start. The problem was that the competition was already halfway through. There were only fifteen minutes left to pick up the pace and by the sound of cheering and whooping, my competitors each had more than half a worm in their buckets.

The clock ticked on and I tried some pitchfork twanging. Miraculously worms began to appear. They were small, skinny and sometimes a bit 'halvy', but they were beautiful, writhing worms none the less.

One, two, three, four, five ... the pile began to mount until the klaxon sounded once again, marking the end of the competition.

'Right, time to count the slippery little suckers.' I smiled for the cameras before disappearing to the counting station, where worm marshals would validate my haul.

'Well done. You have seven worms,' announced my counter.

'I think you'll find it's a little more than that,' I corrected her.

'No it isn't!' she said, holding out the bucket.

'What about that?' I smiled, pointing to another worm in the corner of the bucket.

'That's half a worm!' she said.

'So it's seven and a half worms,' I responded triumphantly.

'We don't count halves.'

'Why not?' I asked, a little miffed.

'Animal cruelty,' she answered.

The weigh-in complete, it was time for the announcement of the winners. The tension in the field was palpable.

'The winner of the World Worm Charming Championships is Leon Holt with two hundred and ninety-six worms.'

'Two hundred and ninety-six!' I nearly choked. 'Two hundred and ninety-six!' I repeated, open-mouthed. This ten-year-old had well and truly whopped me. My dreams of world worm dominance had been shattered, and with that my worm-charming days were over.

And that was the end of that – or so I thought, until the show went out a couple of weeks later and I found myself caught up in a row about the nuances of the English language in a bizarre and truly English way.

'Someone has lodged a complaint against you with the BBC,' warned my agent.

I was puzzled. 'Was it for animal cruelty?' I wondered, anticipating that someone had objected to my half-worm – the English love all animals, great and small.

'No,' she replied, 'for swearing on air.'

What did she mean? I rarely swear, and certainly not on camera – and definitely not on a pre-edited Sunday morning rural affairs show on the BBC. Apart from once getting in trouble for saying I was 'knackered' during a coracle race, I was usually accused of being too prudish, and yet now I was in the midst of a formal complaint against me for bad language.

'The complainant,' began the report, 'alleges that during a *Countryfile* report on the Silver Jubilee World Worm Charming Championships, Ben Fogle said "It's now time to count the slippery little f**kers!"'

What the f@£k? Pardon my language, but really, on a pre-recorded Sunday morning show? Really? The complainant had it in for me and wasn't giving in easily. Despite the BBC's assurance that I had in fact said 'slippery little suckers', the viewer was still not satisfied and took the matter to the Head of Complaints.

The Head of Complaints responded that 'throughout the worm charming the sound quality was less than perfect and there was a loss of sibilants; however, the phrase "slippery little suckers" had an alliteration which the alternative lacked'.

Despite, or perhaps because of, this confusing explanation, the complainant took it to the Governors' Programme Complaints Committee. And so it was that the board of the BBC governors was forced to watch me taking part in the Silver Jubilee Worm Charming Championships. They concluded that I did indeed say 'slippery little suckers'.

If you can't catch worms, you can always try crabs.

'I caught crabs in Walberswick' reads my favourite T-shirt. It is from the time I took part in the World Crabbing Championships in the Suffolk coastal town of that name.

Crabbing is another quintessentially English hobby. It reminds me of my childhood, sitting on the harbour wall in Padstow with a crabbing line in the water. The fear and excitement of catching one of those fearsome clawed crustaceans was overwhelming.

The Walberswick crabbing championships have become something of an institution, attracting thousands of spectators as well as hundreds of competitors. The contest lasts ninety minutes, each crabber armed with a single line and bait of their choice. The person to land the heaviest crab wins. Bait really is the key.

I had done a little research into crab bait and discovered that bacon and sausage seem to be the most popular, followed by bread. My secret weapon … Marmite, of course. Oh, and Jammie Dodgers. I'm not sure how I settled on these, but I felt sure any good crab would be unable to resist the black stuff.

The starting gun fired and a thousand lines dipped into the murky waters. (The scale of the competition is amazing – the peak entry was 1,252 in 2009.) I smeared some Marmite onto a Jammie Dodger. There was a flurry of excitement as each crab was plucked from the lines and placed carefully into waiting buckets of water.

'Haven't you caught anything yet?' asked a young boy, peering into my empty bucket.

I shrugged and watched him walk back to his father and their bucket full of crustacea. His father was disentangling another crab from their line. It was Richard Curtis, the film director. Not any old film director, but perhaps the director of the greatest quintessentially English movie hits, from *Four Weddings and a Funeral* to *Notting Hill* and *Love Actually*. A man who understood the curious customs and attitudes of the English. And now, here he was with his children competing against me in the fiercely competitive crabbing championships.

For ninety long minutes, I dangled my Marmite-smeared Jammie Dodgers into the murky tidal waters. The problem of course was saturation – as soon as the biscuits hit the water they dissolved, leaving my line baitless. And crabless.

All around me families and children were hauling in monster crabs while my bucket remained conspicuously empty. Finally, as I lifted my line from the water, I saw a tiny crab holding on for dear life. I had caught a hitchhiker. Admittedly he was tiny, little larger than a thumbnail, but he was a crab nonetheless.

The clock ticked down and the klaxon sounded. 'Competitors, remove your lines from the water.' We each made our way to the official crab counter and I presented my tiny crab. I was beaten by Richard Curtis and family, who took the championship title. All I left with was the T-shirt. It still makes me laugh.

Sport is an English national obsession. Largely, it has to be said, because we believe we invented most of them. Inventing a sport, or codifying its rules (another English speciality), bestows a superiority which is very useful when we no longer dominate that sport; just think of football, and our fixation with England's one-off 1966 World Cup victory.

The big three sports that originated from these shores are football, rugby (which split into rugby union and rugby league, and led to American football and Australian rules) and cricket (which morphed into baseball on the other side of the pond). In fact, there are twenty-eight other sports that originate from England. Alphabetically, the list runs: association football, bandy, English billiards, bowls, cricket, croquet, Cumberland and Westmorland wrestling, Devon wrestling, Eton fives, extreme ironing, ferret-legging, fives, indoor cricket, Lancashire wrestling, netball, rackets, rally-cross, rounders, rugby fives, rugby league, rugby union, shin-kicking, squash, table tennis, tennis, underwater hockey, walking football and water polo.

A. A. Gill in his book *The Angry Island: Hunting the English* wrote, 'The English have invented almost every game you can think of – and if they didn't invent them, they grabbed and codified them. Far too many games' rules have been constructed by the English for it to be merely coincidental ...' It does seem astonishing that such a tiny island has been responsible for creating so many of the world's biggest sports. I wonder if it is indicative of our inclement weather that we need to run around to keep warm.

The Cotswold Olimpick Games, an event recognized by the British Olympic Association as 'the first stirrings of Britain's Olympic beginnings', were started on the Thursday and Friday of Whitsun week in 1622 by a local lawyer, Robert Dover, with the approval of King James I. They illustrate our historic, long-lasting love of sport and games in general. Dover believed that physical exercise was necessary to strengthen the population for the defence of the realm because, as a maritime nation with plenty of enemies, we always needed to be prepared for an imminent attack. Events were open to rich and poor alike and included horse racing, coursing with hounds, running, jumping, dancing, sledgehammer throwing, fighting with swords, cudgels and quar-terstaff, and wrestling. In booths and tents, chess and card games were played for small stakes. A temporary wooden structure called Dover Castle was erected in a natural amphitheatre, complete with cannons that were fired to begin the events.

Puritans disapproved of such 'pagan' festivities. By the time of James's death in 1625, many Puritan landowners had forbidden their workers to attend. These conflicting attitudes to the Games were symptomatic of the problems in the realm, and increasing tensions between the supporters of the king and the Puritans resulted in the outbreak of the English Civil War in 1642. It's not much of a surprise to learn that this brought the Games to an end. They were revived after the Restoration of 1660, but ended again in 1852, when the common land on which they had been staged was partitioned between local landowners and farmers and subsequently enclosed.

Astonishingly, the Games were revived again in 1966, and except when exceptionally bad weather or an outbreak of foot-and-mouth disease has forced their cancellation, they have been held each year since on the Friday after spring Bank Holiday. Events have recently included tug of war, shin-kicking, dwile flonking, motorcycle scrambling, judo, piano smashing, and Morris dancing. Not events that you'll see Usain Bolt or Mo Farah taking part in.

If there is one sport that truly defines a nation it is football. Wherever I am in the world, I am asked which football team I support. The universal language of football is one that transcends culture, language, and class.

I have an admission to make. I have never really been into football, neither playing nor watching. It has played into my guilty English conscience that I am so illiterate when it comes to our national game. Of course I can reel off a long list of football teams and even players, but don't ask me to put them together correctly. I would argue that a key definition of true Englishness is an ability to talk fluidly and knowledgeably about the beautiful game. I have always seen it as a true indicator of my mongrel genes.

As A. A. Gill wrote, 'After the language, football is England's greatest gift to the world. When all the other inventions are rust and junk, when the discoveries are commonplace, there will still be football. The only truly pan-national human activity, football is played on every continent; there isn't a child in the world who hasn't had a crack at goal …'

When we say football, we mean association football (known as soccer in some countries), but other variations of the game based on kicking a ball evolved and are known as football codes – grid-iron football (American football or Canadian football); Australian rules football; rugby football (rugby league and rugby union); and Gaelic football.

Football appears to have started as a popular peasant game, played between neighbouring towns and villages. Typically, each 'team' would have an unlimited number of players, the purpose of the game being to fight for and move an inflated pig's bladder to markers at either end of the town. It doesn't seem to have mattered how they did it, and games often became mass brawls. The authorities would later attempt to outlaw such dangerous mob pastimes, but some still exist as quaint traditions to this day. For example, in Alnwick in Northumberland, the game begins with the Duke of Northumberland dropping a ball from the battlements of Alnwick Castle, while Workington in Cumbria holds a game between teams named the Uppies and Downies.

These mob games were codified during the nineteenth century at English public schools such as Eton, Winchester, Rugby, Harrow, Charterhouse, Westminster, Marlborough and Cheltenham, so that the schools could compete against each other. Eventually a division between the pure 'kicking' and the 'running' or 'carrying' games became evident. The huge reach of the British Empire allowed these rules of football to spread far and wide – to regions way beyond the borders of the Empire.

By the end of the nineteenth century, distinct regional codes had developed: Gaelic football, for example, deliberately incorporated the rules of local traditional football games to maintain their heritage. In 1859, the Melbourne Football Club codified the first laws of Australian football to develop a game more suited to adults and to Australian conditions. It is as a result the oldest of the world's major football codes. Association football rules were officially drawn up in 1863, and while William Webb Ellis famously (and probably apocryphally) picked up the football and started running with it in 1823, the rules of rugby union weren't codified until 1871; rugby league followed in 1895.

In 1895 the Northern Rugby Football Union was founded. (In 1922 its name changed to the Northern Rugby Football League, while in the 1980s, the 'Northern' was dropped from its name.)

Village sporting rivalries in medieval England have evolved into the world's most popular sports. Who could have predicted that?

My mother is the oracle of all things sporting; she is a true sports fanatic. She would happily spend the rest of her life following sport, a passion she inherited from my late grandmother. As a child, I was pretty hopeless when it came to sport, but my mother, in a vain attempt to get me into cricket, enrolled me at the home of English cricket, Lord's cricket ground. Once a week I would put on my starched whites and make my way to the Mecca of cricket.

Cricket has always struck me as a very formal sport that plays on the English love of queuing: both batsman and bowlers wait patiently for their turn with the ball. It is very orderly and, to be honest, very slow. As the son of a Canadian, I found myself playing baseball in the garden with my dad at weekends in a nod towards my father's baseball heritage. The contrast didn't serve cricket very well and I never really 'got' it. It seemed so strange that we would be forced to wear all white while leaping about on muddy, grassy fields. Why not wear green? I used to wonder. And a cricket box to protect my willy from a heavy leather ball? Any sport that jeopardized the family jewels was never going to take off in my mind.

It is the subject of much mirth to nations where cricket isn't played that we would develop a game that moves at a sloth's pace and can go on for days. There's a wonderful summary of cricket which you can get, printed on tea towels and mugs. It goes like this.

'THE RULES OF CRICKET'

You have two sides, one out in the field and one in.

Each man that's in the side that's in goes out, and when he's out he comes in and the next man goes in until he's out.

When they are all out, the side that's out comes in and the side that's been in goes out and tries to get those coming in, out.

Sometimes you get men still in and not out.

When a man goes out to go in, the men who are out try to get him out, and when he is out he goes in and the next man in goes out and goes in.

There are two men called umpires who stay out all the time and they decide when the men who are in are out.

When both sides have been in and all the men have out, and both sides have been out twice after all the men have been in, including those who are not out, that is the end of the game!

I spent many years playing the game and to be honest I still don't entirely understand it.

Cricket perhaps reflects the optimistic portion of the English mind that hopes for a long string of fine summer days uninterrupted by rain; but it's not difficult to find a sport that provides fun and games in inclement weather.

Bandy, for example, is a team game played on ice with sticks and a single round ball. First seen in London at the Crystal Palace in 1875, it is arguing hard at the moment to be included in the Winter Olympics, claiming that it is the world's second-most popular winter sport. Who knew?! The first recorded games took place in the Fens during the Great Frost of 1813–14. The game's history glories in wonderfully atmospheric names. Bury Fen Bandy Club from Bluntisham-cum-Earith, near St Ives in Cambridgeshire, rejoices in a reputation as the most successful team ever, with a remarkable unbeaten run until the winter of 1890–1. Charles Tebbutt, a member of the club, oversaw the publication of the rules of bandy in 1882. He was also instrumental in taking the game to the Netherlands and Sweden, as well as to other villages in England where it became popular with cricket, rowing and hockey clubs. It is possible to make a pilgrimage to the Norris Museum in St Ives, where Tebbutt's home-made bandy stick is proudly on display.

The English are always resourceful when it comes to inventing sports – using quite literally anything that comes to hand. Perhaps one of our strangest sports is ferret-legging, an endurance test in which ferrets are trapped in the trousers worn by a participant. Contestants put live ferrets inside their trousers; the winner is the one who is the last to release the animals. The world record is five hours and thirty minutes. The origin of ferret-legging is disputed. The sport seems to have become popular among coal miners in Yorkshire in the 1970s, though some Scots claim it first gained popularity in Scotland. Marlene Blackburn of the Richmond Ferret Rescue League claims that ferret-legging originated in public houses 'where patrons would bet on who could keep a ferret in his pants the longest'. The sport may alternatively have originated during the time when only the relatively wealthy in England were entitled to keep ferrets (which were used for hunting), forcing the animal poachers to hide their illicit ferrets in their trousers to avoid detection by gamekeepers.

Having worked with several ferrets over the years, I still bear the scars of their sharp teeth on my hands and arm and I can tell you I would never place one near my nether regions.

One sport in which I have had slightly more success was shin-kicking, also known as hacking or purring. The aim of the game is simple: the two competitors attempt to kick each other on the shin until one is forced to the ground. It originated in England in the early seventeenth century, and was one of the most popular events at the Cotswold Olimpick Games. It also became a popular pastime among Cornish miners. In the nineteenth century the sport was practised by British immigrants to the United States. It was included in the 1951 revival of the Cotswold Olimpick Games, and remains one of its most popular events, run as the World Shin-kicking Championships. The event now draws crowds of thousands of spectators.

In the Cotswold Olimpicks the combatants wear white coats, representing shepherds' smocks. Each contestant holds the other's collar while trying to kick their opponent's shin with both the inside of the foot and the toes. You need to be agile, light on your feet and have an English stoicism which prevents you from giving in to the excruciating pain. When the pain does become too much, you shout (or cry) out 'Sufficient!' Matches are the best of three 'legs'. The referee is called a stickler, which seems appropriate.

The history of the game includes competitors who wore steel-toed boots, which would be one way of winning quickly – though hardly very English, I'd say. Apparently some shin-kickers would try to build up their tolerance to pain by hitting their shins with hammers, a much more English approach. These days it's all a lot safer: competitors wear soft shoes and stuff straw down their trousers for protection. Even so, ambulance crews are in attendance in case some unEnglish cheat wearing boots with steel toecaps turns up.

But my personal favourite English sport is one that was only invented twenty years ago: extreme ironing.

'EI', as it is known, is very simple: people take an ironing board to an extreme or unusual location and ... iron an item of clothing. It is quintessentially English in its simple eccentricity. A man called Phil Shaw is largely credited with its invention. The story goes that he got back to his Leicester home after work one day in 1997 to be faced by a mountain of ironing. He decided that it was too dull to iron indoors, so he took it out to the garden. When his housemate came home, he asked Phil what he was doing and he replied, 'Extreme ironing.' The idea stuck.

A chance meeting with a German man, Kai, took the sport on to the international stage. Kai adopted the name Hot Crease and formed a German branch of the Extreme Ironing Bureau. In

2002, the first Extreme Ironing World Championships were held. Eighty teams from ten countries had to navigate an obstacle course arranged in the shape of an iron, pressing boxer shorts and blouses while scaling a climbing wall, hanging from a moss-covered tree branch and squeezing under the bonnet of a car.

The quality of pressing does actually count. 'Ironists,' Phil wrote in his book, 'are sometimes so absorbed in getting themselves into some sort of awkward or dangerous situation with their ironing board that they forget the main reason they are there in the first place: to rid their clothing of creases and wrinkles.' When it comes to judging, the ironing accounts for 60 of the available 120 points, style for 40 points and speed 20. Of course, the English competitors didn't win any individual medals, but they did win the team event.

There are about 1,500 extreme ironists practising worldwide and some teams have received corporate backing. Calls are now being made for the sport's inclusion in the Olympics. 'If you can have synchronized swimming and curling, I think extreme ironing has as much to offer,' Phil has said.

If included, it would be the first Olympic sport in which the athletes did not use their real names. Apparently, ironists fear ridicule from the outside world, so they adopt pseudonyms. Mr Shaw is Steam; his housemate Paul is Spray. Other competitors are listed as Cool Silk, Iron Mike, Fe (the chemical symbol for iron), Jeremy Irons and Iron Lung. The winner of the gold medal at the 2002 Championships was Hot Pants.

So why should extreme ironing be considered the pinnacle of English sport? The answer is very simple. While it may not be as physically challenging as some sports, the difficulty lies 'in the extreme embarrassment of ironing on a street in front of large crowds', according to Phil. If you combine making a show of yourself in public and a sporting endeavour, that is an extreme challenge for any English person.

CHAPTER EIGHT

OO-ER, MISSUS, IT'S LORD BUCKETHEAD

'Nudge, nudge, wink, wink, say no more …'
Monty Python's Flying Circus

English humour is very odd. Our most successful series – *Monty Python*, *Blackadder*, Benny Hill, the Carry On films, *Mr Bean*, *The Office*, *Fawlty Towers*, *The Two Ronnies* – are irreverent, smutty and surreal; they celebrate the underdog, the bizarre, failure. Just like us, they don't take themselves too seriously.

Our humour touches every aspect of Englishness: our eccentricity, our landscape, our food, our culture. Cheese rolling and Pooh sticks, bubble and squeak, toad in the hole, Marmite, pomp and ceremony, hedgehog-flavoured crisps … It is all tinged with the ridiculous.

It is often assumed, celebrated even, that we have the best humour in the world. That it is unique in its highly developed, sophisticated subtlety. It is littered with sarcasm, teasing, mockery and self-deprecation. We love to laugh at ourselves. It is full of what we would call banter, often indecipherable to foreign visitors. Even for a battle-hardened Englishman it can be difficult to know when humour stops and starts. 'Are they being funny or rude?'

Generally, the more serious the delivery, the more likely it is that it is a joke. 'Lovely weather,' delivered in the midst of a biblical storm, is the benchmark of English sarcasm. We love to say the opposite of what is happening to make a point. In an effort to distinguish ourselves from our North American neighbours, Oscar Wilde once said, 'It is clear that humour is far superior to humor.'

Our humour is often lost in translation, taken literally. A recent example was when the model-turned-actress Cara Delevingne was asked in an interview on US television if she had read John Green's book, *Paper Towns*, before starring in the film. 'No, I never read the book or the script, I just winged it,' she answered deadpan. The US media took her comments literally, while the English had a wry smile on their faces.

We also love understatement. A little like our tendency to apologize, we love to downgrade the situation. 'I'm in a spot of bother' actually means we are drawing our last breath. Famously, Spike Milligan's epitaph reads, 'I told you I was ill'.

The early adverts for Hamlet cigars, in which the hapless protagonist would light up a cigar after finding himself in a life-threatening, embarrassing or awkward situation, was a manifestation of such understatement. One I loved was the cowboy arriving at the Pearly Gates with an arrow sticking right through him; St Peter looks him up and down disapprovingly, checks his list and shakes his head. The Gates close. The cowboy lights up.

Monty Python also played up to this English stereotype. Who can forget the Black Knight proclaiming ''tis but a scratch' after having his arm cut off in *Monty Python and the Holy Grail*?

And it doesn't just happen in films or on television. During the Kuala Lumpur to Perth leg of a British Airways flight in 1982, the plane hit a volcanic ash cloud that caused all four engines to stall. Famously, Captain Eric Moody still managed to make an announcement to the passengers: 'Ladies and gentlemen, this is your captain speaking. We have a small problem. All four engines have stopped. We are doing our damnedest to get them going again. I trust you are not in too much distress.' Arguably one of the finest examples of understated humour was when journalist Henry Morton Stanley finally found Dr Livingstone on the shore of Lake Tanganyika, having searched through 700 miles of impenetrable forest. 'Dr Livingstone, I presume?'

One of my favourite aspects of Englishness is comedy politicians. I don't just mean the comedy of politicians, or even of comedians becoming (or trying to become – yes I'm looking at you, Al Murray) politicians, but the art of the comedic political aspirant. And Lord Buckethead may well be the best practitioner of all.

'Mr Fogle, sir, it is indeed an honour,' announced Lord Buckethead as I emerged onto the roof terrace. Of all the weird and wonderful situations I have found myself in, this must surely have been one of the strangest and most surreal. I was with a man dressed as a cross between Darth Vader and Batman, about to play an urban game of miniature golf on a rooftop in East London. His vast helmet towered above my head as we walked towards the kiosk.

I felt a little giddy and even a little starstruck. I was with *the* Lord Buckethead, the man who had campaigned in general elections against Margaret Thatcher, John Major and Theresa May. In fact, my favourite photograph from the 2017 election is that of May on stage in her Maidenhead constituency, the leader of our country (just, at time of writing) standing alongside her political rivals, Lord Buckethead and someone dressed as Elmo. Lord Buckethead won 249 votes in the Berkshire constituency. Nevertheless he celebrated the result as 'A new Buckethead record!'

Before the election Lord Buckethead proudly informed his 100,000 Twitter followers that he is an 'intergalactic space lord, running to be an independent member of parliament for Maidenhead'. His manifesto promised 'a strong, not entirely stable, leadership'. On a recent visit to another English institution, Glastonbury, he said, 'I just hope the rain stays away for your sake and mine, because on my planet space lords have no need to combat rain. If the storms come I am in big trouble.' And he described Boris Johnson as 'a posh, overblown, full of himself imbecile, who thinks just because he knows a bit of classics he has some superiority over the rest of the species … I say *flocci non facio* Boris Johnson.' (Apparently, it means 'I don't give a hoot …')

I liked him for that and wanted to meet him. On my request for a meeting over a cup of tea, he tweeted, 'Move over G20, this is the top table.'

His real identity remains a mystery as he hides behind his iconic black mask. He is ridiculous and marvellous at the same time.

I had managed to track him down on social media and he had suggested we meet for a game of miniature golf to discuss politics and Englishness. His real identity remained a mystery as he hid behind his iconic black mask. He was ridiculous and marvellous at the same time. 'My vision is a little inhibited,' he said, sweeping back his black cloak to reveal black trousers, cricket pads, a thick black leather jacket and black boots, 'you might have to keep the scores.'

We made our way over to the golf course, designed in swirly, slightly trippy black and white. 'Better take the black ball,' announced Lord Buckethead, before handing me the white one. A young girl handed us our golf clubs without so much as a question or a hint of surprise at the 6ft 5in man beside me, dressed in a black cape and mask.

I looked around me and not a single person was staring. This was incredible and marvellous at the same time. Only in England can someone walk around looking like an extra from *Star Wars* without eliciting so much as a stare or a glance. Another couple on the golf course weren't even distracted from their game as the cloaked politician and I began ours.

'You must be very good at golf,' stated Lord Buckethead, 'it's written in your name. Fogle, golf, it's an anagram.'

I suggested perhaps we might try a game that contained an anagram of Lord Buckethead's name, 'We could eat a bucket of Kentucky Fried Chicken,' he replied.

'What does Englishness mean?' I asked, getting down to the issue at hand.

'It is strange that you ask someone from Gremloids about Englishness. Tea, queuing, roses, binge drinking, vomiting on the high street, louts …'

I asked him about his manifesto, which included free bicycles for all and the nationalization of Adele. 'I'd also like to nationalize Chris Rea,' he replied. 'He knows a thing or two about our transport problems.'

'Road to hell?' I replied.

He nodded gently.

I placed my ball on the putting tee and clipped it with my club while Lord Buckethead looked on.

Also included in his manifesto was the right to hunt fox hunters. 'Would you consider a coalition?' I asked.

'With John Craven, yes,' he answered.

'What about me?'

'What would be in your manifesto?'

'Free umbrellas.'

'Brilliant idea.'

The whole scenario was superbly English, as Buckethead and I worked our way around the putting green while east London hipsters did their hipsterish thing.

Here was a man who, through all his outer space/earthling chat, is the true manifestation of Englishness. Whether he is from Gremloids or just a very clever political satirist, he is the embodiment of English quirkiness and eccentricity. Like all great examples of Englishness he is a living paradox, a box of contradictions. Someone who is deadly serious but is happy to laugh at himself. He confuses and confounds.

For someone with impaired vision, his putting was pretty

good. We finished the eight holes tied – a good English compromise.

'I want to bring back Ceefax, Mr Fogle,' he explained as he returned his golf club to a member of staff, who again acted as if men of six foot five in giant black masks are an everyday occurrence in east London. Maybe they are. 'Fist bump,' he said as he clenched his leather-gloved fist and tapped mine before dropping the metaphorical bomb.

And so ended my extraordinary audience with the legendary Lord Buckethead. 'You must make Englishness great again,' he said as we parted company.

Of course Lord Buckethead isn't the first unusual political candidate. Even in 2017 we had the wonderful Mr Fishfinger, who stood in the constituency of former Liberal Democrat leader Tim Farron, mocking Farron throughout the campaign. When the result was announced, Mr Fishfinger relieved the gravity of the moment by making faces behind Mr Farron's back and then declared that his own tally of 400 votes was a devastating blow. He said, 'I'm absolutely shattered walking back to hotel for a few hours in the freezer then off to London in the afternoon thanks everyone.'

Lord Buckethead and Mr Fishfinger are part of a long tradition. As a child, I have vivid memories of a man wearing a top hat, leopard print coat and huge rosettes and badges screaming into a loud hailer. The legendary Screaming Lord Sutch.

In 1963, he stood for the National Teenage Party – advocating the right to vote for eighteen-year-olds – in the by-election in Stratford-upon-Avon brought about by John Profumo's resignation. He only won 209 votes and lost the first of many deposits, but a pattern was set for the next thirty-five years as Screaming Lord Sutch and the Monster Raving Loony Party became a feature of every British election.

The party's policies and slogans were mostly fanciful – 'Vote for insanity, you know it makes sense' – but the impact on real politicians was far from it. By getting up on the platform with Harold Wilson or Denis Healey, or offering to merge with the Social Democrats in 1980, Lord Sutch and colleagues made sure no one could take things too seriously, at least in front of the cameras.

He stood for Parliament thirty-nine times, garnered 15,000 votes over the course of his political life, lost more than £10,000 in deposits and incurred £85,000 in campaign expenses. His best result was in Rotherham in May 1994 when he gained 1,114 votes, only 200 short of the number required to save his deposit. Perhaps the most politically significant result was when he got 418 votes in Bootle in May 1990. The struggling Social Democrat candidate polled 155. The result convinced the party's then leader David Owen that the breakaway party couldn't carry on. To add salt to the wound, it was then that Sutch offered to merge the Monster Raving Loony Party with the Social Democrats.

There were so many aspects of Screaming Lord Sutch that define him as English. Not only was he clearly eccentric but he drank up to twenty cups of tea a day, and he held victory parties and concerts on the night before polling day to avoid disappointment at inevitably losing yet another deposit. Like I say, the English love to celebrate failure.

Another serial offbeat by-election candidate was Commander Bill Boaks, a retired hero of the Second World War. Boaks stood for election for over thirty years on the single issue of road safety. Ironically, and tragically, he died from head injuries while getting off a bus.

The Official Monster Raving Loony Party might be the most famous of eccentric parties, but there have been plenty more. In fact, over 700 different parties have been represented on the ballot paper in British elections since the 1950s.

I once had a friend, now a prominent writer, who ran for MP under the campaign banner, 'No fruit out of context'. He was trying to ban the use of fruit in savoury food, expressing particular disgust at the Hawaiian pizza with its pineapple. At the time we thought he was as batty as his campaign, but you simply need to look at the recent election of Iceland's Pirate Party, who have only gone and banned pineapple on pizza, to realize his manifesto wasn't so crazy after all.

In 2015 the Beer, Baccy and Crumpet Party suffered a setback after objections were made to their use of the word 'crumpet' (here referring to women, rather than baked goods). After some consideration they rebranded themselves as as Beer, Baccy and Scratchings Party. A Mr Blobby ran as an independent in the 1995 Littleborough & Saddleworth by-election. His policies? A four-day week, fixing wobbly tables in restaurants, and bricking up the Channel Tunnel. Only in England.

Americans describe our humour as very dry, and politics has always been the perfect platform for deadpan, often subtle humour. There is no need in the political arena for great theatrics. The humour is in the man dressed as a fish finger standing next to the leader of a major political party.

How to describe it? Monty Python is considered quintessential English comedy, with its range of deadpan one-liners, absurd physical gags, macabre subject matter and twisted style of comedy that never goes for the obvious, easy jokes. *The Office* is also considered classic English comedy with its 'cringe-comedy' style, based on embarrassment, its humour stemming from inappropriate actions or words. We English tend to feel quite superior about our comedy – it's a mindset that not everyone gets.

Take *Monty Python's Life of Brian* (1979), directed by Terry Jones, and starring Graham Chapman, Eric Idle, John Cleese and Terry Gilliam as well as Jones himself. It is regularly voted No. 1 British comic film of all time. And yet the internet is full of forums, threads and message boards entitled 'Can somebody explain to me the appeal of Monty Python?' People really struggle to articulate what makes it so funny ...

Moving beyond Monty Python, there are rich traditions in other areas: slapstick, gallows humour, the slightly smutty style of Benny Hill. Carry On films combine so many of the absurd, irreverent and slightly naughty aspects of English comedy that they could well be the archetype. Ooo-err, missus!

Benny Hill and the Carry Ons were following in the tradition of Donald McGill's infamous and Englishness-defining saucy seaside postcards. The nudge-nudge-wink-wink humour of the cards caught on in the early 1930s and, until a concerned Conservative government cracked down on them in the early 1950s, were as important a part as a trip to the seaside as candy floss and a stick of rock. At the height of their fame, they were selling 16 million a year.

My attempt to become a weather man. I'm not really that orange.

With Chris Aldridge, reading the Shipping Forecast at the BBC.

The 'World in Action' team making a programme about the pirate radio ship *Caroline* in 1967, filmed by Paddy Searle and produced by Mike Hodges. © James Jackson/Evening Standard/Getty Images

Eddie 'the Eagle' Edwards in action during the Winter Olympic Games in Calgary, Canada in 1988. He achieved celebrity by finishing last in both individual ski jumping events.
© Leo Mason/Popperfoto/Getty Images

In 1912, Captain Robert Falcon Scott's expedition party reached the South Pole, but all died on the return journey. © Hulton-Deutsch Collection/CORBIS/Corbis via Getty Images

With Sir Steve Redgrave at Henley Royal Regatta.

The crowds watching the 2014 Wimbledon championship from Murray Mound, previously known as Henman Hill. © Imagedoc/Alamy

'Saint George and the Dragon'. Fresco in the main arch of the Church of San Giorgio, in Montalto Ligure, Italy. © Seat Archive/Alinari Archives/Mary Evans

Screaming Lord
Sutch was an English
musician who started
his own political
party (the 'Official
Monster Raving
Loony Party'). He
holds the record
for losing the most
elections. © Express
Newspapers/Getty Images

Patrick Macnee, the
actor who famously
wore a bowler hat in
his role as John Steed
in *The Avengers* in the
1960s. © Everett Collection
Inc/Alamy

Inside the South Shields Barbour factory, and with chief designer Gary Janes. Part of the archive can be seen in the background.

Princess Diana wearing a waterproof Barbour-style jacket in the rain during a visit to the Western Isles of Scotland. © Tim Graham/Getty Images

Alexa Chung sporting a pair of Wellington boots and a wax jacket at Glastonbury in 2016.
© David M. Benett/Getty Images

At one of the most famous eccentric sporting events in the world, the annual Cooper's Hill Cheese Rolling. Seen here racing down the vertiginous Cooper's Hill. © PA Images

My 'lucky' blue Pooh stick at the World Pooh Stick Championships. It came last.

The annual worm charming festival in Blackhawton, Devon. © David Pearson/Alamy

Monty Python and the Holy Grail, the 1975 EMI film. © Pictorial Press Ltd/Alamy

With Lord Buckethead, playing miniature golf on the roof of an East London car park.

On Holkham Beach with the Royal Household Cavalry on their summer camp. © James Davidson

Shepherd penning sheep with a sheep dog border collie at a traditional sheep dog trial competition at Bamford in Derbyshire. © David Lyons/Getty Images

With Cedric Robinson and my labrador Storm on the Sands at Morecombe Bay.

Rowing with the Vintners and with Swan Marker David Barber during Swan Upping on the banks of the Thames.

The Wimbledon Queue is not just a queue but The Queue: a curiously beautiful and annually growing tradition. © David Ramos/Getty Images

At the Marmite factory with Mr Marmite St John Skelton, holding my Marmite-tasting pass certificate. I scored 100 per cent.

Our local fish-and-chip shop, combining British humour,
cultural reference and a simple love of fish and chips.

Cooke's traditional
London pie, mash
& eel restaurant.
© Tony Watson/Alamy

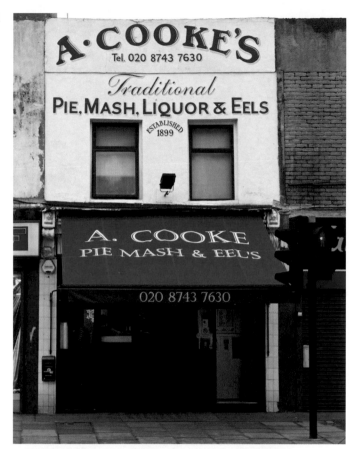

Outside Betty's Tea
Room in Harrogate
with waiters Jemma
and Jack.

Twinings tea shop on the Strand, London. © John Woodworth/Alamy

At the WI meeting in Harrogate.

We love a good sing-song, and there's none better than a song that's funny or bizarre.

As a child, my abiding memory of English humour was borne out in the rather bizarre trend for comedy songs. I can still remember the excitement of waiting for the countdown of the *Top of the Pops* charts and the appearance of a bizarre, often surreally ridiculous song. Neil from *The Young Ones* singing 'Hole in My Shoe' on *Top of the Pops* remains a personal favourite; but we mustn't forget 'Star Trekkin'', which actually made number one. Then there was Kenny Everett's 'Snot Rap'; and, not to be outdone, Roland Rat Superstar, presenter of ITV morning television, who released 'Rat Rapping'.

Meanwhile, Monty Python's 'Every Sperm is Sacred' remains a seminal song about semen:

> Every sperm is sacred.
> Every sperm is great.
> If a sperm is wasted,
> God gets quite irate.

But my favourite, and one in which the lyrics encapsulate the ridiculous of the English, is the 'The Chicken Song', originating in the satirical 1980s puppet show *Spitting Image*, and which remained at number one in the charts for three long weeks. Here's just an extract:

> Skin yourself alive;
> Learn to speak Arapahoe;
> Climb inside a dog

And behead an Eskimo!
Eat a Renault 4
With salami in your ears;
Casserole your Gran;
Disembowel yourself with spears!

The English, eh?

CHAPTER NINE

RAINING CATS AND DOGS

'A horse, a horse, my kingdom for a horse'
William Shakespeare

It is early morning and already the field is heaving with activity as a convoy of army Land Rovers escort three large horse boxes into the dusty car park. Dozens of heavily tattooed men in burgundy polo shirts and jodhpurs are busy pulling on their riding boots as horses are led from the boxes.

The animals ripple with muscles, their coats are brilliantly black: they are as glossy as the soldiers' highly polished boots. Horses snort and hoof at the ground as an army vet (of the equine, animal variety rather than the retired kind) wanders from horse to horse. Meanwhile an army farrier is busy checking all the hooves, inspecting his shoeing.

I am in north Norfolk, on Holkham beach, for the first day of the Household Cavalry summer holiday. Only in England would we give the regimental horses their very own seaside holiday. It's a breathtaking enterprise. For several weeks each July, the entire barracks is packed up from Hyde Park Corner in Central London and relocated to the north coast of Norfolk.

Word has spread and there are already dozens of people milling around on the beach, awaiting the arrival of the holidaymakers. 'I've come from Somerset,' explains one woman, accompanied by her husband, 'it makes me so proud to see these horses and their riders.' As the 24-horse regiment arrive on the sands I see tears streaming down her face.

The horses trot in unison and gather in a perfect line along the beach while the regimental sergeant explains what will happen. By now the number of spectators has swelled to nearly a hundred, all glued in English reserved silence. There is a kind of reverence for the occasion. It is like being in a library.

The cavalry set off on a gentle canter to work the horses in and familiarise them with the conditions. After several turns up and down the beach, the sergeant instructs the regiment to move towards the water's edge. Legs splash in the shallow surf as they form a perfect line, two abreast, and then break into a gallop.

The noise is like thunder. The combination of salty air, horses and that thunderous sound is dizzying. It's primeval, and more than enough to stir the spirit. The crowd watch, open-mouthed, in silent awe as the horses gallop through the sea. Water sprays from their legs as they splash through the calm surf.

This has just been the warm-up. They return to their little beach base, where the soldiers strip off into their swimming shorts. Saddles and boots are removed before the riders mount their magnificent steeds bareback and race into the waves. It's time for the holiday swim. But, just like children, the horses have other ideas. As their hooves and legs disappear into the chilly North Sea waters they rear up and turn around, like children racing from the surf.

It is charming to see the tough, tattooed soldiers trying to reassure their charges and coax them back into the water. Several riders dismount and lead their horses out into the breaking surf. Suddenly there are two dozen horses swimming, their riders whooping with happiness as they cling onto their necks, swimming beside them.

Can there be a greater bond than that between man (or woman) and horse? And particularly between human and working beast? The soldiers form lifelong friendships with their horses; indeed, some soldiers take the horses on in their retirement.

The sight of the Queen's personal bodyguard swimming in the turbid waters perfectly exemplifies the national character. It is glorious and moving and awe-inspiring. It is a scene of pomp and pageantry, with candy floss and a bucket and spade. Here the two great English institutions of pomp and ceremony and the seaside collide.

There are windbreaks and picnic blankets. Children are digging with buckets and spades, building sand castles, while an assortment of dogs race around in the surf. Seagulls screech and wheel overhead. I can taste that unmistakable mix of salt and seaweed in the air. It's a heady mix of childhood with the majesty of occasion. I wade out into the waters, drawn uncontrollably towards this magnificent stirring sight.

Every now and then a horse bucks its rider from its back, a reminder that this is their holiday. The soldiers take it in their stride. 'Horse loose!' shouts one of the officers as his steed gallops, riderless, through the surf. He races through the waves and grabs it by the rein.

It is organized chaos as horses swim and leap and rear and gallop. All around them are human obstacles as spectators and the twelve gathered press photographers move in to get a better view. A *Times* newspaper photographer is dressed in shorts and wellies, the boots long breached by the waves. His legs look like this is the first time they have ever seen sunlight. 'How English do I look?' he asks.

'You just need a hanky tied to your head and you'd have nailed it.'

Here on the windswept expanse of a north Norfolk beach is a demonstration of our unique and emotional relationship to animals.

Animals have been a huge part of my life. As a child growing up in the seventies above my father's veterinary clinic in central London we had an endless menagerie of strange and exotic animals in our house.

My son, Ludo, perhaps unsurprisingly, is obsessed. 'Daddy, there's a kangaroo in the garden,' he once said as he raced upstairs to grab his Lego. It wasn't the fact he had told me there was a kangaroo – not a prolific resident of our countryside – in the garden but the fact that he said it so nonchalantly, as if this was an everyday occurrence.

I should probably try and put this into some perspective. We have a little cottage on the outskirts of Henley in Buckinghamshire. The village itself still has a red phone box and a tiny village green next to a small village hall. It hosts an annual village cricket match. In short, it is quintessentially English.

Our little farm cottage borders the estate of Fawley House, the home of Sir Bill and Lady McAlpine, who in turn share their home with hundreds of exotic animals. There are meerkats and coati, tapirs and ostrich, llamas and alpacas, lemurs and mara, wallabies and kangaroo, to name just a few. It has always amused me, when we take the dogs out along the public footpaths that wind their way through the McAlpine estate, to walk past this extraordinary private collection of animals in the English countryside. Over the years, a number of escapees have ended up in our garden, including on this occasion not a kangaroo but a wallaby.

To be fair, though, an escaped kangaroo or wallaby is nothing compared to the lion once owned by another of our neighbours, John Rendell. And this wasn't any old lion, but Christian the Lion, arguably one of the most famous lions in the world.

Originally bought from Harrods by Rendall and Bourke in 1969, Christian cost them just 250 guineas (about £3,500 in today's money). The lion came to live with them in London's King's Road, where he soon became a celebrity, living in a furniture store and walking in local parks and gardens. The men had permission from a local vicar to exercise Christian in the graveyard of the Moravian church off the King's Road, and they would take him on summer holidays to West Wittering in Sussex where he would gallop along the beach. It was not an uncommon sight to see Rendall driving through Chelsea in his convertible Rolls Royce with Christian peering out the back.

Despite the optimism of London in the sixties it soon became apparent that Christian had outgrown the city and Rendall needed to find him a new home. A chance encounter with actors Bill Travers and Virginia McKenna, who were shopping in the furniture store, led to an audacious plan to have the renowned naturalist and conservationist George Adamson reintroduce Christian to Africa.

Adamson agreed to try and reintegrate Christian into the wild at a compound in the Kora National Reserve. He was accepted by the pride, but the group suffered many twists and turns of fate, leaving Christian the only surviving member. Gradually a new pride was established around him. Some years later, a cautious Rendall and Bourke went to see how the lion had reintegrated into the animal kingdom. In what has become one of the most viewed YouTube clips of all time, we see the lion at first cautiously approach and then quickly leap playfully onto the two men, standing on his hind legs and wrapping his front legs around their shoulders, nuzzling their faces.

It is a peculiarity of the English that we seem to prefer animals to people. You just need to look at the charitable sector, in which the Donkey Sanctuary received almost £21 million last year, over £5 million more than the Royal British Legion. The RSPCA received a massive £64 million and Cats Protection £25 million, beating the NSPCC and Barnardo's by many millions of pounds. But why is it that we care so deeply about our animals?

We pride ourselves on being a nation of animal lovers. We were the first country in the world to consider animal welfare legislation and to start a welfare charity to rescue and preserve the dignity of animals – the Society for the Prevention of Cruelty to Animals, founded in 1824 – which, thanks to Queen Victoria's support, in 1840 became the Royal Society (RSPCA). Funded by the good will of ordinary people, the charity rescues injured and sick animals in a bid to rehabilitate them.

More than half of the British population keep at least one pet. In 2016, a record number of 12 million households had pets, the total pet population amounting to 58.4 million. What are the most popular pets in England? Surprisingly, fish come out on top. If you combine the indoor variety with those in garden ponds (19.9m and 17.1m respectively), you arrive at a figure of 36.1 million, which beats hands down dogs (8.5m) and cats (7.4m).

Despite reports about Britain's ever-increasing population of elderly people, there are more pets than there are people over sixty-five years of age. Brits don't just run with their dogs – they talk to them, watch television with them, buy them holiday gifts and have their portraits painted. Nine out of ten pet owners treat their pets as members of their family.

The extent to which pets are vital members of the family is revealed in various surveys and statistics. We spent more than £4.6 billion on our pets in 2015, an amount per pet of £79 a year (or £219 per pet if you exclude the fish). After that we get into some fascinating territory: 19 per cent of pet owners buy cars with their dog in mind; 65 per cent believe that their pet is more reliable than their partner; and 32 per cent buy their non-human companion more gifts than the other human in their lives. Amazingly, 9 per cent confess that they have created a Facebook page for their pet – and that's just the ones who are prepared to admit it. We love our animals. And it's not just fish, dogs, cats and horses.

Exotic pets have always been prized in England but they are increasingly popular, and the weirder the better: a Mexican red-legged tarantula; a giant African land snail; a wide-mouthed frog; pygmy hedgehogs, sloths, fire-bellied newts, a glis glis, as well as all sorts of reptiles, rodents, butterflies and birds. Articles about unusual pets are read voraciously by the public and are considered a banker by all media outlets, particularly in our summer silly season.

Examples of recent stories range from a shire horse called Lincoln who costs £10,000 a year to feed and devours twenty-four apples a day to a twelve-stone pet emu called Beaky belonging to the Newby family from Essex. The 6ft bird lives in the summer-house in their garden and gobbles 12lb of corn each week, and 5lb of fruit and veg. Wild cat rescuer Dr Terry Moore lives on the outskirts of London with nine snow leopards, three pumas, two Amur leopards and a jaguar: 'The animals love belly rubs, trying to sit on Terry's lap and being read to.'

Low-maintenance yet exotic pets that are legal to own include bearded dragon lizards, chinchillas, crocodiles, piranha fish, scorpions, boa constrictors, the Madagascar hissing cockroach, the green iguana, hermit crabs, bush babies, the Southern Tamandua, the flying squirrel, the Kinkajou or flower bear, the tiny huge-eared white fox known as a Chanterelle fennec, mini donkeys, pygmy goats, axolotl (the salamander beloved of crossword setters), monkeys, Bengal cats, dwarf pigs, skunk, a cat-like carnivore known as the chestnut spotted genet, the semi-aquatic rodent called the capybara, llama, silver fox, turtle, wallaroo, hippopotamus, stick insect, and the beautiful hyacinth macaw. It is a very English fact that more than 300 people are hospitalized each year due to injuries caused by unusual pets.

Dogs of course have a special place in the hearts of the English, including mine. The average British dog owner takes 433 walks a year, covering a distance of 548 miles, which is the equivalent of going from Land's End to John O'Groats. That's a lot of dog walking.

Fifty per cent of dog owners admit to talking to their canine companions when alone. When not talking to our dogs, we spend an average four hours a week talking about our dogs to others. English dog owners spend an average of £400 a year on accessories, food, treats, grooming, holidays, insurance, vets' bills and kennels. One in five dog owners celebrate their pooch's birthday. One in five female dog owners say they would stop going out with a partner who did not like their dog.

Dogs have always loomed large in my own life. Not only did my parents meet through their dogs when my mother brought her sick golden retriever, Honey, in to see my father; but my wife Marina and I also met through our labradors Maggi and Inca while walking in the park.

Dogs have had a long working relationship with man in England, and one of the most obscure activities is hound trailing. Originating in Cumbria, it has been practised since the eighteenth century, but was only formally organized under the auspices of the Hound Trailing Association in 1906. Observers bet on which hound will be the first to complete the course, as the dogs follow a trail of paraffin and aniseed across the landscape. The trail is marked out by two people carrying wooden rags who walk together to the halfway point, then separate and continue to either end, thereby laying a thick scent for the whole course.

Senior dog races have to be completed in less than forty-five minutes. Special trails are laid for veteran racers and for maiden trail hounds. Prizes are also awarded to the dogs with the best appearance. To make sure sly competitors don't swap dogs mid-race, all hounds have a coloured mark placed on their head; to avoid overheating, the dogs are shaved bald, giving them a most peculiar appearance.

I watched as several dozen of them waited on the start line before being given the scent and then released into the mountains. It's a rather odd sight to see all the dogs heading off into the hills alone, a little as if by remote control. But the strangest and arguably the most English sight of all is at the finish line, when the dogs all appear on the horizon for the first time. The owner of each animal holds out a bowl of their dog's favourite food, shaking it frantically while they holler their dog's name.

Despite the colour coding, the hounds all look identical. And I suspect to a galloping, tired hound, all the owners look the same too. And, well, food is food at the end of the day, which leads to a comical scene in which dogs run to the wrong owner and owners grab the wrong dog. There are multiple scenes of dog swapping as animals are exchanged.

From trailing to trialling. Another quintessential English event is the sheep dog trial. Here the dog must perform a range of tasks frequently carried out on a working farm, such as fetching sheep from a distance, guiding them through gates, splitting a group of sheep in two and driving the flock into a pen. The handler controls the dog with a known set of whistled or spoken commands. The trial must be performed within a set time and each of the various tasks is marked by judges. The International Sheep Dog Society, founded in 1906, today holds the worldwide trial once every three years. Sheep dog trials can mean big money, too: in an auction in 2011, £6,300 was paid for a dog called Dewi Fan.

The TV programme *One Man and His Dog* ran on the BBC for twenty-four years, between 1976 and 2000. Its original presenter, Phil Drabble, worked on the show for eighteen years and the original commentator, Eric Halsall, for fourteen. They were subsequently replaced by Ray Ollerenshaw, Robin Page and Gus Darmody. The series reached the height of its popularity in the mid-1980s, getting audiences of up to eight million viewers. It ran regularly before the weekend news, but during the late 1990s it was moved to an earlier slot, much to the distress of many farmers, who could no longer watch it due to the demands of their work.

The series was axed in 2000, but due to popular demand a Christmas special was shown once a year. Clarissa Dixon Wright, the late co-presenter of the equally eccentric and very successful cookery programme *Two Fat Ladies*, had replaced the rather cantankerous Robin Page as presenter. I was invited to join the programme as a guest captain of the England team in 2003. We won, and I still have the winning shepherd's crook. But more importantly I won the coveted role of presenter. The next year, broadcasting from Chatsworth, I returned as host, replacing Clarissa.

In 2006, to celebrate the anniversary of the show, the Duchess of Cornwall came along with her daughter Laura. I still have vivid memories of sitting with the Duchess and her daughter on the hay bales in the early summer Cumbrian sunshine explaining the intricacies of sheep dog trials. It really doesn't get much more English than that. My late maternal grandfather, Dick (another great English name), was a huge fan of *One Man and His Dog*, and I was always sad he never saw me host the show. I know he would have been proud.

We grow up on a canon of children's books in which animals play a magical part. Examples include *Peter Pan*, with Nana the Newfoundland nanny hired by the Darlings to look after their children; *The Wind in the Willows*, about four anthropomorphized characters, Mole, Badger, Rat and Toad; Beatrix Potter's world of Peter Rabbit, Benjamin Bunny, Tom Kitten, Jemima Puddleduck, Squirrel Nutkin, Mrs Tiggywinkle, etc; Paddington Bear; Black Beauty; Winnie-the-Pooh with Piglet, Eeyore, Rabbit and Owl, and so on. From the earliest age we read about lovable creatures and how they are so integrated into our lives. Perhaps it's no wonder that children want pets and we as a nation have so many animals living with and around us.

Safari tourism started becoming popular in the mid-nineteenth century. In 1836 William Cornwallis Harris, a notable early Victorian traveller, led an expedition purely to observe and record wildlife and landscapes. Harris established the safari style of journey, rising at first light, spending an energetic day walking before an afternoon rest, and concluding with a formal dinner and the telling of stories over drinks and tobacco. Jules Verne's first novel *Five Weeks in a Balloon* was published in 1863, and was followed in 1885 by H. Rider Haggard's *King Solomon's Mines*.

Both describe the journeys of English travellers 'on safari' and were best sellers in their day.

One of the most unusual aspects of the Victorian era was the obsession in towns and cities across England with exotic animals, largely imported from the farthest corners of the British Empire. Hippos and tigers were both common sights in England at the turn of the nineteenth century. It has been estimated that single ships sailing from Adelaide to London would carry up to 30,000 parrots to feed the Victorian obsession with the exotic pets.

Private and public zoos and natural history museums thrived during the Victorian era. Touring shows featuring exotic animals from across the world travelled across England, enthralling audiences. Many people simply bought their own animals, either from one of the 118 wild animal dealers in London or from shops in Liverpool, Bath and Bristol. People could walk into a shop and purchase anything from an elephant to a bear to a kangaroo. And the broader politics of the British Empire drove this burgeoning industry into the rest of Europe. Before the Suez Canal was built, for example, almost every ship coming from Asia or Africa touched land first in England. After its construction, Germany steadily overtook the UK in 'the scramble for elephants'.

Perhaps the most famous story of all was of the tiger that escaped in the East End of London in 1857 and ate a boy. It was not even the first time that a tiger had been loose in that very street – one had escaped from a travelling menagerie some years earlier.

The tiger was being delivered to a shop owned by Charles Jamrach, who was at that time the pre-eminent wild animal dealer in the world. He had a network of agents all over the globe. Jamrach stocked all manner of exotic beasts, including elephants, lions, tigers, bears, tapirs and armadillos. And he claimed to be able to obtain his clients any animal they wanted through his network of agents. On at least one occasion he sourced a rhinoceros.

Contemporary accounts of his premises also speak of thousands of parrots and exotic birds packed so tightly together in cages that they were unable to move. But this particular tiger, it seems, was not content to be put on display. As it was being delivered, it put its front feet against one side of the flimsy wooden crate in which it was being transported, and its back feet against the other side. Pushing with all its strength, it managed to burst out and make off down the busy thoroughfare of St George's Street, picking up a small boy named John Wade as it went.

Unwilling to lose his quarry, Jamrach set off after the tiger. In an extraordinarily incongruous scene, he grabbed it by the throat. His account of the event, entitled 'My Struggle with a Tiger', was published in the *Boy's Own Paper* – an illustrated magazine which carried a mixture of factual and fictional stories – in February 1879. In it he describes what happened next:

My men had been seized with the same panic as the bystanders, but now I discovered one lurking round a corner, so I shouted to him to come with a crowbar – he fetched one and hit the tiger three tremendous blows over the eyes.

It was only now he released the boy. His jaws opened and his tongue protruded about seven inches. I thought the brute was dead or dying, and let go of him, but no sooner had I done so than he jumped up again.

In the same moment I seized the crowbar myself and gave him, with all the strength I had left, a blow over the head. He seemed to be quite cowed, and turning tail, went back towards the stables, which fortunately were open.

I drove him into the yard and, and closed the doors at once. Looking round for my tiger, I found that he had sneaked into a large empty den that stood open at the bottom of the yard.

Two of my men who had jumped onto an elephant's box, now descended and pushed down the iron-barred siding of the door; and so my tiger was safe again under lock and key.

In spite of saving young Wade, Jamrach was sued for damages by the boy's father and had to pay £300 – equivalent to more than £30,000 today. But he had one other consolation – he sold the animal to Wombwell's menagerie for the the same amount, where it was exhibited as 'The Tiger that Swallowed the Boy'.

England was a clearing house for the animals of the world and they poured in by the thousand – both alive and dead. The trade in these wild animals was unregulated – there was only the most rudimentary consciousness about the idea of endangered species. The very first animal welfare laws had been passed by this time and, although there were concerns about the extent of the fur trade and the conditions suffered by animals undergoing live export for slaughter, there was neither the systematic legislation there is today nor any international framework to protect wild animals. Demand was high, and it persisted at the end of Queen

Victoria's reign. One Indian-based taxidermy company, Van Ingen & Van Ingen, stuffed roughly 43,000 tigers and leopards between 1900 and about 1950 to supply the European and Indian demand for trophies.

The beasts moved from fair to fair with the travelling menageries, they underpinned new scientific research and they sat glumly in architect-designed cages in the grounds of the most fashionable country houses. The capture, trade and display of exotic animals was one of the many ways in which the British Empire made its influence felt.

After the Great Exhibition of 1851 in London, the English made several improvements in methodology and skill. Much of this can be attributed to the culture of Victorian society. According to Paul Farber, a researcher at the University of Chicago, in his book *The Development of Taxidermy and the History of Ornithology*, the art of taxidermy was first brought into popular regard by the Victorians, who were enthralled by all tokens of exotic travel, and especially by domesticated representations of wilderness. Whether it was a glassed-in miniature rain forest on the tea table or a mounted antelope by the front door, members of the elite class relished the art as a manifestation of one's knowledge, wealth and artistry.

The Zoological Society of London was founded in 1826 by Sir Stamford Raffles with the aim of promoting the worldwide conservation of animals and their habitats – and the society's London Zoo in Regent's Park was established.

Whipsnade Park Zoo opened on Sunday 23 May 1931, the first open zoo in Europe to be easily accessible to the visiting public. Almost 100 years after the opening of London Zoo, Sir Peter

Chalmers Mitchell (secretary of the Royal Zoological Society from 1903 to 1935) was inspired by a visit to the Bronx Zoological Park to create a park in Britain as a conservation centre. Hall Farm, a derelict farm on the Dunstable Downs, thirty miles north of London, was purchased by the Zoological Society of London in 1926 for £480 12s 10d. The site was fenced, roads built and trees planted. The first animals arrived at the park in 1928, including two Lady Amherst's pheasants, a golden pheasant and five red junglefowl. Others soon followed, including muntjac, llama, wombats and skunks. It was an immediate success and received over 38,000 visitors on the following Monday. The brown bear enclosure is a surviving feature from the earliest days of the zoo. The collection of animals was boosted in 1932 by the purchase of a collection from a defunct travelling menagerie and some of the larger animals walked to the zoo from Dunstable station.

It still thrills me to see working horses in the centre of London. I often walk the dogs while heavy horses work the Royal Parks. The sight of shire horses mowing the grass at Kensington Palace or making hay in Hyde Park is curiously uplifting. You can also see them rolling the bracken in Richmond Park. For the past twenty-five years, Historic Royal Palaces and the Royal Parks have worked with Operation Centaur, based at Holly Lodge in Richmond Park, to help maintain their estates while promoting the conservation of iconic native breeds.

Operation Centaur works with shire horses and Cleveland bays – traditional English working breeds which are now on the rare breeds watch list, having been dramatically reduced in numbers as a result of post-war agricultural mechanization. The aim is to provide the horses with sustainable work in contemporary society to help secure them a future.

If you live in the Greater London area, you will be familiar with the incongruously exotic colours and aggressive sounds of flocks of parakeets. They can roost in one tree in huge flocks. This bird – technically a ring-necked, or rose-ringed, parakeet – is Britain's most abundant naturalized parrot and became established in the wild in the 1970s after captive birds escaped or were released. The population is concentrated in south-east England, though sightings are often reported in other parts of Britain, and are likely to be local escapees.

What is extraordinary is that the ring-necked parakeet's native range is a broad belt of arid tropical countryside stretching from western Africa right across lowland India, south of the Himalayas. In these climes the birds are common, but despite their tropical origin, parakeets are able to cope with cold British winters, especially in suburban parks, large gardens and orchards, where food supply is more reliable. They feed on a wide variety of fruit, berries, nuts, seeds, grain and household scraps.

People argue that a cull of parakeets is necessary, due to their potential impact on native bird species such as woodpeckers, starlings and nuthatches through competition for nest holes. Here is the RSPB's view:

> The RSPB is not in favour of a cull of parakeets at this time, but believes that it is important that the spread of the ring-necked parakeet is monitored, and its potential for negative impacts on our native bird species assessed.

The Government is obliged to ensure that non-native species do not adversely affect native wildlife, and has developed a policy framework for addressing the possible risks associated with such species becoming established. This includes the production of evidence-based risk assessments of non-native species already in, or likely to reach, Great Britain. Decisions on the type of action necessary is based on the outcome of these risk assessments.

Ring-necked parakeets, like all birds living in the wild in the UK, are protected by law. The species can be controlled under licence in England, but only in isolated cases where the birds pose a serious threat to conservation of a native species, are causing serious damage to crops, or for air safety purposes.

Perhaps the strangest animal story of all is that of the Hartlepool Monkey. During the Napoleonic Wars, a French ship was wrecked off the coast off the north-eastern port of Hartlepool. There was only one survivor: a monkey. Apparently a mascot, it was dressed up in a little uniform. When the villagers found the monkey, they noticed its uniform, and the fact that it didn't respond to questioning. Understandably suspicious of this hairy little man, according to folklore the locals, not knowing what the French looked like, naturally decided that the monkey was a French spy and hanged it after an impromptu trial on the beach.

But did it really happen? There's another possible source for the story in a song written by Geordie songwriter Edward Corvan, and called 'The Monkey Song':

In former times, mid war an' strife,
The French invasion threatened life,
An' all was armed to the knife,
The Fishermen hung the Monkey O!
The Fishermen wi' courage high,
Seized on the Monkey for a spy,
'Hang him' says yen, says another, 'He'll die!'
They did, and they hung the Monkey O!
They tortor'd the Monkey till loud he did squeak
Says yen, 'That's French,' says another 'it's Greek'
For the Fishermen had got drunky, O!
'He's all ower hair!' sum chap did cry,
E'en up te summic cute an' sly
Wiv a cod's head then they closed an eye,
Afore they hung the Monkey O!

The song apparently refers to a real event in 1772 in the village of Boddam, Aberdeenshire, when a ship was wrecked off the coast and the villagers hanged the sole, primate, survivor. But their reasons were actually far more reasonable. The villagers could only get salvage rights if there were no survivors; therefore, the monkey had to go. To this day, people from Peterhead still taunt the people of Boddam with 'Fa hangit the monkey?!' ('Who hanged the monkey?') Needless to say, Hartlepool has embraced the legend far more than the Boddamers. But why that might have happened is another mystery.

Of course, sometimes truth can become stranger than fiction. In 2002 Hartlepool made national headlines when a monkey became the town's first directly elected mayor. H'Angus the

Monkey, the mascot of Hartlepool United Football Club, was elected on the slogan 'free bananas for schoolchildren'. Having originally stood as a joke, Stuart Drummond, the man in the monkey suit, went on to win two more elections, stepping down only in 2013. In 2008 the Audit Commission gave Hartlepool the top four-star rating for performance against other councils and said it was 'improving strongly'.

We LOVE our animals.

CHAPTER TEN

THE QUEEN'S SANDMAN AND SWANMAN

Heavy grey cloud clings to the horizon as a wicked wind whips off the turbulent waters. Shafts of light from the sun occasionally cut through and illuminate the erratic water, which appears to be running in all directions. It is slightly disorientating as I walk across the gelatinous, sticky mud. Or is it sand? I can't quite tell.

I have no idea if the tide is rising or falling. In places, the water has carved deep channels. The sand has been sculpted into steep cliffs that break off and collapse with a mighty thud into the grey waters, which are now beginning to resemble white water. The water becomes a chaotic, bubbling cauldron as large patches of glistening mud and sand appear. The water thins, and before you have time to comprehend what you are seeing, disappears, to be replaced by a vast, limitless expanse of nothingness. It is like the parting of the Red Sea as the ocean disappears.

Welcome to Morecambe Bay, one of the most extraordinary and dangerous geographical wonders in England.

Historians argue that the route across Morecambe Bay has in all probability been used for more than five thousand years. Almost certainly, it was used by monks who would go 'over sands' to reach the religious houses of Furness and, by the mid-nineteenth century, at low tide routes opened up across the bay for farmers to drive cattle and packhorse trains to ferry people and cargo. Today, Morecambe Bay may have lost its significance as a major trade route, but it can still be crossed.

I am here to meet the legendary Cedric Robinson. He knows more about these sands than anyone and, it has been calculated, the miles he has clocked up walking them could have taken him twice around the world. For half a century he has been the Queen's Guide to the Kent Sands of Morecambe Bay, with a fixed salary of £15 per year. He has one of those jobs that could only exist in England.

The dangers of the shifting sands have always been known. Even in Roman times, no one attempted a crossing without the help of local fishermen. The official job wasn't created until 1501 when a certain Edmondson was appointed. Cedric took over from William Burrow in the 1960s.

Cedric's love of the sands is lifelong. He left school at fourteen to sell shrimp from a horse and cart, crossing the bay with his father and sister. He first led a group over in 1964 and the walks afterwards became more and more frequent, as did the size of the parties – sometimes the group would be 1,000-strong or more at a time. His dedication to the job has earned him an MBE and local celebrity status.

Cedric has never guided the Queen across the sands, but he has met her, and he escorted Prince Philip across once, in 1985.

As they reached the other side of the bay, a crowd had gathered and started to applaud. The often-told story goes that the Duke turned to Cedric in their carriage and said, 'Stand up, Mr Robinson. It is you they are clapping, not me!'

'Hello Ben,' he smiles warmly as we greet at the bay's edge, opposite Grange-over-Sands. We strike out across the sands. It has been nearly fifteen years since I first walked across the bay with Cedric.

'Apart from three trips to London to visit the Queen, I have never left the sands,' he explains as we gently walk out into the waterless bay. On his hand is scrawled '3.15' in pen. 'I have never left the house without writing down the next high tide,' he says. He has a shepherd's crook that he uses to probe the sand.

'I can't tell you how many people just think they can cross the sand without knowledge,' he explains. 'I've seen horses and tractors swallowed by the sand.' He used to be a prawn fisherman and he told me that once, his horse and cart got stuck in the quicksand. 'We couldn't free the horse,' he recounts with horror. 'I got away just in time to watch the water swallow the horse.'

His face brightens as he continues, 'But the water must have freed the sand, because the horse suddenly appeared on the surface and swam to safety. This is a dangerous place, and no one can read the sand like me.'

As those poor cockle pickers who tragically drowned several years ago found out.

We are now far out in the bay. The grey horizon and the grey muddy sand merge in a grey blur. It's difficult to tell which way is up. All around us is the crackle of tiny shrimp-like creatures in the moist sand.

Some days, when he has a walking group, it can take Cedric days to map a safe route across the bay. Sometimes it is simply too dangerous and he has to cancel. Quicksand is notoriously difficult to predict and spot. Cedric knows this better than anyone.

We stop in the middle of the bay. It is at once moonlike and beautiful. The sky is mottled with blue sky and grey cloud that reflect off the puddles of water scattered across the bay like a dalmatian's spots. There is not another person around. We are alone. I am in Cedric's world.

'Do you know I've never taken a holiday,' he states proudly.

'Never?' I repeat.

'Why would I need a holiday when I have this?' He gestures around us. To the north-east are the fells of the Lake District and to the west is the Irish Sea.

'I remember seeing icebergs in here when I was a child,' he recalls. 'They were big enough to stand on. The whole bay would be covered in an icy froth that my father called "snow broth".'

I ask him if he actually still receives his nominal £15 a year. 'They present me with a cheque,' he smiles mischievously.

I wonder who would be willing to take on the dangerous, life-long job for £15 a year. 'The Duchy [of Lancaster] are going to advertise for a new Queen's Guide,' he explains.

'Who could replace you?' I wonder.

Cedric shrugs his shoulders. 'It's got harder rather than easier to cross the sands,' he says. 'The tides, the wind and the weather have all changed and it's harder to read the sands.'

'So what kind of person could do this job?' I press him a bit.

He looks at me and gestures with his hands. 'Someone like you,' he smiles.

I honestly think it is one of the greatest compliments I have ever had.

While I might not make the final cut for Queen's Guide to the Sands, I am the proud holder of another great English honour: the Freedom of the City.

I received it in the Chamberlain's Court at Guildhall, accompanied by the Beadle, wearing a top hat and frock coat. The clerk of the court wore a silk gown, and instructed me to read the 'Declaration of a Freeman':

> I do solemnly swear that I will be good and true to our Sovereign Lady Queen Elizabeth the Second; that I will be obedient to the Mayor of this City; that I will maintain the Franchises and Customs thereof, and will keep this City harmless, in that which in me is; that I will also keep the Queen's Peace in my own person; that I will know no Gatherings nor Conspiracies made against the Queen's Peace, but I will warn the Mayor thereof, or hinder it to my power; and that all these points and articles I will well and truly keep, according to the Laws and Customs of this City, to my power.

My certificate – a parchment document on which my name was beautifully inscribed by a calligrapher – was handed over and I was formally a 'Citizen of London'. Looking down proudly at the certificate, I noticed that the inscription read 'Ben Fogle, TV Company Director'.

I had been away in Antarctica when I was nominated for the honour for my services to adventure and exploration, so my wife had had to fill in the documents for the ceremony. I think she missed both the mood and the significance of the occasion by describing my work so blandly. She could have chosen ocean rower, mountaineer, writer, traveller, polar explorer or broadcaster, but decided on the least exciting option. 'Well, you are a TV company director,' she snapped upon presentation of my framed certificate, which now has pride of place in our loo.

That's another English thing. Placing anything of sentimental value in the loo.

The City of London website describes the Freedom of the City like this: 'The medieval term "freeman" meant someone who was not the property of a feudal lord but enjoyed privileges such as the right to earn money and own land. Town dwellers who were protected by the charter of their town or city were often free – hence the term "freedom" of the City.' Murray Craig, Clerk of the Chamberlain's Court at the City Corporation of London, says the apocryphal belief that it allows freemen the right to drive sheep and cattle over London Bridge probably comes from the exemption from tolls and charges given in earlier times. Today the status is only symbolic, but it carries an enormous cachet. And the ceremony is supposedly one of the oldest traditional ceremonies still in existence today, dating back to 1237.

The legal system in Britain is the product of centuries of creation, alteration and destruction, and England still has many archaic items of legislation to prove it. We as a nation have accrued so many laws, bylaws and conventions over the centuries that it would take several lifetimes and many thousands of hours of parliamentary time to debate and repeal them. And some are just not true, but we have persevered in our belief that they must be because we really want them to be written down on vellum somewhere.

One that does certainly exist, though, is that 'all beached whales and sturgeons must be offered to the Reigning Monarch'. It was passed by Edward II, who was concerned by 'overly conspicuous consumption' in the realm. That was in 1322. The law was even tested in 2004. Robert Davies caught a 9lb sturgeon off the coast of Wales and in an act of commendable patriotism offered it to the Queen, who politely (of course) allowed him to 'dispose of the fish as he saw fit'.

And who knew that a 1872 Licensing Act states: 'It is illegal to be drunk in the pub'? The Act goes on to explain, 'Every person found drunk … on any licensed premises, shall be liable to a penalty.' Originally brought in to encourage lower levels of drinking, the law is still in use today as a means of dealing with unacceptable public drunkenness.

Hangovers in other parts of our legislation include the illegality (since 1313) of wearing armour in Parliament, or allowing your dog to mate with any dog belonging to the royal household. You can be arrested for being in charge of cattle. Finally, and most recently, a poaching law was introduced in 1986 that pronounced it illegal to 'handle a salmon in suspicious circumstances'.

Our country abounds with archaic institutions and rules. It's an essential ingredient of the recipe for Englishness. 'Freedom of the City' or 'Queen's Guide to the Kent Sands of Morecambe Bay' are great examples of the respect we pay to our past lives. Another example is that of the New Forest Verderers.

The Verderers are a body of ten persons appointed to administer the law concerning the New Forest. Five are elected and five are appointed as representatives of the Crown, the Forestry Commission, the Countryside Agency, Hampshire County Council and The Department for the Environment, Food and Rural Affairs (DEFRA). The Verderers sit in open court at regular intervals throughout the year and any member of the public may make a 'presentment' to them, raising any issue concerning the forest. They employ 'Agisters' to tend to the New Forest's population of ponies.

Evidence suggests that the Verderers date back to the thirteenth century, when they were the legal guardians of the sovereign's hunting ground now known as the New Forest. I travelled down to the New Forest to meet them.

Climbing aboard a Land Rover, we headed for our first call, the ancient court in which the Verderers sit once a month to hear from members of the public. While the Agisters wear ceremonial jodhpurs and hunting jackets for ceremonial and court appearances and often patrol on horseback, for my introduction they were dressed a little less formally in green fleece jackets. They showed me around the 219 square mile National Park.

The ponies are all owned by individuals or 'commoners' who exercise their right to allow their ponies to roam and graze the forest. They are the resident gardeners, maintaining the vegetation through grazing. Their heavy footfall also helps to turn the soil and maintain the forest. The Agisters' primary role is to keep an eye on these ponies and ensure that they are healthy and happy.

Fallow deer grazed on the open meadowland as we meandered along the Park's highest point. Through ancient forest and across heathland we bounced across country in search of the famously hardy ponies. Once a year the ponies are gathered in a series of 'drifts', during which each animal is checked, wormed, vaccinated and has its tail trimmed to the pattern of the Agister responsible for that area of the National Park. To qualify as a New Forest pony, the animal must fulfil a set of requirements: the upper height limit is 148cm and the ponies can be any colour except piebald, skewbald, spotted or blue-eyed cream.

William the Conqueror used the New Forest as his hunting ground and commissioned Domesday Book to document the ownership of all the property in the kingdom at the time of his conquest. If you do a little bit of research, our current Queen has some pretty astonishing powers.

She can drive without a licence, she doesn't need a passport to travel, she can create lords and she doesn't have to pay taxes. She has the power to form governments. She has knights. She has the ability to fire *sniggers* the entire Australian government. She is also head of state in Antigua, Barbados, the Bahamas, Belize, Canada, Grenada, Jamaica, New Zealand, Papua New Guinea, Saint Kitts and Nevis, Saint Lucia, the Solomon Islands and Tuvalu. She is head of a religion and she is immune from prosecution. She also has some extraordinary privileges.

The town of Hungerford has to present a red rose to the sovereign in exchange for its fishing and grazing rights. The owner of Fowlis Castle must deliver her a snowball in midsummer. The City of Gloucester pays the Queen for its holdings with an enormous eel pie, while Great Yarmouth must provide a hundred herring baked in twenty-four pastries to the Sheriff, who sends them to the Queen. The Duke of Marlborough has to present a small satin flag bearing the fleur de lys on 13 August, the anniversary of the Battle of Blenheim, and the Duke of Wellington a French tricolour before noon on 19 June every year. But perhaps one of the most extraordinary privileges is that she owns all swans, whales, dolphins and, as we have seen, sturgeon.

According to *Commentaries on the Laws of England*, the 'superior excellence' of whale and sturgeon made them uniquely suited to the monarch's use. The porpoise was later added to the list of Royal Fish. Henry de Bracton, the thirteenth-century author of *On the Laws and Customs of England*, further refined the law by stating 'the King owns the head of the whale and the Queen owns the tail'. To this day, even beached whales belong to the Queen.

I know this for a fact because I had to ask her for one. Well, I didn't personally say 'Hello Ma'am, can I please have one of your dead whales?' because that would have been both weird and inappropriate. But I did formally request one.

You're probably wondering what I wanted with a dead whale. Several years ago, I joined a team of zoologists and marine experts on an unprecedented natural history experiment in which we planned to return a dead beached whale, known as a whale fall, to English waters to see what would come and feast on it. There was some hope that we might record the first great white shark in English waters as we dragged the whale off the coast of Devon. Of course, we had first to find our beached whale, and then ask Her Majesty if we could borrow it – or have it, I should probably say.

I can't profess to know the exact protocol used, but thankfully the Queen granted us her dead whale and the experiment was a huge success. We ended up attracting a shiver (what a wonderful collective noun!) of nearly two hundred blue sharks, though we failed to find a great white.

Queen Elizabeth II is also known as Seigneur – meaning Lord – of the Swans. And the title means that by tradition she owns all mute swans (so named, apparently, because they make a lot less noise than other swans) found on Britain's open waters, although in practice she only exercises that right along the River Thames.

Once a year, under the stewardship of the Queen's Swan Marker, a small flotilla of rowing boats in full regal dress set out to count, measure and check the conditions of all Her Majesty's swans, in an event known as swan upping.

It takes five days to check all the swans. The term 'swan upping' comes from the direction in which the boats travel upstream from Sunbury lock to Abingdon in Oxfordshire.

Over a decade ago I joined the swan uppers for a day. Ten years on, the Swan Marker, David Barber, invited me and my family to follow this ancient tradition again as they worked their way up the Thames. Aboard boats of all shapes and sizes we made our way downstream, the blue-shirted Royal Dyers in two skiffs, the white-shirted Vintners in another two, while the Queen's Swan Uppers were all in royal crimson red with the monarch's insignia emblazoned across the front.

Until the sixteenth century, the ownership of the swans in a given body of water was commonly granted to the relevant land-owners. The only bodies still to use such rights are the two livery companies of the City of London, the Vintners' Company and the Dyers' Company. The Worshipful Company of Vintners dates back to the twelfth century and gained its royal charter in 1364 when it acquired the rights to sell wine without a licence. The Dyers, a trade association of companies involved in the dyeing industry, received their charter in 1471. That wine and dyeing should now be involved in the royal protection of swans is both brilliant and bizarre.

As a special privilege I was given one of the oars on the Queen's boat. Seated aboard his white 'throne', the Swan Marker sat in his velvet crimson jacket with captain's hat and swan feather, behind him a huge white flag bearing Her Majesty's insignia and crown. This was true English pomp and circumstance. Next to us, the Vintners' and Dyers' skiffs with their ornate swan flags escorted us along the river. Behind us were an armada of other boats, all here to witness this historical spectacle.

Gently and methodically we worked our way upriver. Huge crowds had gathered along the towpath and bridges in support of the protectors of the swans. 'All up' was the cry as the first family of swans came into view.

The six skiffs all came together as we approached the swans in a kind of pincer movement. Carefully we created a sort of horse-shoe around the cob and his family, penning them close to the bank while we surrounded them, making a temporary pen with our wooden skiffs.

Slowly, the Swan Marker closed the gap, until the family of swans was encircled within reach. 'It's yours, Ben,' smiled David, instructing me to grab one of the cygnets. I enveloped it with my hands and scooped it from the water. One of the Vintners handed me a piece of rope to tie its flippers together, before we gently carried each swan ashore and placed it on the lawn of a house.

There were two swans and two cygnets. Each was inspected before having a ring placed on its leg. They were then weighed and had their bills and heads measured.

In the 1970s, the river's swan population suddenly declined. The culprit was lead poisoning from the lead used as weights by fishermen on their lines. The weights were banned and swan numbers soon improved, but the swans still face many risks, mainly from dog attacks, but also from the worst of human nature. 'We find lots have been shot by air rifles,' explains David. Pollution, population and increased boating traffic have all put pressure on the magnificent swan. 'We have things like mink now on the Thames, and they take young cygnets, so the conservation side is extremely important. Last year, we only marked eighty-three cygnets. The year before it was a hundred and twenty, so you can see the downturn.

'Hopefully, this year, we can go back up to round about the hundred mark, that we would be happy with. But we'll just have to see. It's one of those things, there's lots of attacks have been going on, so until we get through the week, we won't know.'

There are five days, around eighty miles of river and a whole lot of swans to be counted. The ancient tradition is now about conservation and education. In the past it meant a hearty dinner – swan was once a food served at feasts and banquets. But today it is all about the welfare of the swan.

Once they have been documented and checked by the vet, it is time to return them to the water. We held the four swans side by side at the water's edge before releasing them together on the word of the Swan Marker. 'Make sure you hold their bottoms away from your body,' advised one of the Vintners in their starched white shirt, white trousers and white plimsolls, streaked with green guano.

'Don't hold that bum towards me,' worried David in his crimson royal jacket. It's tough to work with animals while wearing ceremonial clothes. We boarded our little skiffs and took to the oars once again as we worked our way towards Marlow.

Rowing gently upstream is a journey into the heart of England. There is something quintessentially English about rivers, with their weeping willows bowing into the water, the perfectly manicured lawns and English rose gardens of the small houses that line the banks of this iconic river. This is the world of *Wind in the Willows* and *Three Men in a Boat*.

'All up' came the call once again as a larger family of seven swans was corralled between the skiffs. This time it was the turn of my children Ludo and Iona to help with the tagging and measuring. The joy and fascination on their little faces was a joy to behold, and their happiness at holding a small grey cygnet in their arms was enough to make me weep.

There is something emotive about swans, with their bleached white feathers and their long necks. They glide elegantly on the surface of the water. When it comes to flight they are slightly more ungainly, but they have a magnificence becoming of a queen. Perhaps some of these ancient quirks and foibles have elegance as well as eccentricity?

CHAPTER ELEVEN

I'M SORRY,
I HAVEN'T A QUEUE

'Manners makyth man'
William of Wykeham (1320–1404)

It's 4.30 a.m. and daylight is just breaking over South London, but already I am surrounded by a swarm of people, shuffling intently, all focused on one thing … the biggest Queue in the world.

I am in Wimbledon, London SW19, where the world's greatest tennis tournament is held; but while most might associate the venue with tennis, strawberries and cream and Pimm's, it is also famous as the venue of the world's most extreme queuing.

A little before 5 a.m. I reach the gates of the All England Lawn Tennis and Croquet Club; there, a huge sign points me in the direction of a small park, beyond the tennis courts. The sign bears two words: THE QUEUE.

The Wimbledon Queue is an institution. Venerated and celebrated, it combines two of Britain's great hobbies: tennis and queuing.

The sign, and its capitalization, tell a story. This is not just a queue but The Queue: a curiously beautiful and annually growing tradition. Although the majority of the tickets to watch the tennis have already long sold out or been shared between VIPs, the Queue offers a unique last-minute chance to participate in this prestigious tournament, a biff on the nose for elitists and lucky ticket holders. Some people will spend days and even weeks in the Queue, returning each evening after the day's tennis to rejoin for the following day.

There is a festival-like atmosphere as I join the marching tide of Queuers on their way to celebrate one of England's greatest achievements. Hundreds of tents are neatly ordered along marked lines. The overnight Queuers are still asleep, but not for long. I am presented with a Queue card and the all-important 'Guide to Queuing'. Yes, there is bureaucracy and a codified set of rules for the Queue. Within the pamphlet is a Code of Conduct.

CODE OF CONDUCT

The AELTC, in accordance with statutory authority, reserves the right to refuse entry to anyone adopting unreasonable social behaviour or who causes obstruction, danger or annoyance and/or commits any action against the spirit of this Code of Conduct. Please have regard for our neighbours, the facilities and others in The Queue and adopt reasonable social behaviour at all times.

1. You are in The Queue if you join it at the end and remain in it until you have acquired a ticket.
2. Your position in The Queue cannot be reserved by the placing of equipment – you must be present in person and hold a valid, numbered and dated Queue Card. Queue Cards are issued one per individual and are strictly non-transferable.
3. You may not reserve a place in The Queue for somebody else, other than in their short term absence (e.g. toilet break, purchase of refreshments etc.). Temporary absence from The Queue should not exceed 30 minutes.
4. Queue jumping is not acceptable and will not be tolerated.
5. There are no left luggage facilities inside the Grounds; only one bag per person will be allowed into the Grounds and any item/bag exceeding 40cm x 30cm x 30cm (16in x 12in x 12in) in size or hard-sided bags of any size must be left in one of the facilities outside the Grounds (please note that bags deposited in left luggage should be no bigger than 60cm x 45cm x 25cm).
6. The turnstiles accept cash (Sterling) only; if necessary, please ask a Steward for directions to the nearest ATM (cash point).
7. Do not leave bags or other items unattended at any time; they will be removed and may be destroyed by the Police.
8. Confiscation of a Queue Card constitutes refusal of entry to The Championships' Grounds.

9. Anti-social behaviour likely to cause annoyance or offence to other queuers will not be tolerated.

SPECIFICALLY:

- Barbecues or fires are not permitted in The Queue, in Wimbledon Park, the Golf Course or on pavements outside the Park or Golf Course
- Overnight queuers should use tents which accommodate a maximum of two persons.
- Please do not bring or erect gazebos.
- Do not play music or ball games etc. after 10.00pm. At this time all queuers must be close to their tents and settling down for the night, recognizing that other queuers will be going to sleep. This rule is strictly enforced.
- Pizza/'take-away' orders must be arranged for delivery at the Wimbledon Park Road gate only.
- Excessive consumption of alcohol and/or drunken behaviour will not be tolerated and will result in the confiscation of your Queue Card and removal from The Queue. There is a limit of alcohol allowed into the Grounds of one 75cl bottle of wine, or two 500ml cans of beer, or two cans of premixed aperitifs per person. Bottles of spirits or fortified wines will not be allowed into the Grounds.
- Please use the litter bins provided.
- Loud music must NOT be played at any time (use personal headphones).

> – The Stewards have the AELTC's authority, supported by Security Officers and the Police, to confiscate your Queue Card and therefore refuse entry to the Grounds.

By 5.45 a.m. the stewards are beginning to wake the overnight Queuers. 'Morning,' they whisper gently. The Queuers emerge from their tents slowly, then start to brush their teeth and their hair. Women of all ages are busy applying make-up while Queue officials wander round. We Queuers are preparing for the day ahead. The officials commence the process to 'consolidate' the Queue. The tents are taken down and we start to close up into tighter formation. There is a grace and natural ease with which we English can form a queue; it almost feels like synchronized swimming, so adept and well-trained are we. A recognizable Queue rapidly emerges. A man with a huge yellow flag bearing the letter 'Q' marks the back of the Queue. It's both fantastically complicated and highly organized.

Despite the long, winding, snaking line of people, there is never a question of where the Queue begins and ends. Everyone adheres to the strict code and there is a jovial pride in our unique ability to organize chaos into structure.

We respect the queue, but we also love to hate it. We have a strict social code that is fantastically nuanced, and woe betide anyone who transgresses the set-in-stone conventions.

We queue for everything. Buses, trains, tubes, tickets, at restaurants, sporting events, for ice cream, even to have our cheese cut at the supermarket counter. In his 1944 essay, *The*

English People, George Orwell imagined that a foreign observer would be struck by English crowds' 'willingness to form queues'; while the Hungarian-born English writer George Mikes wrote in his 1946 book *How to Be an Alien* that 'an Englishman, even if he is alone, forms an orderly queue of one'. In 1947 the historian Ernest Barker said, 'There will be some bad manners and a little thrusting but the institution for the queue is of that order will be made to work.'

If there is one thing at which the English excel, it is the art of queuing. Some would say that the British are good at organizing themselves into a queue but not so good at waiting in it. This is perhaps the reason we are so intolerant of queue jumpers. We have all been overseas, where, shall we say, they have a more liberal code of conduct when it comes to queuing. Where someone has 'pushed' in front of us, we tut and sulk and try to make it difficult for them, but we will rarely confront them. That would be terribly unEnglish.

Queuing is what the English are renowned for doing – and doing very well. We do it better than anyone else in the world: we are the world champions of queuing.

Queues are, or have been, a symbol of our own society: polite, orderly and hierarchical. If there was one single national trait that demonstrates our social etiquette, it is queuing. The word itself comes from the Latin word *cauda*, meaning 'tail'; in fact in the mid-eighteenth century the word 'queue' meant primarily a plaited ponytail hairstyle. The earliest use of the word in the context of a line was in 1837 by the historian Thomas Carlyle, in which he complimented the French for their talent of 'standing in a queue'.

It's not known where the idea really came from, but the sense of 'first come, first served' always prevails; whether the same was true centuries ago we can't be sure. One theory is that queuing became a necessity as shops sprang up with the growth in town and city populations. An informal chat with the butcher at a market stall became a more anonymous transaction when there were many other people around. To ensure fairness, people stood in a line. And then, as cities became tougher and tougher to survive in, the queue took on a social dimension. 'Queuing started to become associated with extreme hardship as the poor had to queue to access handouts and charity,' says Dr Kate Bradley, a lecturer in social history and social policy at the University of Kent.

The government formally encouraged queuing during the Second World War. 'Propaganda at the time was all about doing your duty and taking your turn,' says Bradley. 'It was a way the government tried to control a situation in uncertain times.' There was a guilt trip associated with not waiting your turn, which was considered very unEnglish. This carried on after the war until, again, queues, like the dole queue, started to become indicators of low class.

More recent research shows that not all English queues are the same. There is a difference between a regulated queue like that at the supermarket checkout, at a bank or a restaurant waiting to be taken to a table, and a bus-stop queue, or sometimes at the pub. Where people aren't shown the way to queue, the system breaks down and it becomes more of a free-for-all.

The thing about queues is that we love to hate them. According to research from University College London, the English wait for an average of just six minutes in a queue before giving up in frustration. The study also revealed we are unlikely to join a queue if there are more than six people in it … but the likelihood of giving up on a queue disappears if the number of people *behind* us has grown to more than six. And there is nothing – and I mean nothing – the English like more than the satisfaction of knowing they are at the head of a lengthy queue. Just look at the anxiety on people's faces in the supermarket as they check if they are in the fastest-moving queue, and the look of relief when they realize they are.

We also value our personal space. Indeed we require a six-inch radius as the minimum afforded to a person in a queue, to avoid increasing our stress or anxiety.

There are a few other important cultural notes to be observed about queuing:

Queue jumping, skipping or barging, sparks a huge sense of injustice amongst all members of the queue. We hate unfairness and injustice more than we do queuing. It is also unEnglish and therefore inappropriate to engage in conversation whilst queuing. Another recent study found that accepting an offer to go ahead of someone in the queue is not welcomed by other queuers. It is thought of as impolite, and will lead to a lot of shuffling and grumbling behind.

Finally, as we've seen at Wimbledon, there are festive queues and everyday queues. According to a study, in festive queues 'we eat, drink and make merry. We play games. We sing songs. In a total inversion of normal English etiquette, talking to a stranger is actively prescribed: you will be regarded as rather snooty and frowned upon if you "keep to yourself" in the usual English manner. There is an atmosphere of camaraderie, a sense of solidarity ... Lifelong friendships and even marriages have been initiated in these queues.' Not so much at the hand-baskets-only checkout at the supermarket, unfortunately.

When it comes to English quirks and traits, the one that most defines our nation apart from queuing must be our love of apologizing. Sorry ...

A recent article by Robin Edds included a list of sixty-five things that will make an English person say 'Sorry':

1. Walking into someone.
2. Nearly walking into someone.
3. Being walked into.
4. Nearly being walked into.
5. Walking into a door.
6. Not hearing what someone has said.
7. Thinking you heard what someone said but being so scared of being wrong about what they said that you ask them to repeat it, just in case.
8. Calling someone on the phone.
9. Answering the phone in someone else's presence.
10. Being late.
11. Being early.
12. Being predictably punctual.
13. Using too much milk.
14. Not using enough milk.
15. Walking across a zebra crossing.
16. Letting someone walk through a doorway before you.

17. Coughing.
18. Sneezing.
19. Swearing.
20. Spilling your pint on someone.
21. When someone spills their pint on you.
22. When you pay for a packet of chewing gum with a tenner because you don't have anything smaller.
23. When the bartender mishears your order.
24. When the bartender drops your change as they pass it back to you, even though it's clearly their fault.
25. Checking your phone.
26. Not replying to an email.
27. Replying to an email too quickly.
28. Replying to a work email over the weekend.
29. When offering your seat to someone a millisecond late.
30. Not offering a drink to someone within the first ten seconds of them entering your house.
31. Asking a shop assistant for help.
32. Not having a stamp, lighter, and pen on your person at all times.
33. Paying in coins for something.
34. Asking someone in the street for anything at all (directions, lighter, etc.).
35. Not having something or knowing something someone on the street asks you for.
36. Sending something back to the kitchen/bar if it's raw/ wrong/likely to kill you.
37. Making an early taxi driver wait until the agreed time you wanted to leave at.

38. Piers Morgan.
39. Making a joke.
40. Making a joke someone else doesn't get.
41. Not getting someone else's joke.
42. Someone else's baby being sick on you.
43. Someone else's dog trying to bite you.
44. Someone else's car trying to run you over.
45. Someone else's partner trying to chat you up.
46. Drinking too much.
47. Not drinking enough.
48. Lying.
49. Telling the truth.
50. The weather.
51. Centuries of colonial oppression and exploitation.
52. Taking slightly too long to board a bus.
53. Ordering any drink at the bar more complicated than a beer or glass of wine.
54. Ordering any drink at a bar.
55. Wanting the attention of a waiter in a restaurant.
56. Asking for your bill in a restaurant.
57. Walking in on your flatmate doing something ordinary in the kitchen.
58. When you need to get to the fridge and someone is standing between you and the fridge.
59. Coming down with an illness.
60. Doing poorly on an exam.
61. Doing very well on an exam.
62. Asking someone on a date.
63. Accidentally making eye contact with a stranger.

64. Accidentally making eye contact during sex.
65. Sex.

'Sorry'. Can there be a better word that sums up the art of Englishness? We are eternally sorry. We are sorry about everything. We are sorry for being sorry. More often than not, we begin our sentences with it: 'Sorry for asking, but ...' Sorry seems to reflect our feelings of inadequacy. It's also a way of showing reverence and politeness.

If it is the weather that defines Englishness, it is the word 'sorry' that describes our nation. It seems that even if we haven't broken a rule – and we are sticklers for rules and protocol – we have to say 'sorry'. Apologetic to a fault, we shout 'Sorry' all the time; for example, as we've been talking about Wimbledon, when playing tennis you are expected to apologize if your shot is a winner and proves too good for a rally to continue; or if your shot goes out or is a mishit or too short, wide or long for your knock-up partner to reach with ease; or lands in the next court disrupting their game – just moments after their ball has inter-rupted yours.

I can remember the time I took part in a charity boxing bout for BBC Sport Relief. I couldn't help apologizing every time I threw a punch. I even found myself apologizing when on the receiving end of an uppercut, as if it were my fault that my face was in the way – which of course it was.

We don't like to deliver opinions harshly. We load our sentences so they don't cause offence. We use please, thank you and sorry as punctuation. Business English colleges, forums and websites are devoted to subjects like 'How to be Polite in English', with tips on softening tools for turning down invitations or proposals and saying 'no' euphemistically.

We ask permission when we don't really have to. 'Do you mind if I … Would it be a problem if I …? I was wondering if I could … sit here/exist/breathe the same air?' We use a softer tone of voice because we are so worried about offending the other person, and perhaps also in order that a negative reply will be similarly softly delivered. We don't like being rejected or spoken to harshly either.

The English don't want to offend anyone, so we tend to mask our true feelings behind a host of euphemisms. There was a lovely little chart circulating online recently which tried to clarify the true meaning of certain English phrases, see overleaf.

Politeness forbids us from being direct and saying what we mean. No wonder we had such a reputation for being devious negotiators in the nineteenth century.

But being a polite nation makes for a quieter life. We have none of the drama of the Italians, or the gruffness of the Germans. We are calm, stiff-upper-lipped and polite. Lord Shaftesbury, writing in the first decade of the eighteenth century, said: '"Politeness" may be defined as a dext'rous management of our words and actions, whereby we make other people have better opinion of us and themselves.' He was determined to make English society a more polite, genteel and cultured place and came up with the idea that 'All Politeness is owing to Liberty. We polish one another, and rub off our Corners and rough Sides by a sort of *amicable Collision*.'

I like to think of English politeness as an amicable collision. But most definitely not in a queue.

WHAT THE ENGLISH SAY	WHAT THE ENGLISH MEAN	WHAT FOREIGNERS UNDERSTAND
I hear what you say	I disagree and do not want to discuss it further	He accepts my point of view
With the greatest respect	You are an idiot	He is listening to me
That's not bad	That's good	That's poor
That is a very brave proposal	You are insane	He thinks I have courage
Quite good	A bit disappointing	Quite good
I would suggest	Do it or be prepared to justify yourself	Think about the idea, but do what you like
Oh, incidentally/by the way	The primary purpose of our discussion is	That is not very important
I was a bit disappointed that	I am annoyed that	It doesn't really matter

WHAT THE ENGLISH SAY	WHAT THE ENGLISH MEAN	WHAT FOREIGNERS UNDERSTAND
Very interesting	That is clearly nonsense	They are impressed
I'll bear it in mind	I've forgotten it already	They will probably do it
I'm sure it's my fault	It's your fault	Why do they think it was their fault?
You must come for dinner	It's not an invitation, I'm just being polite	I will get an invitation soon
I almost agree	I don't agree at all	He's not far from agreement
I only have a few minor comments	Please rewrite completely	He has found a few typos
Could we consider some other options	I don't like your idea	They have not yet decided

CHAPTER TWELVE

GRUB

If there is one food that defines the nation, it is Marmite. The dark brown yeasty savoury spread manages to divide our usually compromise-seeking nation. Like the weather, it has the power to provoke conversation. There can be few other foods so unusual, and with such a polarizing effect on people.

I never travel without a jar of Marmite. Like a cup of tea, there is a consistency in its unique flavour that can take you back to your childhood. I have a cameraman friend who has a special Marmite travel case. My wife was given a silver Marmite kid for her eighteenth birthday.

Even Bill Nighy was stopped at the airport trying to take an extra-large jar through in his hand luggage. In fact, so numerous are the number of people trying to take jars of Marmite past security that London City Airport recently introduced a Marmite swap programme in which the airport exchanges a 100ml jar for any larger jar of Marmite. Marmite is the only product on Jeremy

Clarkson's dressing room rider; and it was also, incredibly, the centrepiece of the floral tribute at the funeral of the late reality star Jade Goody. Marmite's name has now even become an official part of our everyday language: the label of the 'Marmite effect' is applied to anything that people either love or loathe; something for which there is no middle or neutral ground.

Whether you are for or against it, Marmite is us. It is as English as they come. If a jar of Marmite could grumble, it would. It is rigid, sturdy and sensible; hardy but unsure of its social standing.

Marmite is a thoroughly modern food. A product created from up-cycling waste.

It was discovered in the nineteenth century with the realization that brewers' yeast could be eaten. Burton upon Trent was the home to several large breweries, all of which produced vast quantities of yeast as a by-product. In 1902, the Marmite Food Company was founded to 'feed' off this yeasty effluent. The recipe was simple; it combined the concentrated yeast with salt, spices and celery to produce the first variant of Marmite. According to Marmite historians – and they do exist – the spread was named after the unusual shape of the earthenware pots in which it was sold, which looked like the French cooking pot of the same name.

Marmite's big moment came during the First World War, when it was included in soldiers' rations. The men loved it, and it continued to be a part of the army's fighting chest until the end of the Second World War, leading some observers to conclude that it helped us win two world wars. Even in more recent times, homesick British peacekeeping troops in Kosovo asked for supplies to be sent out. The company duly obliged.

Marmite had taken off to such an extent that the Burton upon Trent factory couldn't keep up with supply and a second factory was built in London in 1927. The London factory eventually closed in the 1960s but the Burton factory still exists, producing more than 50 million jars a year. That's almost one for every household per year.

Up until the 1960s, a jar was included in the 'maternity kits' for new mothers, given away free by the NHS to help fight anaemia and help heal tissue after any heart damage. Isn't it amazing that our taxes were used to supply not only soldiers but new mums with Marmite? Powerful stuff.

I have spent many years travelling the globe accompanied by the bulbous black jar and its iconic yellow lid. I have eaten the spread atop mountains, on oceans, in deserts and in the jungle. I once spread it all over my skin in Alaska to ward off mosquitoes, a trick repeated in other regions of the world. Scientists have validated the defensive effect against mozzie bites, which is due to the high quantities of B12 vitamins. New research has even suggested that the high B12 content can prevent premature ejaculation, and eating just five grams of Marmite provides a quarter of our daily vitamin intake.

Five grams? Any Marmite aficionado will recognize that that is quite a lot: most fans will tell you that one of its wonders lies in the need for only the tiniest amount for your daily 'hit'. And as a result, the jar is a little bit like the Tardis – a lot goes into a seemingly small space.

*   *   *

The oracle of all things Marmite is St John Skelton, also known as Mr Marmite. Growing up to the tangy smell in the local air, once so acrid that locals complained, St John started work at the bustling factory at the age of twenty-two. In the forty-two years since he has been responsible for tasting every single batch of Marmite to leave the factory, the equivalent of 24,000 jars. If you break down the batches, that is in fact equivalent to 840 million jars of Marmite. Okay, so he doesn't physically eat every single jar, but due to the variability of the ingredients, his taste buds have been responsible for the uniformity of flavour in close to a billion jars. That's a lot of yeast extract.

'When I came to Burton, it was the bright lights to me, as Lindsey' – his home town – 'is very small. There were very different people in Burton too, as they were much more prepared to be friendly to people they didn't know.'

'If people have been brought up on Marmite, they tend to be fond of it throughout their lives,' explains St John. 'I've always loved it. From when I was a baby, I liked savoury foods over sweets. At kids' parties, while everyone else was eating jelly and blancmange, I preferred the Marmite sandwiches they made for the grown-ups.' According to St John the quality of Marmite has improved over the years. The best way to eat it, he insists, is between two slices of white bread, with a thin layer of butter and slices of cooked chicken.

St John has stepped out of retirement to show me round the cavernous factory. It feels a little like a school during the holidays. A building that should contain far more people than it does. Like many across the country, the Marmite factory workers have succumbed to technology, been replaced by robots.

Now just fifty people work in a factory that once employed thousands.

Dozens of 'yeast tankers' are lined up in the yard ready to be 'milked' of their yeast, harvested from the huge Coors and Marston breweries nearby. Industrial hoses suck the yeast into massive silos. It's like a dairy farm for robots as up to a dozen trucks are relieved of their yeast. The yeast is then transferred into copper vessels where it is spun by a centrifuge into which water and salt are both added. The solution is then heated.

As the yeast begins to digest itself with the heat, it starts to break down into a rich fluid which is then sieved to remove the hops; the resulting by-product of slurry is sold off as a fertilizer for the agricultural industry. The remaining fluid effluent is converted into a flammable gas which is used to heat the factory. I told you it was ahead of its time.

The soup simmers for several hours before it is thickened into a paste in tall towers in a process of evaporation which turns the liquid from 6 per cent solid into 50 per cent solid; and the process is repeated until it reaches a solidity of 75 per cent solid. Now stable, the paste is transferred into one tin vat. These are then used as the blends to ensure the consistency of the product.

Consistency is a huge factor in Marmite production. There are so many variables: the varying quantities and qualities of yeast from various breweries is an obvious challenge. But there are some unusual – perhaps unique – social factors too, because Marmite is directly affected by the nation's consumption of alcohol. Christmas and World Cup football matches all instigate a rise in the consumption of beer, with the result that there is more yeast to work with.

Once the product is stable, the blending can begin. Like all the best products, of course, the exact ingredients of Marmite remain a tightly guarded secret. The secret blend is hidden in a plain box marked 'Premix 8897523'. This is the magic that converts the yeast extract into the nation's most loved – or loathed – spread. It has an aroma of roasted vegetables, herbs and citrus. Even Marmite stalwart St John doesn't know the exact ingredients. As the secret mixture is added, a large label announces that from this point the product is known as Marmite. Without the secret premix, the naked product becomes another iconic brand, Bovril. The factory divides production between the two in an 80/20 split, producing 6,000 tons of Bovril every year.

Once the Marmite has been piped it is warmed once again to 40°C so that the brown, sticky paste is runny enough to be packaged. In its 'shelf' form, it would be too solid to pack. Here robotic arms swing and glide effortlessly and efficiently as hundreds of empty black jars are unpacked from boxes ready to be filled.

While Marmite itself has a unique taste, the jars too have an unmistakable appearance. In fact they are pharmaceutical-quality jars that have been made by the same German company, Gerresheimer, for many years. Two hundred and fifty jars are swept down the line by giant robotic arms that then check every single jar for the tiniest flaw. Twenty-eight filler heads carefully fill each jar, the lids of which are then screwed on faster than the human eye can see. Above me a vast tower of Marmite jiggles and wriggles around a circular machine as this latest batch makes its way to the final packing area.

*   *   *

St John was such a fixture that to celebrate his forty-two years at the factory he was presented with a limited-edition jar of Marmite bearing his face. His colleagues had organized the manufacture of 3,000 jars of Marmite XO, and St John said he was honoured by the gesture. Despite retirement he continues in his role of Lord Marmarati – leader of a secret group of Marmite fanatics, The Marmarati, which now claims to have 350 members. When he retired in November 2016, he created a tasting vacuum and had to search for a new dedicated group of tasters with buds refined enough to taste the minute differences between batches. Marmite developed an exam in which you need to get at least 19 out of 24 points to become a taster. Did I take it? Of course I did.

I was ushered into a small, stark, white laboratory. Eight small beakers of colourless liquid had been carefully placed on the surface, in front of which was an examination paper. Men in white lab coats walked around looking scientific and important. 'You must identify each liquid before rating them in order of strength,' explained St John, suddenly looking fearsomely academic.

The paper in front of me bore strict instructions:

1. Please do not communicate with, or distract other people taking part.
2. Please do not consume food, sweets or chew gum whilst the screening is in progress.

For each colourless liquid I was given four options: acid, bitter, salt and sweet. Once I had identified the flavour I had to rate them in order of intensity, from weakest to strongest. I was surprisingly nervous, all sweaty palms and racing heart.

I regressed to my childhood loathing of exams. I hated them because I was so bad at them, hopelessly unacademic. I failed them all. I have tried to avoid exams as much as possible in recent years but now, here I was surrounded by Marmite royalty and about to put my love of one of our most iconic brands to the ultimate test. I picked up the first glass cup and sniffed the colourless liquid to discover it was also odourless.

'Make sure there is no distraction in your mouth,' advised St John, offering me a glass of water. 'Rinse your mouth regularly.'

I sipped a small mouthful. Salty, I was sure. I picked up another beaker and this one was stronger, but was it salty or sugary? How could I mix up sweet and savoury? This was ridiculous. Under pressure my mind started playing tricks on me.

I took another sip of the first cup, which now tasted sweet. But was it the dregs of the previous cup that I'd failed to 'cleanse' with fresh drinking water? Arrrrggh. How was I going to make it as a professional Marmite taster if I couldn't even distinguish between salt and sugar?

'It's definitely sugar,' I whispered to myself, before reaching for the other beakers.

I swished the fluid around my mouth. This cup was rank. It wasn't a salty flavour after all and it certainly wasn't bitter. I quite like bitter; this was acidic and disgusting – and strong, very strong. I raced to the sink to spit out the noxious substance. St

John smiled a little as I wiped the spit from my mouth and returned to the concoctions.

'Think rationally,' I reminded myself as I sipped each cup methodically and allowed the sweetness to caress the front of my tongue. I divided them into their two groups and then returned to have another taste before placing them in ascending order. First flavour screening complete, I was presented with the second batch of flavours.

What if I had got the first set wrong? By my reckoning the remaining ones had to be 'bitter' and 'salt', but if I had been wrong the first time then I would fail the whole exam.

I began to doubt my ability to distinguish between acidic and bitter. We rarely try many of these flavours on their own in their raw, visceral nakedness, but now in a laboratory in northern England I was forcing my taste buds to work to Olympic standards.

Once again I gingerly sipped one of the cups. This one was definitely salty. I have drunk enough salt rehydration sachets over the year to know what it tastes like when mixed with water. Interestingly, the more dehydrated you are, the less you taste the salt; the more hydrated, the more you can taste it.

The other substance was unfamiliar. Was it bitter? Once again I trusted to instinct and carefully marked them all off the list before handing in my paperwork and walking to the small meeting room.

I waited nervously before St John returned. 'I want to be fair,' he smiled, 'you failed to mark one of the categories. Have a good look at the paper,' he said, 'and think carefully about what you've done. And make sure you are still happy with your decision.'

Suddenly his words sounded like an ominous warning. Had I messed up that badly? I returned to the lab for reassurance, sipping the liquid again. Now I was sure it was salty, but why had St John questioned my judgement? Was he playing with my mind?

I handed over the now complete but unchanged papers and returned to the waiting room.

St John returned looking serious before placing the papers in front of me. 'You scored twenty-four out of twenty-four. Full marks!'

'One hundred per cent!' I marvelled. I had never got full marks for anything in my life, and now here with Mr Marmite I had finally obtained academic excellence in … Marmite. It seems a rather fitting tribute to living Englishly.

The press seem to agree. Marmite has provided our newspapers with manna from heaven. A quick look online revealed hundreds of Marmite-related stories.

After a spate of Marmite thefts from a Spar store in Northamptonshire, the manager was forced to keep the Marmite behind the counter. There have been dozens of stories of Marmite being banned from British prisons because prisoners were using it to make home brew or hooch. Apparently, at Dartmoor prison the prisoners were making a drink called the 'Marmite Mule'. In 2011, Marmite was banned in Denmark because it fell foul of the country's law restricting products fortified with added vitamins.

But my personal favourite came from the *Daily Mail* under the headline, FACE OF JESUS FOUND IN JAR OF MARMITE. According to the story,

A family breakfast turned into a religious experience when they spotted what appears to be the face of Jesus in the lid of a Marmite jar. Claire Allen, 36, was the first to notice the image, on the underside of the lid, as she was putting the yeast spread on her son's toast.

And husband Gareth, 37, said he could not believe his eyes when she showed him.

Mr Allen, of Ystrad, Rhondda, south Wales, said: 'Claire saw it first and called her dad to come and take a photo of it.

'When I first looked at it I wasn't sure, but when I moved it away from me it started coming out. I thought Christ, yeah, she's right – that's the image of Jesus.

'The kids are still eating it, but we kept the lid.'

Mrs Allen said her 14-year-old son Jamie had also remarked on the likeness. She told the *South Wales Echo*: 'Straight away Jamie said, "That looks like God", and my other boys Robbie, four, and Tomas, 11, even said they could see a face.

'People might think I'm nuts, but I like to think it's Jesus looking out for us.

'We've had a tough couple of months; my mum's been really ill and it's comforting to think that if he is there, he's watching over us.'

According to another story, one Marmite superfan has revealed an immense collection of Marmite memorabilia which included more than 200 *jars* of Marmite:

Shelly McClellan, a self-confessed lover of the iconic Burton-made product, only began collecting items four years ago. And in that time the 45-year-old, whose obsession with the black spread began when she was a child, has amassed more than 200 different jars, and memorabilia ranging from jewellery and clothing to lamps.

Shelly McClellan went to a pop-up Marmite shop in London dressed as a jar. She said: 'I've also done several Marmite projects which have included me knitting a hat and painting a gnome.

'My most treasured item is a gold Marmite jar celebrating 100 years. It also came with a knife and was only given to employees. I managed to get my hands on one as someone was selling one on eBay. My dad went and picked it up for me.'

Yet another story was about a man from Etwall who 'hates' food, and says that he only eats to stop himself from starving to death and believes a daily dose of Marmite has been keeping him alive.

In 2016, a post-Brexit Marmite row, or 'Marmageddon' as it was dubbed, caused panic buying. A very public spat between Tesco and Unilever saw the supermarket giant refuse to accept price rises on hundreds of Unilever products caused by the falling pound, which resulted in Marmite disappearing from Tesco's shelves. No one meddles with our Marmite! Smaller supermarket chain Morrisons, however, quietly hiked the price of the iconic British toast-topper by 12.5 per cent, setting off new fears about food price rises in the wake of the Brexit vote. Tesco struck a deal to keep price rises to about 5 per cent. I even got caught up in the Marmite crisis myself, As jars went online for more than £1,000, I bought a jar for £50 just in case.

If every country in the world were asked to assemble a capsule of iconic national food staples, there is no doubt that the box labelled 'England' would contain a distinctly shaped pot of Marmite, a caddy of Twinings teabags, a small slim bottle of Worcestershire sauce, and a tall jar of Branston pickle. Interestingly, if you break down the assortment of flavours they all have things in common. They all have an emphasis on strong, piquant flavours, and arguably they are all best with something else … e.g. Marmite and toast, Branston and cheese, Worcestershire sauce with Welsh rarebit or a Bloody Mary, tea with biscuits. They all now have iconic branding, which suggests people love the homely familiarity of the product as well as its taste.

Marmite to me is the epitome of English food. Widely derided and sneered at abroad and by half the people at home, it stoically and quietly grinds on in the face of opposition and unpromising odds. As a result it makes a lot of people very happy. For the naysayers, we can just repeat the classic phrase 'You can't please all the people all the time …'

Can there be a dish any more English than fish and chips?

If there is a spiritual home of fish and chips it must be Whitby. The home of Dracula and the annual Goth Festival, the Yorkshire seaside town has also become a Mecca for fish and chip aficionados.

I love Whitby. It has a faded, gothic glamour with its ruined abbey and its grand Victorian façades. While the most famous fish and chip shop is arguably Magpies, which boasts a year-round queue for a table, I paid the town a visit in order to work in the newly crowned hero of fish and chips, the Quayside restaurant.

Long before the sun had risen on a hot summer's morning, I joined a small trawler, the *Providor*, as we motored out of Whitby harbour into the North Atlantic ready to catch the fish of the day. The trawler swayed gently on the benign water. It isn't always like this. Fishing remains one of England's most dangerous professions.

We laid the long nets and trawled up and down the coast. Several hours later we hauled the brimming nets onto the deck before returning to harbour with our bountiful catch.

It was still early but already Whitby was alive with visitors sitting on the quay wall watching the returning trawlers unload their catch while munching on fish and chips. Seagulls wheeled overhead, threatening to steal the contents of their white paper wrappers.

Our shining cargo was unloaded and ferried to the local fish merchant, Dennis Crooks, where I helped clean and fillet the haul before finally delivering it to Quayside, the winner of the 2014 annual Fish and Chip awards – the Oscars of the chippie. Quite an accolade. More than 2,000 of Britain's 10,500 chippies enter the competition.

As I walked into the bustling, proud establishment, the owner, Stuart Fusco, to whom I was apprenticed for the day, handed me a long white apron and a chef's hat.

The secret to the perfect fish and chips, of course, is in the batter, and Stuart was certainly not giving away his award-winning secret recipe. The preferred fish divides between our nations within the United Kingdom: haddock, favoured by the Scots, must be sweet, flaky and soft in the mouth while cod, England's favourite, should be subtle, firm and flaky.

Using a pair of tongs, I gently dipped the freshly filleted fish into the creamy batter mix, allowing it to steep for several minutes before dropping it with a fizz into the bubbling cauldron of fatty oil. The queue was already snaking around the corner as visitors, many of whom had travelled for hours, waited patiently for the national dish.

Fish and chips are synonymous with the seaside. Eaten in newspaper, drowned in vinegar and smothered in salt, they have become a staple for a generation. Winston Churchill described them as 'the good companion'.

No good Englishman or -woman can avoid the temptation of a chip. We consider it the bedrock of our culinary experience, but of course the chip is not a chip at all; it began life as the French fry. The story of the chip dates to seventeenth century France where it is reputed to have been created as a substitute for fish.

In times past, rivers in France froze just as readily as our English ones. The fish couldn't be caught and the French, in a pique of resourcefulness, resorted to carving potatoes into the shape of fish which they then fried as an alternative.

This coincided with the introduction of fried fish to England from Jewish refugees coming from the Mediterranean. One of the earliest references in literature was in *Oliver Twist*, in which Charles Dickens referred to a 'fried fish warehouse'.

No one knows for sure who married the fish and the chip to create our culinary triumph. While some credit John Lees, an entrepreneur from Lancashire who sold fish and chips from a wooden hut at Mossley market, most still attribute the Jewish immigrant Joseph Malin, who opened a fish and chip shop in East London in 1860. In the nineteenth century, working-class diets were pretty bleak and unvaried, so when fish and chips arrived, it provided a new taste sensation and shops sprang up across the country. Italian migrants passing through English towns and cities saw the growing queues outside the chippies and sensed a business opportunity. Within years, fish and chip shops were a fixture on the High Street, with over 25,000 operating by 1910. The dish became so popular that during the First World War the government prioritised its protection, worrying that if the enemy cut off supplies, the effect would hamper public morale. According to Professor John Walton, author of *Fish and Chips and the British Working Class*, 'The cabinet knew it was vital to keep families on the home front in good heart. Unlike the German regime that failed to keep its people well fed and that was one reason why Germany was defeated […] fish and chips played a big part in bringing contentment and staving off disaffection.'

By the late 1930s and the advent of the Second World War, the government ensured fish and chips were never included in the nation's rationing, once again fearing the effect on morale, and George Orwell agreed. In *The Road to Wigan Pier* (1937), he suggested that fish and chips helped to quell uprising and avert revolution.

Today, fish and chips has lost a little of its culinary hero status, diluted by the nation's love affair with the North American burger and the Italian pizza. Burgers, fried chicken, pizza, Indian and Chinese dishes all now outsell fried fish. Cost is part of the problem. Strains on stocks of cod and haddock have pushed prices up, while health concerns about deep-fried food have turned many consumers away. According to statistics, our annual takeaway consumption breaks down as follows: 748 million burgers, 569 million Chinese and Indian meals, 333 million fried chicken dinners, 249 million pizzas and 229 million portions of fried fish. The fall in popularity is reflected in the number of chippies: 25,000 in 2010 and fewer than 10,000 by 2017.

You are what you eat. You can tell a lot about a nation from their diet. As well as the land of Marmite and fish and chips, we are also the land of Worcestershire Sauce, HP sauce and Twiglets. We get through an estimated six billion packets of crisps and 4.4 billion bags of savoury snacks a year – around 150 packets per person – and you do wonder what our love affair with crisps is doing to us. Looked at by tonnage, we consume more crisps, crackers and nuts than any other European country. And this is where our own touch of eccentricity shines through.

In the UK in 1981, Hedgehog Foods decided, as a joke, to produce hedgehog-flavoured crisps (potato chips). To everyone's surprise, the crisps were a huge success. I have vivid memories of the phenomenon. We, as kids and as a country, were intrigued and outraged in equal measure, and I can remember the mad scramble to get hold of a packet of the most coveted crisps in the country. Hedgehog-flavoured crisps were actually flavoured with pork fat – no hedgehogs were used in the manufacturing process. Consequently, it wasn't long before Hedgehog Foods Ltd ended up in court (1982) up against the Office of Fair Trading, on a charge of false advertising. Bizarrely, a settlement was finally reached when Mr Lewis of Hedgehog Foods interviewed gypsies who actually ate baked hedgehogs, to ascertain the flavour of hedgehogs. Mr Lewis then commissioned a flavouring firm to duplicate the flavour as closely as possible and changed the labels from 'hedgehog-flavoured' to 'hedgehog flavour'.

Our national taste buds can be as eccentric as our customs, clothing, humour and habits.

CHAPTER THIRTEEN

ENGLAND'S GREEN AND PLEASANT LANDS

If there is a landscape that sums up our nation it must surely be the lawn. From the English garden lawn to the bowling green, grass tennis court and cricket field, the green strips of finely cut grass are unequivocally English. When I think either of my father or my father-in-law, the most vivid image that comes to mind is that of them mowing the lawn.

There are 15 million lawns in Britain. Last year we spent £54 million on lawn fertilizers. We then forked out another £127 million on lawnmowers. There is even an English lawn awards and a lawnmower museum. Except perhaps a dog, there is nothing an Englishman loves more than a lawn.

The earliest lawns were probably found in medieval monasteries, where contemplation was helped by their greenness. But the first mention of the English lawn was in a 1625 essay on gardens by Francis Bacon. Bacon referred to lawns as 'the greatest refreshment to the spirit of man', and he was quite firm about what made a proper garden. It should be square, surrounded by a 'stately, arched hedge', a distant patch of wilderness (thickets of sweet briar and honeysuckle) and, in the foreground, a lawn. 'Nothing is more pleasant to the eye than green grass kept finely shorn,' he wrote.

The earliest domestic lawn is at Chatsworth House in Derbyshire, where Capability Brown designed Salisbury Lawns in 1760 – so named because they seemed as big as Salisbury Plain, the vast rolling green plains of Wiltshire. Enormous lawns at houses such as Chatsworth demonstrated your wealth, for the lawns were expensive to keep. Many large estates used sheep and goats to keep the grass short; indeed, visit almost any stately home today and you will be sure to find vast flocks of sheep, 'organically mowing' the huge lawns that surround the old piles. If you didn't want animals littering your idyll, you needed gangs of men with scythes.

It wasn't until 1830 that lawns really took off when Edwin Budding, an engineer from Stroud, Gloucestershire, patented an invention which would transform our country – not just socially, but also in the way it looked and sounded. It was the first mechanical lawnmower. The Budding marked the end of the skilled men with scythes, and meant everyone could now cut their grass into a short green oasis.

The first petrol mowers appeared in the late 1890s. Then someone came up with a steam mower, and electric jobs came in the 1920s. And herein lies a smudgy-cheeked point of lawns for many a bloke: the chance to play with machines. The lawn became the pride of the English home. I still have vivid memories of the noise and the smell as my father emptied the big green collecting bucket from the front of the mower into a huge pile of grass cuttings at the end of the garden.

I can't imagine how many hours my father and father-in-law have dedicated to mowing, trimming, weeding and perfecting their lawns. In a sense lawns are a way of taming and controlling Nature; they give a sense of control and order that is deeply English. Neat and tidy.

In Britain, we tend to be quite private about our lawns, often keeping them hidden behind the sort of hedges stipulated by Bacon. 'Keep off the Grass' was a familiar sign in my youth. It always struck me as strange to be kept away from such an inviting landscape. Surely a lawn was for walking on, not just looking at?

The French laugh at us for our obsession with lawns. In one of the Asterix cartoon books, a suburban Englishman loses his temper when Roman soldiers are about to march across his lawn. He holds them up with a bristling pitchfork, one indignant moustache facing an entire legion.

I wonder whether it is the 'greenness' of the lawn that is so evocative. When I think of England, I imagine a green landscape, lush and heavily watered from our high rainfall. There has to be some positive from our damp climate. And that's greenness. On an island with such geographical diversity it is difficult to pick a landscape that sums up Englishness. We have an extraordinarily varied coastline, from the dramatic cliffs of Cornwall to the vast flat expanses of northern Norfolk. We have the chalky South Downs, the glorious lakes of Cumbria and the wild moorland of Dartmoor and Exmoor, not to mention the forests and the world-class National Parks. Our landscape is unique and yet undefinable. It is like our weather, unpredictable and changeable.

But there is one phrase that has entered our everyday conversation when we talk about our landscape. 'England's green and pleasant land'. The phrase comes from William Blake's *Milton: a poem* – not, strangely enough, from 'Jerusalem', which is the name every one associates with it.

> And did those feet in ancient time
> Walk upon England's mountains green?
> And was the holy Lamb of God
> On England's pleasant pastures seen?
>
> And did the Countenance Divine,
> Shine forth upon our clouded hills?
> And was Jerusalem builded here
> Among these dark Satanic Mills?
>
> Bring me my Bow of burning gold;
> Bring me my Arrows of desire:
> Bring me my Spear: O clouds unfold!
> Bring me my Chariot of fire.
>
> I will not cease from Mental Fight,
> Nor shall my Sword sleep in my hand
> Till we have built Jerusalem,
> In England's green & pleasant Land.

The poem was set to music by Sir Hubert Parry in 1916 at the request of poet Robert Bridges. Sir Edward Elgar arranged it for orchestra and ever since, it has been played at stirring English occasions like the Last Night of the Proms. And it is, of course, the WI's hymn of choice. It was always my favourite hymn at school and shall forever remember it being sung in Westminster Abbey at the wedding of Prince William and Catherine Middleton. It was also used with particular poignancy as the opening hymn for the London Olympics in 2012.

England doesn't have a national anthem. Isn't that incredible? Of course we have 'God Save the Queen', but that is Great Britain's anthem. North of the border they have 'Flower of Scotland', Wales have 'Hen Wlad Fy Nhadau' (Old Land of My Fathers). But England doesn't have one. The fact that we don't have a national anthem is symbolic of our loss of identity and our shame at displays of our English heritage.

Yet 'Jerusalem' is the official hymn of the England and Wales Cricket Board; it was used as the England football team's official Euro 2000 song, becoming a top ten hit; and most famously it is sung at the Last Night of the Proms. Giving 'Jerusalem' official status as England's national anthem is frequently mentioned as an option but no government will decide. It would get my vote.

Our lawns, fields and rolling hills are our 'green and pleasant land', but we are an island. And so we have cliffs, beaches and of course, seaside resorts.

Blackpool, Redcar, Bognor Regis, Margate, Whitstable, St Ives, Brighton, Bournemouth ... the names of the English seaside towns are synonymous with smutty seaside postcards, slightly dodgy B&Bs and tooth-breaking 'seaside rock'. They are where we go crabbing while seagulls mug us of our chips; they are synonymous with slot machines on the end of the pier and the promenade. My late grandmother, Jean, lived in Brighton and the city still evokes happy memories of my childhood: the smell of the sea mixed with the vinegar of chips and sweet scent of candy floss. But beyond our shoreline is another world.

It is perhaps a little-known fact that my full title is Lord Fogle of Sealand; however, it was not bestowed by Her Majesty the Queen but by King Bates of Sealand. If you've never heard of Sealand, then you've missed out on one of the strangest and most eccentric English stories of the last few decades. Did you know that just an hour from the Suffolk coast lies one of England's strangest and most eccentric kingdoms? A tiny principality sitting in the North Sea, defiantly proclaiming its independence.

A cross between a bizarre steampunk sea monster and the alien tripods from *The War of the Worlds*, the 'sovereign nation' soared from the ocean as I approached. The word SEALAND was painted on the side of one of the buildings, with its black, red and white national flag fluttering in the stiff breeze. As I reached the bottom of the platform I scanned the structure for a ladder or a staircase. There was nothing, just barnacle-encrusted steel dipping sheer into the stormy ocean, pounded by the waves.

'How do we get up there?' I asked Prince Michael.

'You'll see,' he answered with a smile, handing me a life jacket.

High above, tiny heads appeared over the parapet as people manoeuvred what looked like a very old crane over the side. A thick cable descended to our rocking boat, a short plank of wood on the end acting as a sort of bo'sun's chair. 'Do you want to go first?' asked the Prince. Before I could answer, I was ushered on to the contraption and soon I was dangling high above the North Sea. Buffeted by the wind, the boat disappeared below me and all I could see was the angry swirl of the ocean.

As I reached the deck, a surly man came to meet me. 'Passport.' I handed over my passport, complete with the visa that I had acquired at a Harwich pub. I told you this was an eccentric story.

The Principality of Sealand is an old Second World War fortress, seven and a half miles off the Suffolk coast. Its total area is 0.0015 square miles, or perhaps a couple of squash courts placed back to back. Former British Army major Paddy Roy Bates and his wife, Joan, declared Sealand a state in 1967, although it has never been recognized by the British government or any other international body; in fact its status has been derided by just about every legal opinion in the field of international law. Its relatively short but rich history is littered with court battles, international intrigue and even an attempted coup by armed mercenaries. In those five decades of existence, only 106 people have been given 'citizenship'. I was joining an elite club.

When Roy Bates died in 2012, his 63-year-old son 'Prince' Michael Bates succeeded. He continues to rule, but is doing so from his land-based home in Essex where he runs a business – even monarchs have to make a living these days. And the future of the nation is in doubt as there are repeated reports of it being sold.

That is for the future, though. As I was winched on to the platform, I was more interested in its past.

The story begins in 1943 at the height of the Second World War, when the government built anti-aircraft forts off the Kent and Suffolk coasts for protection against the waves of German bombers. The forts were decommissioned in the 1950s but, because they lay outside British waters, in the 1960s they attracted pirate radio operators who were banned by the government from broadcasting on the mainland.

In the decade of peace and love, the fight for the forts was very physical. Roy Bates attacked and ousted a station already broadcasting from HM *Fort Roughs* – Sealand's previous designation – intending to set up his own radio station. Before they could transmit, though, a new law banned broadcasting even from these forts outside British territorial waters. So Roy's radio station was never heard. As it happened, the day the law came in was also the birthday of his wife, Joan. So he proclaimed Fort Roughs a sovereign state, renamed it Sealand and bestowed the title of Princess of Sealand on her as a birthday present.

'It was not long before the British government decided they could not have what ministers described as a possible Cuba off the east coast of England,' Sealand's website says. Helicopters and destroyers were sent by the government to destroy the other forts and Bates was threatened that Sealand would be next. Roy and Michael fired shots at one Royal Navy ship and were prosecuted, but the judge in the case ruled that, as Sealand was in international waters at the time, the UK had no jurisdiction over it. Bates declared that the judgement was 'de facto recognition' of Sealand's sovereignty. Most of the rest of the world sniggered.

In 1982, the United Nations Convention on the Law of the Sea extended the UK's waters to include the platform. It was a crushing blow but Roy, with true plucky English underdog spirit, retaliated by extending Sealand's own territorial waters to twelve miles, thereby annexing Felixstowe. To this day, the annexation has not been challenged.

There have since been kidnappings, international smuggling operations and attempted coups, with armed troops dropping on to the platform at midnight from helicopters. One final bizarre incident happened in 1997. When police in Miami discovered the body of Andrew Cunanan, who had committed suicide after murdering fashion designer Gianni Versace, they also found a Sealand passport and Sealand diplomatic plates.

It really is a study in English eccentricity.

After my first visit I was honoured with a knighthood for services to Sealand, and I returned to the rusty wreck to receive my title. It was strange to return in a suit and tie to be honoured out on the helicopter deck. Ed Sheeran also received a knighthood, and he has promised to do a highly exclusive concert on Sealand.

While I haven't managed to set up my own micro nation, I did once try to buy a lighthouse.

I have always been fascinated by lighthouses and their keepers, and over the years I have been lucky enough to explore countless lighthouses around Great Britain, but in 2004 a friend told me about a lighthouse for sale down in Kent. I had just started seeing a new girlfriend, and I thought I would romance her with my lighthouse shopping.

The Old Lighthouse is now a historic building, its lighthouse duties long replaced by newer self-automated models. Opened with great ceremony by His Royal Majesty the Prince of Wales in 1904, it survived two world wars before it was decommissioned in 1960.

Dungeness is a vast expanse of shingle ridges, built up over the centuries by longshore drift. By the end of the medieval period it had grown into a promontory reaching out into the English Channel and had become a lethal shipping hazard. Advances in marine technology during the sixteenth century had led to a large increase in both the number and size of ships in the English Channel. It is said that during one winter gale over a thousand sailors lost their lives and many valuable cargoes sank with them. The name Dungeness derives from the Old Norse *nes*, 'headland', the first part of the name probably being connected with the nearby Denge Marsh – although the name is popularly held to be of French origin, the meaning being 'dangerous nose'.

The first lighthouse, a wooden tower with an open coal fire on top, was licensed to private ownership by King James I in August 1615. As time passed, the sea continued to retreat as the shingle banks grew. A second brick lighthouse 110ft high was constructed around 1635. This second lighthouse lasted over 100 years, but it too became victim of the growing shingle banks and after complaints about poor light visibility at sea another new light-house was built in 1790. This third lighthouse, some 116ft tall, was lit by Argon lamps, fuelled first by oil and finally petroleum. The light was magnified by silvered concave reflectors. Towards the end of the nineteenth century the shingle bank had grown to such an extent that an additional smaller Low Light near the water's edge became necessary. A siren-type foghorn was housed in the same building.

In 1901 Trinity House commissioned Patrick & Co of London to build a new, taller fourth lighthouse, approximately 150ft high. It was this lighthouse which was ceremonially opened by the

Prince of Wales in 1904. For fifty-six years it provided a welcome landlight to vessels negotiating the perils of the English Channel. Constructed of more than three million engineering bricks with sandstone inner walls, the lighthouse features in Nikolaus Pevsner's *Buildings of Kent*.

During the late 1950s work began on Dungeness power station and it became apparent that, due to the height of the new building, the light would be obscured from the sea. Subsequently a fifth, automatic lighthouse was built closer to the water's edge, where it still operates today.

Now the Old Lighthouse was on the market and I was looking to live out my *Fraggle Rock* fantasy. But while the lighthouse was my motivation, Dungeness is the real star. It's one of the most eccentric landscapes in England.

Often called the desert of England, Dungeness is a crazy, odd, surreal landscape. It is open and bleak and weird in a slightly post-apocalyptic kind of way. Not that it's devoid of life: on the contrary it is a thriving nature reserve, and home to a third of Britain's plant species. But even the rich flora and fauna can't quite detract from the sheer surreality of this odd environment.

The landscape itself certainly divides people – a broad, echoing flatness, the vast planes of shingle dipping into the ocean. What makes it so surreal though is the eclectic range of dwellings. Railway carriages and upturned boats have been turned into quaint and spooky homes, while there are a wide range of alternative buildings, from cabins and shacks to tiny cottages standing alone in the vast shingle plain. The unique structures have attracted modern artists and architects to create a mind-boggling array of futuristic and post-apocalyptic dwellings that prickle the senses.

Bleak black rubber houses and stark concrete boxes bring a Mad Max edge to the landscape. But perhaps the most famous house is Prospect Cottage, a black (of course) cottage that belonged to the late Derek Jarman. In the 1990s, people went to Dungeness because Jarman, the seminal arthouse film-maker, lived there: fashion shoots regularly took place in his front garden, and there's now a note in the window saying: 'No fashion shoots in my front garden without prior written permission'.

Jarman's garden is still intricately tended, around beds of intensely weird vegetation that can't decide if it's seaweed or something else. Unsurprisingly, Dungeness has become a popular location for music videos as well as fashion shoots. The surreal landscape appears on the cover of Pink Floyd's *A Collection of Great Dance Songs* and The Thrills' *So Much for the City*. The Prodigy shot one of their videos, 'Invaders Must Die', here, a rather appropriate name for a landscape that looks like the set of *The War of the Worlds*. Danny Boyle and Michael Winterbottom have filmed here and Athlete wrote a song about the place, but my most vivid memory is of a 1970s episode of *Doctor Who* located in the otherworldly landscape that gave me nightmares for months.

As if the area wasn't weird enough, the area is also home to the Denge acoustic mirrors, known as listening ears, built between 1928 and 1930. These huge concrete structures were designed as an experimental early warning system to detect aircraft by capturing their sound waves. Dungeness was chosen because it was one of the quietest spots in England. The acoustic mirrors didn't work, and were abandoned when radar was invented, but they remain as huge 'ears' emerging from the already odd surroundings.

This really is a Marmite landscape, and my girlfriend squirmed as we drove across the desolate desert towards the imposing lighthouse.

The owner met us at the door before ushering us up the vertiginous, spiralling staircase. Internally there are a series of mezzanine floors made of slate and supported by steel beams and massive rivets. Each floor is linked by circular concrete stairs which hug the walls and have decorative wrought-iron banisters. There are viewing windows on all floors.

We squeezed around the lens of the long-decommissioned magnifying glass encasing the light, and through a tiny metal door onto the surrounding balcony. A stiff breeze blew off the ocean, but it was clear enough to see France in the distance. It was the most breathtaking view as tiny fishing boats puttered across the relatively calm waters. The vast shingle desert stretched out far below. I could make out the railway tracks, and dozens of fishing boats hauled up on the shingle by rusty old bulldozers.

Three hundred degrees of beautiful perfection. It was the other sixty degrees that presented a small problem.

'Will workers from Sector A please report to the plant office,' boomed a Tannoy from the nuclear power station behind. The power station is now arguably the area's most famous and controversial landmark. The local fishermen fought a long battle against its construction ... but lost. Today it stands out like a vast wart on the landscape.

In fact, there are two power stations. The first was built in 1965 and the second in 1983. One of the positive aspects was that the warm water created by the station's outflow turned the desert into a wildlife haven, even leading to its classification as a Site of Special Scientific Interest.

Apart from the obvious reason that locals didn't want a nuclear power station on their doorstep, another unforeseen problem was the noise attenuation of shingle. You can hear somebody talking half a mile away. So they must know their neighbours pretty well.

The windswept 468-acre estate, on Romney Marsh, in Kent, has been owned by a family trust since it was established in 1964 – but several years ago the entire Dungeness estate was put on the market.for £1.5m. It includes the ground rent on twenty-two cottages, but didn't include the pub, the power station or either of the two lighthouses. Perhaps unsurprisingly, it was eventually bought by the owner of the power stations, French energy company EDF, who have become the landlords to this bizarre landscape.

And perhaps you won't be surprised to hear that my girlfriend – Marina, who latterly became my wife – didn't share EDF's vision for the marsh. She didn't fall for the charms of the light-house either. She felt a nuclear power station behind our house might detract from those 300-degree views.

The blustery wind battered the trees as torrential rain enveloped the countryside. Over the course of a car journey, the Indian summer had transformed itself into an English autumn.

I drove through some simple gates and into an estate of green rolling hills. Then, out of the gloom, loomed what is arguably one of the most famous houses in the world, the splendid Highclere

Castle, known to millions as Downton Abbey from the epony-mous TV series. Though I must admit to being a Downton novice, the house has a startling familiarity. Even on a rain-soaked, autumnal day, it shone like a beacon amid the Capability Brown gardens.

It was here that the 5th Earl of Carnarvon brought many of the Egyptian artefacts that he and Henry Carter returned with from their archaeological excavations, work that led to the discovery of Tutankhamun's tomb. The earl later succumbed to the bite of a mosquito, often attributed to the curse of the tomb, and the castle fell into disrepair, but the house itself seems to have escaped the curse. It has now found fame as the home of Hugh Bonneville and the cast of Julian Fellowes's drama.

Lady Carnarvon met me at the door, surrounded by labradors. While Isis is the series' fictional labrador, the real dogs of the castle are under the matriarchy of Bella, the yellow lab. The entire house is used for filming, except for the family portraits, which are replaced by those of the show's fictional characters. The worldwide fame that comes with an estimated 150 million view-ers has brought an unexpected bounty of transatlantic visitors keen for the quintessential stately home experience.

When I visited an American shooting party was exploring the house. The visitors' enthusiasm seemed undiminished, despite the wind and rain, as they posed for photographs. Lady Carnarvon and I sipped tea while her labradors rolled on their backs beneath the famous fireplace and demanded affection.

Highclere is just one of a long line of grand stately homes that have had to diversify with the times to maintain the pricy upkeep of these crumbling piles. Over the years I have been fortunate enough to visit and explore many of these magnificent homes. I have been on the roof of Castle Howard with the lord of the manor, Nick Howard, helping him regild the impressive dome with gold leaf. I was fortunate to be guided around Chatsworth House by the late Dowager Duchess of Devonshire.

I once went out with the niece of the Duke of Norfolk, whose family home is Arundel Castle in West Sussex, during which time I played cricket on the lawn and spent several happy Christmases in the magnificent castle. I have spent time with Lord March, the Lord of Goodwood House, also in Sussex, who has diversified his estate into the home of high speed with the Goodwood Festival of Speed and the Revival, as well as making it the home of Bentley. But while England's grand stately homes may dominate the country's architectural heritage, one of my personal favourites is Ebberston Hall in North Yorkshire.

Ebberston Hall has had a colourful history of ownership. Described as a lodge, a folly and England's smallest stately home, the tiny house is both charming and eccentric. It was built for William Thompson, the MP for Scarborough and warden for the Royal Mint, in 1718 by Colen Campbell, a pioneer of the Palladian revival in England. Campbell described it as 'a Rustick Edifice'.

With its carved friezes, panelling and moulded cornices it is like a doll's-house version of Chatsworth. The proportions of the Lilliputian rooms give it a TARDIS-like grandeur of unexpected space and a surprising feeling of height. Elaborate water features, pools and waterfalls surround the house like a miniature Capability Brown landscape.

The house eventually passed to the 'squire of all England', George Osbaldeston, a sportsman celebrated for his achievements with guns, swords, whips, fists, bats and oars. Osbaldeston stocked the water garden with trout, demolished the two pavilions and was about to knock down the 'little fairy house' itself when his luck ran out on the Turf; he was reduced to carrying his furniture down the drive to the Grapes Inn to barter it for drink.

The house was sold to Major William de Wend Fenton in 1941 for £5,000. But it was his son West De Wend Fenton who was the real saviour of the house. West was a renaissance man with a love of adventure. A wildly romantic figure, he was described as passionate and impulsive with no comprehension of convention. He proposed nine times to Margaret Lygon before descending into a three-day drinking binge that culminated in him flying to Paris and enlisting in the French Foreign Legion.

West saw action against the fellagha in the mountains of Tunisia; he deserted, was captured, imprisoned and made to dig his own grave before finally being rescued. His escapades in North Africa not only earned him the nickname 'Beau West', due to his stature and handsomeness, but also the hand of Margaret Lygon. A restless adventurer, he ended up in Greece, where he built a house on a plot of land bought in exchange for a .410 shotgun; and in the Soviet Union, where he ran charabanc tours.

Back in Ebberston the family lived an eccentric life with a menagerie of goats, chickens, pot-bellied pigs, deer, llamas, peacocks, and a baleful turkey called Henry. Some of the paying visitors were shocked. West farmed his remaining fifty acres on loosely organic principles ('It's just easier, you don't have to buy fertilizer'), grew his own vegetables, made his own wine, and shot his own rooks, which he would throw into the freezer with their feathers on.

There is no shortage of homes propped up by modern-day aristocrats who have slipped down the monetary scale. Perhaps the most famous are the Fulfords, more commonly known as the Fucking Fulfords.

Fulford House has been owned by the Fulford family since 1190. 'We peaked in about 1530 and it's been a slow decline ever since,' says Francis 'Fucker' Fulford. The house now relies on house tours, photoshoots and, in a thoroughly twenty-first-century take on diversification, reality television to pay for the repairs and upkeep of the house. The star of TV series *The Fucking Fulfords*, *How Clean is Your House* and *Life is Toff*, to name just a few, Francis Fulford is one of a number of aristos who have turned to celebrity as a means of preserving their family architectural heritage. Once described as 'the Osbournes in Tweed' due to their colourful language, their shows captured the public imagination and highlighted the extraordinary lengths to which the landed gentry will go to retain their ancestral homes.

It's also reputedly one of the most haunted houses in the county. Francis Fulford has seen one twice: 'The first time I was five. She appeared on my bed; I thought it was my sister so I tried to hit her, but my fist went straight through and she passed through a wall above my head.' Thirty years passed till he spied her again. This time around, Francis awoke thinking, 'Oh bugger, I need to pee,' only to be confronted by a silhouette by the door, which he assumed was an intruder. Once again, he considered attack – until he realized it was 'the girl from years ago, wearing the same nightie, with a candle in her hand and dark hair'. Fulford now considers himself a ghost expert. 'It's bollocks that people see white or grey ladies – they look like you or me. The only difference is that you put your fist through them.'

Of course, our architectural heritage and eccentricity is not restricted to the aristocracy. One of my favourite stories in recent years was that of Robert Fidler, who built a castle on his farm in Surrey. The problem was that he didn't have planning permission, so he exploited a unique legal loophole. Honeycrock Farm was built on green-belt land, in breach of national planning rules. The planning regulations also stipulate that any building whose presence remains uncontested for four years automatically becomes legal.So Fidler decided to hide the castle behind a 40ft haystack to sit out the four-year period, after which it would become lawful.

In true English eccentric style he built the 'turrets' from old grain silos placed in each corner with a sturdy timber frame between. He then clad the whole building with brick, complete with crenellations around the top. The house was pure English whimsy: one half was mock Tudor, half-timbered and gabled. In the central hall was a salvaged Victorian stained-glass skylight.

After four years, Fidler proudly removed the hay bales to reveal his castellated folly. The authorities were less impressed, and despite the legal loophole he was made to rip it down. A victory for the rural British landscape, perhaps, but a defeat for English eccentricity.

* * *

We like to think of ourselves as a nation that embraces the peculiar and the unorthodox, especially when it comes to architecture. A look around our eclectic architectural achievements is testament to our creativity. But, a little like society in general, our architecture is becoming increasingly homogenized.

We once celebrated the work of our architects: Joseph Paxton's revolutionary Crystal Palace, or John Nash's Brighton Pavilion, or the Tardis-like cabinet of curiosities built by John Soane, architect of the Bank of England. Fidler's treatment by the state is perhaps testament to our changing attitudes to eccentricity, and to the slow creep of fence-sitting homogeneity.

CHAPTER FOURTEEN

THE WORD

'The greatest legacy the English have bequeathed the rest of humanity is their language … It is the medium of technology, science, travel and international politics. Three quarters of the world's mail is written in English, four fifths of all data stored on computers is in English and the language used by two thirds of the world's scientists is English.'

Jeremy Paxman, *The English*

See what you can make of this:

Well enow, I wilt admit t. I has't nev'r very much hath understood Shakespearean English. I findeth it a little santimonious. I'd beest like, Heigh-ho broth'r. Do you bandy looks with me, you rascal art these strange words. Those gents behold the same but different. To beest honest those gents wast complete gobbled gook. S'wounds what is that gent trying to sayeth. Spit t out lad. Don't tryeth and beest so ponsy. That gent at each moment hath seemed to useth ten words whither that gent could has't hath used just one. Id beest like, well enow broth'r, thee might beest a very valorous story writer but its the way thee telleth t. I hath used to thing, hang on, I speaketh English and yet your meaning escapes me what thee art talking about. Thee sure maketh a meal of thy language …

Baffled? Well, now you know how I felt about studying Shakespeare at school. In the passage above I ran my words through an online Bard Translator and it spewed out that text. Looking back at it I have no idea what it says, which was kind of how I felt about his literature.

I should probably admit that the first language I learnt at school was not English but French, after my parents decided it would be a brilliant idea to send me to the French Lycée in London. I hated every minute of it and left after two years with a complex about the French and an English language deficit. This was then beautifully combined with several months each year in Canada to leave me with a sort of backwards, north American lilt. Oh, and did I mention I was dyslexic? The result was a highly confused awareness of language and an uncertain grasp of English.

At school I was teased for my 'Canadian' accent, which was so subtle as to be almost extinct, but to the ears of young boys I was a fully paid up plaid-shirt-wearing Canadian Mountie, and I was teased mercilessly.

As a child my favourite word was *supercalifragilisticexpialido-cious*. I always assumed it was the longest word in the English dictionary, until I began my research for this book and discovered that it is in fact *pneumonoultramicroscopicsilicovolcanoconiosis*, a word that refers to a lung disease contracted from the inhalation of very fine silica particles, specifically from a volcano; medically, it is the same as silicosis. It's not quite as catchy, is it? (Although, if you take it literally, it is quite catchy.) You see, our language is as complex and nuanced as every other aspect of Englishness.

If there is one person who has shaped and crafted the English language, it is our most famous writer, William Shakespeare. It seems incredible that one man can have had such a profound effect on a nation. It's even more incredible when you think that he lived more than 450 years ago and he is still relevant. In his fifty-two years, Shakespeare enriched the English language in ways so profound it's almost impossible to fully gauge his impact. He gave us unique ways in which to express our emotions, he allowed us to define moods and feelings, hope and despair, sorrow and rage, love and lust.

As I said, I have always struggled with Shakespeare. As a child I can remember reading his books at school; to my dyslexic eyes, the words were a confused jumble of words that hardly resembled the English language I knew. But whether you love him or not, he's almost impossible to avoid. We quote him, often unwittingly, on a daily basis. Without him, our vocabulary would be very different. He was a true wordsmith, an artist of the word.

The Complete Works of Shakespeare is always given, along with the Bible, to castaways on *Desert Island Discs*, as they are abandoned on the lonely island in the middle of nowhere. In the case of Nelson Mandela, it really was. He said that it was the complete works of Shakespeare that had sustained him through his twenty years' incarceration on Robben Island: 'Shakespeare always seems to have something to say to us.'

Hamlet alone has inspired other writers in numerous genres, at far-flung ends of the literary spectrum. It provided the titles for Agatha Christie's theatrical smash, *The Mousetrap*, and Alfred Hitchcock's evocative spy thriller, *North by Northwest*. And then there's David Foster Wallace's iconic novel, *Infinite Jest*, Ruth Rendell's *Put on by Cunning*, Philip K. Dick's *Time Out of Joint* and Jasper Fforde's *Something Rotten* … Even contemporary bands like Mumford and Sons named their album *Sigh No More*, borrowing a phrase from *Much Ado About Nothing*. And how many of Iron Maiden's fans recognize that the title of the song 'Where Eagles Dare' is a quote from *Richard III*?

Our language is filled with familiar phrases that influence every corner of our lives. The jealousy of 'the green-eyed monster' is from *Othello*'s arch-villain, Iago. If you've ever been 'in a pickle', waited 'with bated breath' or gone on 'a wild goose chase', you've been quoting from *The Tempest*, *The Merchant of Venice* and *Romeo and Juliet* respectively. That favourite English pastime, to 'gossip', came from *A Midsummer Night's Dream*. 'The be-all and end-all' is uttered by Macbeth as he murderously contemplates King Duncan, and 'fair play' falls from Miranda's lips in *The Tempest*. He even invented the knock-knock joke in the Scottish play.

Some phrases have become so well used that they're now regarded as clichés – surely a compliment for an author so long gone. 'A heart of gold'? You'll find it in *Henry V*, while 'the world's mine oyster' crops up in *The Merry Wives of Windsor*. The list is lengthy: the latest count is somewhere around the 1,000 word mark added to the English language. Here are some more of them:

All our yesterdays (*Macbeth*)
All that glitters is not gold ('glisters')(*The Merchant of Venice*)
All's Well That Ends Well (title)
As good luck would have it (*The Merry Wives of Windsor*)
As merry as the day is long (*Much Ado About Nothing/King John*)
Beggar all description (*Antony and Cleopatra*)
The better part of valour is discretion (*I Henry IV*; possibly already a known saying)
Brave new world (*The Tempest*)
Break the ice (*The Taming of the Shrew*)
Breathed his last (*3 Henry VI*)
Brevity is the soul of wit (*Hamlet*)
Refuse to budge an inch (*Measure for Measure/The Taming of the Shrew*)
Cold comfort (*The Taming of the Shrew/King John*)
Come what may ('come what come may') (*Macbeth*)
Comparisons are odorous (*Much Ado about Nothing*)
Dead as a doornail (*2 Henry VI*)
A dish fit for the gods (*Julius Caesar*)
Cry havoc and let slip the dogs of war (*Julius Caesar*)
Dog will have his day (*Hamlet*; quoted earlier by Erasmus and Queen Elizabeth)
Devil incarnate (*Titus Andronicus/Henry V*)

Eaten me out of house and home (*2 Henry IV*)

Elbow room (*King John*; first attested 1540 according to
Merriam-Webster)

Faint hearted (*I Henry VI*)

Fancy-free (*A Midsummer Night's Dream*)

Fight till the last gasp (*I Henry VI*)

Flaming youth (*Hamlet*)

Forever and a day (*As You Like It*)

For goodness' sake (*Henry VIII*)

Foregone conclusion (*Othello*)

Full circle (*King Lear*)

The game is up (*Cymbeline*)

Give the devil his due (*I Henry IV*)

Good riddance (*Troilus and Cressida*)

Jealousy is the green-eyed monster (*Othello*)

It was Greek to me (*Julius Caesar*)

Heart of gold (*Henry V*)

Hoist with his own petard (*Hamlet*)

Improbable fiction (*Twelfth Night*)

In my heart of hearts (*Hamlet*)

In my mind's eye (*Hamlet*)

It is but so-so (*As You Like It*)

It smells to heaven (*Hamlet*)

Itching palm (*Julius Caesar*)

Kill with kindness (*The Taming of the Shrew*)

Knit brow (*The Rape of Lucrece*)

Knock knock! Who's there? (*Macbeth*)

Laid on with a trowel (*As You Like It*)

Laughing stock (*The Merry Wives of Windsor*)

Laugh yourself into stitches (*Twelfth Night*)

Lean and hungry look (*Julius Caesar*)

Lie low (*Much Ado about Nothing*)

Live long day (*Julius Caesar*)

Love is blind (*The Merchant of Venice*)

Melted into thin air (*The Tempest*)

Make a virtue of necessity (*The Two Gentlemen of Verona*)

The makings of (*Henry VIII*)

Milk of human kindness (*Macbeth*)

Ministering angel (*Hamlet*)

More in sorrow than in anger (*Hamlet*)

More sinned against than sinning (*King Lear*)

Much Ado About Nothing (title)

Murder most foul (*Hamlet*)

Naked truth (*Love's Labours Lost*)

Neither rhyme nor reason (*As You Like It*)

Not slept one wink (*Cymbeline*)

Once more into the breach (*Henry V*)

One fell swoop (*Macbeth*)

One that loved not wisely but too well (*Othello*)

Own flesh and blood (*Hamlet*)

Star-crossed lovers (*Romeo and Juliet*)

[What] a piece of work [is man] (*Hamlet*)

Play fast and loose (*King John*)

Pomp and circumstance (*Othello*)

Pound of flesh (*The Merchant of Venice*)

Salad days (*Antony and Cleopatra*)

Sea change (*The Tempest*)

Seen better days (*As You Like It*)

Send packing (*I Henry IV*)

Make short shrift (*Richard III*)

Sick at heart (*Hamlet*)

Snail paced (*Troilus and Cressida*)

Something in the wind (*The Comedy of Errors*)

Something wicked this way comes (*Macbeth*)

A sorry sight (*Macbeth*)

Sound and fury (*Macbeth*)

Spotless reputation (*Richard II*)

Stony hearted (*I Henry IV*)

The short and the long of it (*The Merry Wives of Windsor*)

Set my teeth on edge (*I Henry IV*)

Thereby hangs a tale (*Othello*; in context, this seems to have
    been already in use)

There's the rub (*Hamlet*)

Too much of a good thing (*As You Like It*)

Tower of strength (*Richard III*)

Truth will out (*The Merchant of Venice*)

Wear my heart upon my sleeve (*Othello*)

What the dickens (*The Merry Wives of Windsor*)

What's done is done (*Macbeth*)

Wild-goose chase (*Romeo and Juliet*)

Witching time of night (*Hamlet*)

Working-day world (*As You Like It*)

The world's my oyster (*The Merry Wives of Windsor*)

Yeoman's service (*Hamlet*)

Where Shakespeare forged the path, dozens of English writers have continued to define through literature the English language and what it means to be English. And in my mind, nowhere is this better displayed than in the books written for our children.

As a child I grew up on Enid Blyton, Roald Dahl and Kenneth Grahame. All of them had the ability to paint a picture of an idyllic England, one of Fair Isle sweaters, dandelion and burdock, green lawns and long idyllic summers. It's probably not surprising that a nation obsessed with the weather has consumed literature in which existence is a perpetual summer of picnics, sailing, rowing and spiffing adventures. *Winnie the Pooh*, *The Wind in the Willows*, *Three Men in a Boat*, The Famous Five, the tales of Beatrix Potter were all quintessentially English and still conjure a time of simple happiness. For me it was the backdrop of 'traditional' or 'old-fashioned' England that made them so charming.

Several years ago, Enid Blyton's publisher decided to make some 'sensitive text revisions' to her classic Famous Five books. So 'tinker' was changed to 'traveller', 'mother and father' to 'mum and dad' and 'awful swotter' to 'bookworm'. The suggestion that tomboy George needed 'a good spanking' became 'a good talking to', while girly Anne's assertion, 'You see, I do like pretty frocks – and I love my dolls – and you can't do that if you're a boy' had its final clause removed, rendering the sentence throwaway rather than poignant. Unsurprisingly, given that all the charm had been stripped out of them, the revised editions flopped, and the publisher reverted to the originals, conceding that the updates had proved 'very unpopular'.

Of course, our language has gone through many changes. The *Oxford English Dictionary* has been the *Vogue* magazine of our language fashion for hundreds of years, and each quarter, the dictionary publishes an update that includes new words and 'retirees' – words no longer deemed relevant. The OED, as it is often referred to, is a reflection of Englishness through language.

Anything new that goes into the dictionary is drafted and researched by a team of fifteen lexicographers on the 'new word' team. They work year-round analysing corpuses – basically great big bundles of electronic text collections containing billions of words – online databases as well as submissions from members of the public. The OED waits for ten years of evidence before adding a word to the huge and growing body of English. The quarter ending December 2016 saw around 500 new words, phrases, and senses enter the dictionary, including the following:

> *bralette* – A tight-fitting crop top with thin straps
> *glam-ma* – A glamorous grandmother, especially one who is relatively young or fashion-conscious
> *gobby* – (of a person) tending to talk too loudly and in a blunt or opinionated way
> *tombstoning* – Jump into the sea from a cliff or other high point
> *upstander* – A person who speaks or acts in support of an individual or cause, particularly someone who intervenes on behalf of a person being attacked or bullied
> *YouTuber* – A person who uploads, produces, or appears in videos on the video-sharing website YouTube

Of course, our language in both written and spoken form has often reflected our obsession with the weather. Just take a look at some of our weather proverbs:

> *a bolt from the blue* – something that happens unexpectedly
> *a ray of sunshine* – someone or something that brings great joy
> *right as rain* – perfect, very good, healthy, correct, factually accurate
> *to weather the storm* – to reach the end of a very difficult situation without too much harm or damage.

Inevitably, plenty of expressions that use the weather metaphorically are negative in tone:

> *to chase rainbows* – to try to accomplish something that can never be achieved, to go on a useless quest
> *dry spell* – a period or time where there is little activity, productivity, low income, etc.
> *to have one's head in the clouds* – when someone has unrealistic or impractical ideas
> *under a cloud* – in trouble or difficulties; out of favour
> *under the weather* – not feeling well

'Ee ba gum'. 'My lover.' 'Gan canny.' 'Ey oop'. 'Awlraght'. Our nation's language is made up of so many regional dialects. I have spent time in Yorkshire and Lincolnshire where I haven't had a clue what has been said. Within the geographical boundaries of England today, the English language is spoken in nearly thirty dialects, a form of a language which is peculiar to a specific region or social group. No other nation in the world can boast so many variations on the same language.

Northern dialects include Cheshire, Cumbrian (including Barrovian in Barrow-in-Furness), Geordie (Tyneside), Hartlepudlian (Hartlepool), Lancastrian (Lancashire), Mackem (Sunderland), Mancunian (Manchester), Northumbrian (rural Northumberland), Pitmatic (Durham and Northumberland), Scouse (Liverpool), Smoggie (Teesside) and Yorkshire (also known as Broad Yorkshire). In the Midlands, you have dialects particular to East Midlands and West Midlands, and most notably Black Country, Brummie (Birmingham), Potteries (north Staffordshire) and Telford (east Shropshire).

In East Anglia, the dialect shifts between Norfolk and Suffolk. In the south, you have Received Pronunciation (RP or BBC English), Cockney (working-class London and surrounding areas), Essaxon (Essex), Estuary (Thames Estuary), Kentish (Kent), Multicultural London (London) and Sussex. The West Country has a recognizable variety of languages and accents, with Anglo-Cornish and Bristolian distinctly different again.

When I was in the Royal Naval Reserve I became fascinated by yet another dialect, Jackspeak. This is the humorous and colourful slang of the Royal Navy, the Royal Marines and the Fleet Air Arm. The Royal Navy has a heritage all of its own: a cryptic everyday lingo. Mysterious, fascinating and a closed book to the most erudite civilian …

Jackspeak is constantly refreshed, just like the OED's huge database, and is also influenced by current events. Although much of the naval slang is old, there are many modern examples.

You can hear sailors talking about 'Dagenham Dave' (an unstable person – just this side of Barking, London) or someone 'going Harpic' (clean round the bend). Here are a few more of my favourites:

> *the cat is out of the bag* – 'The secret is out'. It comes from keeping the cat o' nine tails (a naval whip with nine chords to flog miscreants) in a red bag. Only when the naughty sailor was tied up ready to be flogged was the 'cat' removed from the bag.
>
> *the cut of his jib* – a person's facial appearance. A long time ago, a ship's nationality could be told at a distance by the shape of one of her sails (the jib) at the front of the boat.
>
> *touch and go* – uncertainty. It refers to a ship touching the sea-bottom and then slipping off, i.e. not running aground.

Arguably the most famous 'slang' dialect is Cockney rhyming slang, in which words are replaced by other words or phrases they rhyme with. It dates back to the mid-1800s and originated in the East End of London. No one really knows how or why it came about, but there are plenty of theories. One suggestion is that its use became popular in the marketplace to allow traders to talk amongst themselves without customers knowing what they were saying. Another suggestion is that it may have been used by criminals to confuse the police.

Some of the associations are ingenious though. For example, 'bees and honey' means money. Bees are seen as very hard-working and hard work brings money; having money is sweet – just like honey.

The English language has spread far and wide. Wherever it settles it adapts to the local conditions and local people. One of the most intriguing places I have ever been was Pitcairn Island in the South Pacific, the home of the mutineers from the *Bounty*. Today the island language, Pitkern or Pitcairnese, continues to use many expressions no longer in use in modern English, as the language on this isolated atoll in the middle of the Pacific has been frozen in time. I travelled there to research my first book, *The Teatime Islands*, a travelogue to Britain's last remaining outposts, the last pink bits of the Empire. It took me the best part of two weeks to sail from Tahiti to the remote and mysterious British Overseas Territory. When I arrived, it was fascinating to listen to what was being said and try to work out what it meant.

Here are some common phrases:

Whata way yee? – How are you?
About yee gwen? – Where are you going?
You gwen whihi up supa? – Are you going to cook supper?
I nor believe – I don't think so
Yee like-a sum whettles? – Would you like some food?
Do' mine – It doesn't matter. I don't mind
Wa sing yourley doing? – What are you doing? What are you
   up to?
I se gwen ah big shep – I'm going to the ship
Humuch shep corl ya? – How often do ships come here?
Cum yorley sulluns! – Come on all you kids!

I se gwen ah nahweh – I'm going swimming
Lebbe! – Let it be!
Cooshoo! – Good!

English, our language, is an amazing invention and an amazing tool. Perhaps it's our greatest gift to the world. We, as users, are endlessly inventive and it's difficult to know whether the language allows us to be that creative or whether it comes from our peculiar mindset. Whichever way it is, English seems set fair to thrive in the decades to come. We seem to have no problem at all coming up with and then adopting new words. In this great tradition I should like to present to you my own word (combining 'English' and 'angst') to be added to the great lexicon of the English language:

Engst – the complex of being English

CHAPTER FIFTEEN

TEA AND SYMPATHY

Betty's Tea Room in Harrogate is an institution.

It is an English phenomenon. People make pilgrimages to this Mecca of tea rooms. Fortnum & Masons or the Ritz are also-rans when it comes to the quintessential afternoon tea. I first visited Betty's when I was a small boy and my parents took us on a holiday to North Yorkshire. Even then, I was struck by its essence of Englishness.

For nearly 100 years Betty's has been a Yorkshire landmark. It was founded in 1919 by Swiss-born Frederick Belmont, who had trained in confectionery-making and baking, after he settled in Yorkshire. Where he got the name nobody knows, although there is speculation it was from Betty Lupton, a local girl who served the town's famous spa water to visitors; others suggest it might have been the Victorian actress Betty Balfour. While the provenance of the name will probably never be known, Betty's was a huge success and there are now six Betty's tea rooms across

Yorkshire; but it is the Harrogate Betty's that revels in world acclaim and to which people flock from all over the world.

When Anna, 7th Duchess of Bedford, started taking tea and sandwiches between lunch and dinner in the 1840s, she began one of our most delightful traditions. Soon she was joined by her friends at Woburn Abbey, and this afternoon pause for tea became a fashionably social event. During the 1800s, upper-class and society women would change into long gowns, gloves and hats for tea, which was traditionally served in the drawing room between four and five o'clock. By Edwardian times, afternoon tea, served in the finest china and silverware, had become a byword for sophisticated and elegant gatherings.

There is some confusion between high tea and afternoon tea. High tea was the main meal of the day for the working class (which is why many still refer to their evening meal – supper – as tea). It originated during the industrial revolution for workers who returned home after a long day's physical work and needed a hot, hearty meal. It was called 'high' tea to differentiate it from the 'low' afternoon tea. Confused? I was about to be. In the spirit of immersion, I decided to join staff for an afternoon serving tea and scones to the genteel folk of North Yorkshire.

The tea queue stretched around the corner. Can there be two more beautiful words to the English ear than 'tea' and 'queue'? Here the two happily link as patient devotees wait their turn to be seated. Betty's has gained a worldwide reputation for the finest afternoon tea, and no list of things to do in Yorkshire is complete without reference to the iconic tea rooms.

In the staff room I changed into my Betty's uniform: black trousers and waistcoat, white shirt and maroon tie. I joined the other staff in the bustling kitchen where a chef was busy preparing for the 1 p.m. sitting in the grandly named Imperial Room. 'Tarragon sandwich, egg sandwich and Yorkshire ham sandwich,' explained Jen, pointing to the three-tier sterling silver afternoon tea stands.

On the next level were the scones. 'Sc-*ons* or sc-*oans*?' I asked. 'Sc-*ons*,' she smiled.

'Which first? The clotted cream or the jam?' I added.

'It's down to taste, but I think the clotted cream makes a fantastic base for the jam to sit,' she explained.

On the third tier was a dizzying array of tiny cakes. I could recognize a Battenberg and a meringue but the rest I'd have to leave to Mary Berry.

Next she introduced me to the huge choice of teas. 'These are the most popular, afternoon tea and Tea Room tea. Then there is the Assam, Lapsang Souchong, Pure Ceylon, Betty's Blue Sapphire, Gunpowder ...' Her words disappeared in a caffeinated blur. 'It's loose tea, of course,' she added. 'All the teas have a different brewing time of between three and five minutes,' she explained.

'Which should you pour first? The tea or the milk?'

'Well,' Jen replied diplomatically, 'there is no right or wrong. But the customer is always right.'

When tea was at its most popular, it became practical to pour a little cold milk into the cheaper china cups to prevent them from cracking when the warm tea was added. Essentially it became a class division between those who could afford the more expensive, non-crackable bone china who added milk after, and the working class who added milk first. Only in England could the consumption of tea become a battleground of social etiquette and class.

And with that, I had been given my tutorial. Now it was time to meet my customers. 'Don't forget this,' smiled Jack, handing me an apron that I tied around my waist.

'Tuck in the ends,' added Jen.

The room was already full. There were a few tables of couples and several of groups. While the afternoon tea ceremony appeals to many for special occasions (including, surprisingly, hen and stag dos), there are plenty of regulars who have been coming daily for years. While afternoon tea has remained a popular ritual, places like Betty's have had to keep up with the times and most now include the option of a glass of champagne to accompany the sandwiches and tea which is of course served on the finest bone china from the Royal Crown Derby.

I had a table of six women. They looked to be in their forties, and it turned out they were celebrating a birthday. At twenty-one and thirty years old respectively, Jen and Jack looked a little, ahem, younger than most of those enjoying afternoon tea. Jack had been working in the tea rooms since he was sixteen. That is almost half his life.

I walked to the first table. 'Good afternoon. Lovely weather,' I added for extra Englishness before taking their order.

Tea and weather. Two of my favourite topics in one greeting.

In the corner, a pianist, the same one who has performed in this hallowed tea room for decades, quietly played on the keys to accompany the gentle tinkle of bone china cups meeting their saucers. Tea flowed and scones were gently spread with clotted cream. The jam, or rather 'preserve', is specially produced and has a bespoke consistency to complement the rose and lemon scones. You cannot underestimate the evocative power of that sound of cup on saucer. It reminds me of my late grandmother. It is a soothing, calming, stabilizing sound. There is something terribly reassuring about tea.

The tea room was picture-postcard perfection as I moved from table to table, carrying tiers of sandwiches and scones and trays of brewing tea.

I wonder what kind of people still take afternoon tea? 'We had Russell Brand not long ago,' Jen told me as she glided elegantly to one of the tables. Does that make afternoon tea ironic or iconic?

Of course, there would be no afternoon tea without the revered leaves themselves.

When I think of tea, the song 'Everything Stops for Tea' automatically starts playing in my head. It's one of the songs that helped the British through the Second World War, the Blitz etc …

> Every nation in creation has its favourite drink
> France is famous for its wine, it's beer in Germany
> Turkey has its coffee and they serve it blacker than ink
> Russians go for vodka and England loves its tea
> Oh, the factories may be roaring
> With a boom-a-lacka, zoom-a-lacka, wee
> But there isn't any roar when the clock strikes four
> Everything stops for tea
> Oh, a lawyer in the courtroom
> In the middle of an alimony plea

Has to stop and help 'em pour when the clock strikes
     four
Everything stops for tea.
It's a very good English custom
Though the weather be cold or hot
When you need a little pick-up, you'll find a little tea
     cup
Will always hit the spot
You remember Cleopatra
Had a date to meet Mark Antony at three
When he came an hour late she said 'You'll have to wait'
For everything stops for tea.
Oh, they may be playing football
And the crowd is yelling 'Kill the referee!'
But no matter what the score, when the clock strikes
     four
Everything stops for tea.
Oh, the golfer may be golfing
And is just about to make a hole-in-three
But it always gets them sore when the clock yells 'four!'
Everything stops for tea.
It's a very good English custom
And a stimulant for the brain
When you feel a little weary, a cup'll make you cheery
And it's cheaper than champagne
Now I know just why Franz Schubert
Didn't finish his unfinished symphony
He might have written more but the clock struck four
And everything stops for tea.

Tea is the most quintessential of English drinks, but it only really arrived in the mid-seventeenth century, much later than you might expect. And, strangely, it was the London coffee houses that were responsible for spreading the word about tea to England. One of the first tea merchants was Thomas Garway, who owned a house in Exchange Alley. He sold both liquid and dry tea to the public as early as 1657, but the prices were outlandish – between sixteen and fifty shillings per pound. Even so, tea soon gained popularity and by 1700 over five hundred coffee houses served it.

It has been estimated that 84 per cent of the British population drink tea every day. That works out at 165 million cups a day or 60.2 billion cups of tea a year; an average of 900 cups for every man, woman and child per year, or three cups a day. Yikes. That really is a lot of tea.

Typhoo, Tetley, PG Tips, Yorkshire Tea, Twinings ... all are iconic English brands of tea, but what you may not realize is the art that goes into making the perfect cuppa. Behind all the great English teas is the hidden army of 'tea tasters' who, depending on your attitude towards tea, might have the best jobs in the world. Indeed a recent job advertisement for Tetley tea described it as 'the best job in the country, but one that few know exists'.

I first learned about tea tasting when I went to spend a day with Typhoo's master blender in their factory in the Wirral.

Tea is a natural crop, which means there is always variety between different harvests; which in turn means that the taste of the leaves will change. The tea manufacturer must constantly adjust and tweak the recipe for each bag to ensure consistency and 'brand taste'. This makes tea tasting as demanding on the palate as wine tasting or whisky blending.

Across the world, every day, from East Africa to Sri Lanka and China, tea plantations harvest their precious leaves and send the bales to huge tea markets, upon which buyers from across the globe descend to buy the leaves. The key is ensuring the correct mix of leaves are bought to ensure the perfect blend, and this is where the 'master taster' comes into their own. Every day they must sip, slurp and swirl hundreds of varieties of tea, in tiny samples couriered in from across the globe before they come to auction. It is a race against both time and fellow tea companies to ensure a ready supply of the right blend of tea leaves.

You see, to the connoisseur, tea really is like wine: the soil, rainfall, even the gradient of the hill can affect the flavour of the leaves. Any change in the weather will alter the taste. Even tea that comes from the same bush will vary in flavour over time. We Brits are pretty fussy when it comes to tea and our highly refined taste buds can detect even the subtlest of inconsistencies; therefore the blenders must perform their magic to create a perfect consistent blend, using thousands of different leaves from all corners of the globe.

When I arrived at the Typhoo factory I was shown into a huge room that looked like a cross between an old school kitchen and a science lab. On the benches there were more than a hundred cups. At the end of the room were two huge industrial gas stoves, on which stood the same metal kettles for boiling water that have been used for decades. It's all about consistency.

I stood next to the counter with the hundreds of cups and little sachets of tea leaves next to them, each one with a market code.

Each cup of tea has a slightly different colour and cloudiness, although appearance is just one aspect of a multi-sensory experience. The taster is looking for impact, liveliness, and zestiness. My mind boggled at the idea of drinking hundreds of cups of tea each day, until I realized they merely slurp a tiny sample from a spoon, the same spoon that has been used – again for consistency – for many years.

'Slurp it into your mouth so you can feel the consistency and texture,' the taster tells me. 'Look at the sparkle. Is it thick or thin?' he asks, while peering into the cup. We swirl the tea in our mouths and feel the flavour.

As with wine, the art is in the way the leaves are tasted. 'Don't swill the tea too much,' the taster insists, after I have already gargled it like mouthwash. The key is in the spit; this is when you get the full impact of the flavour.

The provenance of the teas plays a large part in the flavour. Sri Lankan is citrus and floral, while Indonesian tea can be spicy and even sulphuric-tasting, possibly as result of the volcanic soil in which the tea plant grows.

The blending must also factor in the international variations of taste. In the same way that chocolate will be made with varying amounts of sugar, milk and cocoa according to the part of the world it's being manufactured for and the corresponding variations in sweet tooth, tea also changes. The English prefer a smooth flavour, for example, while the Australians like a bitter tea. Tea bags must be altered according to the export market.

As we work our way up the long counter, sipping dozens of samples of tea, I marvel at the taster's descriptions, which range from yeasty to fruity. There are more than 2,500 tea plantations across the world and a tea taster will often sample anything from 200 to 1,000 cups a day. Careful notes are taken with each sip as the team of tasters move along the benches. To taste is to understand the philosophy of tea and how it should be served. For example, black tea must be piping hot when tasted; the tea must not be diluted with milk as this takes possession of the tea's properties and flavours. Green and fruity teas must be tasted once the temperature has cooled down; this allows one to evaluate the fresh, floral flavours.

So precious are the tea tasters to this billion-pound business that one tea manufacturer recently insured the tastebuds of its master blender for £1 million, about the same sum as Heidi Klum's legs. The company values its tasters so highly that, like the royal family, they are not allowed to travel on the same plane together for fear of losing a whole generation of tasters and the secrets of the perfect char.

I wonder what he drinks between tastings, on his tea break.

'Tea, of course.'

So we now know what goes into the bag, but we still have the age-old question of how to brew the perfect cuppa.

According to the most recent scientific study of tea-making (only in England would scientists spend time researching tea-making rather than, say, studying cancer), the most important factor, it seems, is patience. After exhaustive testing, scientists discovered that the key to the best-tasting brew is to let it sit for six minutes before drinking. A university research team spent more than 180 hours testing volunteers with hundreds of cups of tea. They concluded that the best method was to add boiling water to a tea bag in a mug and to leave the bag for two minutes. They then suggested removing the bag before adding milk and leaving it to rest for a further six minutes until it reached the optimal temperature of 60°C; leave it any longer and it drops below 45°C destroying the flavour.

Of course, everyone has their own idea on how to make the perfect cuppa. For Jamie Oliver, for, example, it is all about the vessel from which you drink the tea. I agree that getting the right cup is important. Never use plastic as the tannins stick to the side of the cup; don't use metal as the tea will taste metallic. While most might assume ceramic is best, this can be too porous, allowing the tea to cool down too quickly. Jamie suggests a porcelain cup, just as the Chinese used to serve their tea.

According to Twinings, it is about the water. They suggest always using freshly drawn, filtered, *cold* water in the kettle. The tea loves oxygen, which can help it develop a deep flavour; and you must never reboil water that has been boiled already. Then of course you must choose between an electric kettle and gas-heated water, but that's a whole different subject.

Kate Fox, in her excellent anthropological study *Watching the English*, noted that the strongest black tea is drunk by the working class, while the brew gets progressively weaker as you move up the social ladder. She observes that even milk and sweeteners have their own codes:

'Taking sugar in your tea is regarded by many as an infallible lower class indicator: even a spoonful is a bit suspect (unless you were born before 1955); more than one and you are lower middle at best; more than two and you are defiantly working class.'

According to one recent study, 98 per cent of tea is taken with milk.

According to Fox, 'Tea-making is the perfect displacement activity: whenever the English feel awkward or uncomfortable in a social situation, they make tea.' It reminds me of the famous Second World War poster, 'If in Doubt Brew Up'. Tea, like the weather, is a cornerstone of English culture and society. It is the first thing you will be offered when you enter someone's house. 'Oh it's cold, would you like a cup of tea?' 'Oh it's hot, how about a cup of tea?'

Tea acts as a unifier, breaking down social barriers. Of course, there has been the slow creep of Americanization and we will sometimes hear the addition, 'Or would you prefer coffee?' But any Englishman or woman worth their salt will offer a cup of char.

A close contender to the cuppa is the pint, our other national drink.

The pub is a quintessential ingredient of our national identity. If you don't have a local then you haven't lived. 'When you have lost your inns, drown your empty selves, for you will have lost the last of England,' said Hilaire Belloc in 1912. The pub is a uniquely British institution – a place to drink beer, wine, cider or spirits and to enable people to meet. The 50,000 or so pubs in the British Isles are often the centre of community life – in cities, towns, villages and rural hamlets – and contribute significantly to the sum of the nation's happiness. A British pub or boozer is uniquely social compared to European or North American bars. The pub is a place people go to chat to others, and it therefore plays a huge role in social cohesion.

We have the Romans to thank for our beloved local. When the Roman army invaded, they brought with them the idea of shops by the roadside that sold wine. They adapted these to cater to our local taste for ale or beer – the Latin word for these shops was *taberna*, which was corrupted to 'tavern'. The popularity of taverns never looked back. King Edgar, who was on the throne around AD 970, introduced drinking restrictions including a limit to the number of taverns, or alehouses as they were now also called, in a town or village; he allegedly bought in a maximum quantity that could be drunk by a villager. This was called a 'peg' and led to the expression 'to take someone down a peg or two'. A wish in government to restrict our drinking habits has a familiar ring to it.

As people became more mobile, moving around the country on horses or in carriages, inns sprang up offering accommodation as well as food and drink. These three institutions (alehouses, taverns and inns) were given the collective name 'public houses' at some point in the sixteenth century, and that of course was rapidly shortened to 'pub'.

It's one of those facts that always surprises me, but beer was the staple drink throughout this period because the water was unsafe to drink. So it was normal for everyone – including children – to drink beer for breakfast. Even when tea and coffee were introduced, they were so expensive that ale continued to be the national drink for many years. When spirits arrived, in the form of gin from Holland and brandy from France, the extra potency of these drinks caused huge public order problems, which King George II tried to control with the Gin Acts of 1736 and 1751. He was perhaps more successful than anyone before or since, reducing consumption by three-quarters and sobering up the population before the disorder got completely out of hand.

Since then, the pub has been a staple of our social lives and has been woven into this country's and the world's history. For example, Karl Marx drafted *The Communist Manifesto* above the Red Lion in Great Windmill Street in London; Sir Thomas More was tried in a pub in Staines; the discovery of the structure of DNA was announced by Francis Crick and James Watson at the Eagle in Cambridge; and the Bell in Peterborough was the first pub to sell Stilton cheese, when the owner (in the 1720s) paired it with beer and the combination ensured the success of the cheese.

Pub names themselves are familiar, comforting, entertaining and sometimes disturbing. For example, the name of the Dog & Duck refers to an old sport where dogs chased a duck that had had its wings clipped. (I told you we create sports out of whatever is to hand!) The Three-Legged Mare was actually a gallows that could hang three people at a time. The Red Lion (the second-most popular pub name after The Crown) refers to the heraldic red lion of Scotland, which James I (James VI of Scotland) insisted be displayed on all buildings of importance when he assumed the throne from Elizabeth I. Naturally the pub was a place of great importance, and James felt that it would remind his English subjects that the Scots were now in power. Likewise the White Horse is named after the sign of the House of Hanover.

The Dolphin meanwhile displays pride in English military achievements. Dolphin actually comes from the French *Dauphin* – we have always had problems pronouncing French words – and the pubs commemorate victories over France. There is a Dolphin pub in Wellington, Somerset that celebrates the win at the Battle of Waterloo. Others like the Three Tuns and the Brewers refer to livery companies. Pub names take inspiration from anything, and it's that which gives them such a rich variety.

Our two national drinks are still going strong.

England is a country fuelled on tea and grog.

CONCLUSION

I am on the edge of a cricket green in Oxfordshire watching my child race around in cricket whites. There is a waft of freshly cut grass and the unmistakable sound of leather against wood as the cricket ball thuds against the willow bat. Behind us a couple of rowers are sculling quietly down the Thames, while a few people walk their dogs and a family of swans glide along.

It is a picture-postcard image of Englishness. When I am in faraway places, this is how I see my nation. Green grass and weeping willows; cricket whites and cream teas; picnic rugs and hampers. Clichéd? Perhaps, but that doesn't make it any less real. It is a projection of what it means to be English, a timelessness borne out in art, literature and film, a distillation of our hopes and aspirations

I am from the British Isles, I hold a UK passport. I am European and I'm a part (just) of the European Union. I am

British but I am also English. I hold a Canadian passport and my grandfather was born in Scotland. It's confusing.

I drive a Land Rover and have a labrador retriever. I wear a cloth cap, a Barbour and I am *obsessed* with the weather. I listen to *The Archers* and the Shipping Forecast on Radio 4. I love Marmite, tea and Digestive biscuits. I own a pair of cords and I enjoy fish and chips. I grew up on a diet of Enid Blyton and Roald Dahl and was inspired by the derring-do of the Boys' Own adventures, by the great heroics of Scott and Shackleton.

Yet some parts of being English make me feel queasy. I would never fly the St George's cross, preferring the idea of the Union flag. The St George's cross has become a symbol of jingoistic nationalism. Even our English rugby team prefers to use the English rose rather than the red and white flag. We hide our Englishness, and that is something you don't find anywhere else in the world.

But, then again, nothing about Englishness is straightforward. We are a people of contradictions and juxtapositions. A nation of contrary oddities.

When did we get a complex about our identity?

Billy Bragg has been discussing questions about England since the early 1980s in both his writing and his songs. In 2002, he released *England, Half English*, an album that stole its title from George Orwell, and was adorned with a St George's flag. Its title track found him tentatively exploring what his home country was:

My mother was half English and I'm half English too
I'm a great big bundle of culture tied up in the red
   white and blue
I'm a fine example of your Essex man
And I'm well familiar with the Hindustan
'Cos my neighbours are half-English, and I'm half-
   English too.

In many ways, the only time we are ever allowed to proudly cele-brate our Englishness is during national sporting events. The European Championships and the World Cup are two of the world events in which Britain is allowed to break up into its nation states. Suddenly the community of millions becomes a real team of eleven. Sport is that rare opportunity for the nation to cohere around a single cultural event, however basic and, traditionally, masculine.

Other nation states within the United Kingdom proudly proclaim their borders and their identities. Since devolution the differences between us have perhaps been accentuated. Now the Scots and Welsh have parliaments to give their identities shape, form and fact. But what about England?

The English regularly confuse Englishness and Britishness, as though the semantics mark a distinction without a difference – but the Welsh and the Scots rarely see it that way. According to the British Attitudes Survey, only 14 per cent of Scots chose 'British' as the best or only way to describe themselves, compared to 44 per cent of English people asked.

Peter Mandler, a professor of modern cultural history at the University of Cambridge, says: 'For most of the nineteenth and twentieth centuries, when people described British values, they said "English" instead of "British". People weren't sensitive, they didn't care. But since the mid-twentieth century they became more sensitive. Being British and English should not be a confusion. They are not mutually exclusive categories.'

George Orwell shared with the rest of us an acute difficulty about what to call ourselves. 'We call our islands by no fewer than six different names, England, Britain, Great Britain, the British Isles, the United Kingdom and, in very exalted moments, Albion.' But he preferred the first: England. The English, he found, shared 'an unconscious patriotism and an inability to think logically'. We were 'inefficient but with sound instincts', chief among which were 'gentleness' and 'respect for constitutionalism and legality'. We had an intense sensitivity to class ('I was born into what you might call the lower-upper-middle class'). Our patriotism was thick-headed – the bulldog is 'an animal noted for its obstinacy, ugliness and stupidity' – and proudly insular: 'nearly every Englishman of working-class origin considers it effeminate to pronounce a foreign word correctly'. Yet we have given so much to the world through our inventiveness, creativity and willingness to take on challenges few others would attempt.

Daniel Defoe's poem, 'The True-Born Englishman', in contrast reflects how many see England – as a 'mongrel' nation forged from Celts, Angles, Saxons, Danes and Normans. Successive waves of immigration since the twentieth century have given rise to the notion that England is unique in its composition, a mixture of all things good from all countries. However, this is simply wrong, according to Professor Mandler:

'The English are no more mongrel than any other European country – it's a story that people tell themselves, but it doesn't describe the country.'

So where and when did our identity go?

Football during the 1980s and 90s arguably has a lot to answer for. It was the football fan of that time who confirmed all the reasons why unionists of both the left and the right preferred to keep questions of English identity unanswered.

The huge rise in numbers of travelling football fans during the 1980s projected Englishness onto the map. There were outbreaks of fighting at both the 1980 European Championships and the 1982 World Cup. After the Heysel disaster in 1985, in which thirty-nine people died in a stadium crush before the Liverpool–Juventus European Cup final, UEFA banned English clubs from European football. Without the option of following their club abroad, the hard core switched their travel arrangements: there was a perceptible growth in the numbers and volatility of the England team's away fans.

The 'English disease' of hooliganism was born and has arguably tarnished the St George's cross and the very sense of Englishness ever since. It was during this period, too, that England's support became a recruiting ground for right-wing organizations such as the BNP.

In some ways, Englishness has never been able to sever its links to hooliganism. Nor lose the sense of shame that we felt about it as a nation. To a child of the 1980s, Englishness and hooliganism were inextricably linked and something to be ashamed of. The St George's cross became a symbol of violent radicalism. During international football, it springs up everywhere. Sold in supermarkets, flown on family cars, we enjoy seeing it flutter, for a fortnight or two, uniting the country in hope if not expectation – since we all know about what happens in the penalty shoot-out. But when the tournament ends, the banners are put away, to be replaced by a curious and unhealthy unease about the flag of St George.

Englishness needs to be more than a football match. We are more than the hooligans of the 1980s. We are not the BNP or Nigel Farage.

We are a nation built on a unique set of principles based on a muddled sense of belonging.

We are the sum of our regions, but our identity has been collectively moulded by a number of traits.

Instantly definable and yet confusingly mysterious, we are a nation of individuals who keep their cards close to their chest. A stiff-upper-lipped people who will say sorry for apologizing.

We are also a nation of eccentrics. We have an underlying quirkiness that is hampered by our desire to fit in and to sit on the fence. We are terrified to be different, and yet we celebrate and encourage eccentricity. Perhaps we lost our ability to celebrate Englishness when we started to examine the ills of our empire and what it inflicted on other countries, taking part in self-flagellation to apologize for our previous military and entrepreneurial success and as a way of erasing the character trait of superiority.

Over and above everything else, though, the weather has helped shape who we are. We are the climate: unpredictable, changeable and mild. You see, Englishness is based on polite hopefulness. For an Englishman the grass is always greener. We are all eccentrics clinging to a wind-swept, rain-lashed isle hoping for better weather, but rather reluctantly rather enchanted with what we've got.

We are of course far more than the sum of a flag. Englishness is both glaringly simple and infuriatingly contradictory. We are a nation that supports the underdog and celebrates failure. I wonder if it is a deep-rooted socialist core that makes us suspicious of success. We are largely unshowy. We don't like to show off expensive cars or diamonds. We are the masters of understatement. The tweed jacket with holes and the clapped-out Land Rover Defender are as likely to be worn and driven by a Yorkshire farmer as a Suffolk banker.

I'd argue we are largely a tolerant nation. A little like the proliferation of green parakeets, we are a nation built on multiculturalism and immigrants. Englishness is not the white face and buzz cut of the BNP but every colour and hue of those who have settled on this sceptred isle and called it their home.

We consider the curry one of our national dishes even though it has been plagiarized from India. We consider the cup of tea quintessentially English, though I can assure you we have no tea plantations.

We really are a nation defined by our weather. It consumes our daily routine and our conversations. It is like a mirror to us. We are the weather.

As the world becomes smaller we may have been diluted by the allure of teeth whitening, the exoticism of Vegemite and the Americanization of our language, my bad, but deep down we have retained the traits of Englishness that have defined our nation in history. We are a collective drizzle. Deeply judgemental, we are quick to make social assumptions. The accent, haircut, clothes, job, car, house: all of these can be used to define social status. In many ways we have become a nation of tribes. The Essex Girls. The Newcastle Lads. The Scousers. The Cornish Fishermen. The 'Normal for Norfolk'. The Chelsea Toff. Geographically, as a nation, we can sweepingly divide England between the North and the South.

The South may be climatically warmer but it tends to be harder, busier, colder. The North, while chillier, tends to be happier, warmer. It doesn't take itself too seriously. It is the underdog of the nation. It is no surprise that Yorkshire as a county consistently wins more Gold medals in the Olympic Games than Australia.

The English weather has made us a hopeful nation. We cling to our weather reports in the hope of good news. We are slaves to the rarity of the sun. The elusive sun and the bountiful rain have a lot to answer for, but just think how different we would be if we had the climate of California. To paraphrase that Monty Python quote: What did the Romans ever do for us? What did the weather ever do for us?

What would we talk about? We would become even more socially inept than we already are. We would never have invented the wax jacket or the Wellington boot. We would never have built the Land Rover or invented badminton to escape the rain. We wouldn't have pioneered the drainage of football pitches. A cup of tea wouldn't be half as satisfying. We wouldn't have green lawns and I doubt we would have strawberries and cream half as good as we do. Our produce would be different. Our landscape would be different and our personality would be different. We would stop being a nation of apologists and become a smug nation. Safe and secure in its weather. We would become softer, and I don't mean that in a good way. We would no longer be walking rain clouds with bursts of thunder and lightning but the eternal sunshine of California 'homogeny', the boob-implanted, lip-plumped, teeth-whitened perfection of guaranteed weather.

So why is it that we still find it so hard to celebrate our Englishness? I wonder if it is a hangover and self-flagellation from the shame of our colonial past? I can't help but feel there is more to it.

As a child I was brought up and educated in the importance of the collective union. The troubles of Northern Ireland focused on the value of the United Kingdom and the promise of the European Union had the exoticism of the unknown. England sort of fell by the wayside. It was forgotten.

Let us forget her no more. Like the runt of the litter or a shower on a sunny day we should nurture her and celebrate her. We should collectively lift our cups of tea and raise them to England, my England, our England. A nation shaped by its weather: unpredictable, changeable and mild. You see, Englishness is based on polite hopefulness. For an Englishman the grass is always greener on our neighbour's lawn.

In the end, though, we are all eccentrics clinging to a rain-lashed isle hoping for better weather but reluctantly rather charmed with what we have.

God save the Queen.

INDEX

BF indicates Ben Fogle.

slang) 254–5; *Oxford English Dictionary*
9, 251–3; regional dialects 253–4,
255–6; Shakespeare and 243–51;
worldwide spread of/Pitcairn Island
256–7
lawns 223–6
Lees, John 220
legal system: archaic institutions and rules
181–2; Freedom of the City 179–80;
New Forest Verderers 181–5; Queen's
Guide to the Sands 175–9; Queen's
Swan Marker 185–8
Lephard, Robert 82
Leslie, Sir John ('Jack') 95
Livingstone, Dr 143
Lock & Co., St James's 113
London Olympic Games (2012) 20, 49,
227
London Zoo 168
Longleat, Wiltshire 86–9
Lord Buckethead 143–7
Lord's Cricket Ground, London 73, 120,
134
Love Your Garden (TV programme) 79
Lovell, Tony 119
Lupton, Betty 259
Lygon, Margaret 239

Macintosh, Charles 102
Mackintosh coat 102
Malin, Joseph 220
Mallory, George Herbert Leigh 64
Mandela, Nelson 246
Mandler, Professor Peter 277–9
March, Lord 238
Markov, Georgi 116
Marmite 10, 11, 12, 14, 57, 128, 129, 141,
205–17, 221, 276
Mary Poppins (film) 89–90, 112
McAlpine, Sir Bill and Lady 157
McClellan, Shelly 216
McGill, Donald 150
McGowan, Mark 90–2
McKenna, Virginia 158
Merle, William 32
Merryweather, Dr George 32
Met Office 39, 42, 46, 48, 80
Mikes, George: *How to Be an Alien* 194
Mildmay, Audrey 77
Mill, John Stuart: *On Liberty* 85, 97
Milligan, Spike 142

Mitchell, Sir Peter Chalmers 168–9
Monster Raving Loony Party 148, 149
Monty Python 141, 143, 150, 151, 282
Moody, Captain Eric 143
Moore, Dr Terry 160
Morecambe Bay 7, 175–9, 181; Queen's
Guide to the Kent Sands of Morecambe
Bay 175–9
Moss, Kate 107, 108, 110
Mr Fishfinger 147
Murphy, William 32
My Fair Lady (film) 31
Mytton, Mad Jack 85, 92–3

New Forest Verderers 181–5
Newton, John 36
No. 10 Downing Street 7
Norman Conquest (1066) 37, 51
North British Rubber Company 109
North, Lord 95

Oates, Laurence 63
O'Brian, Patrick 52
Old Lighthouse, The, Dungeness 231–6
Oliver, Jamie 269
One Man and His Dog (TV programme)
163–4
Operation Centaur 169–70
Orwell, George 276, 278; *The English
People* 193–4; *The Road to Wigan Pier*
220
Osbaldeston, George 238–9
Oxford English Dictionary (OED) 9, 251–3

Page, Robin 163
Parry, Sir Herbert 226
Paxman, Jeremy: *The English* 9, 243
pets 159–61, 164, 165–6, 170
Philip, Prince 28, 106, 118, 176–7
Pile, Stephen: *The Book of Heroic Failures*
55
Pinsent, Sir Matthew 70, 71
Pitcairn Island, South Pacific 256–7
place names, eccentric 86
politeness viii, 12, 181, 194, 196, 200–3,
280, 283 *see also* apologizing
Portland, William John Cavendish-
Bentinck-Scott, 5th Duke of 95–6
Portsmouth University 46–7
Prescott, John 49
Proms, The ix, 72, 227

ACKNOWLEDGEMENTS

Special thanks to everyone who helped me along the way.

Chris Aldridge

Julian Alexander

Polly Arber

Myles Archibald

David Barber

Betty's Tea Room

Philippa Broderick

Lord Buckethead

Eddie Edwards

Sarah Edworthy

Julian Humphries

Julia Koppitz

Cedric Robinson

Heike Schuessler

St John Skelton

Martin Toseland